Dorothy

£1.50

To the two people who have brought
the most joy into my life:
my daughters, Dorothy and Lisa

Dorothy
Revelations of a
Rejected Soprano

Dorothy Paul

MAINSTREAM
PUBLISHING

EDINBURGH AND LONDON

First published in Great Britain in 1997 by HarperCollins

Published in Great Britian in 2002 by
MAINSTREAM PUBLISHING COMPANY (EDINBURGH) LTD
7 Albany Street
Edinburgh EH1 3UG

ISBN 1 84018 646 1

Reprinted 2003

A catalogue record for this book is available from the British Library

Typeset in Chancery and Van Djick
Printed and bound in Great Britain by
Antony Rowe Ltd, Chippenham, Wiltshire

ACKNOWLEDGEMENTS

Grateful thanks to John Bett for believing in me, and helping me to realise that belief.

Thanks to Michael Boyd, Giles Gordon, Robert Marsack and Meg Henderson for nudging me on.

To Frank B.S. Mitchell for help with research and all my friends and family who have given me support and strength.

FOREWORD

The first time I ever saw Dorothy Paul in the flesh, so to speak, though she hates me saying it, was as I was leaving STV's studios at the Coo'caddens after watching a live *One O'Clock Gang* show. I was still at school and wearing the dreaded uniform, and there stood the resident soprano, obviously looking for someone and none too pleased about it. I have an impression of tapping toes and an angry expression, but I also remember thinking how sophisticated and gorgeous she was close up and made-up in theatrical slap – extra impressive to a spotty schoolgirl. She was wearing what every female of that era still secretly regards as the true badges of glamour – sticky-oot dress with voluminous net underskirt underneath, backcombed hair and stiletto heels, and she was a star, she worked on the most popular show on TV – you have to remember that we were a more innocent lot in those days. Looking back now I realise that she wasn't that many years older than I was, but the gulf between me and that vision seemed immeasurable at the time. I suppose I imagined her as coming from some far distant, glittering world I would never get near; it was many years before I discovered that we were brought up within a few miles of each other in Glasgow, me in Blackhill, Dorothy in Dennistoun.

After the *Gang* show disappeared there was the odd scrap of information in the newspapers from time to time, that Dorothy, husband Gerry and daughter Dorothy had moved to Ireland, their second daughter Lisa was born there and finally, a tiny paragraph stating that Gerry had died, leaving her with two children. All over the country people who remembered the earlier days felt sorry for her loss while deciding that she would be fine, she'd have loads of money, unlike your average young widow she'd never have to work again, after all, she was part of the other half who live in a different and

7

more opulent world. At that time the public still didn't allow 'stars' to be like themselves, somehow they wanted to believe that celebs led charmed lives quite unlike their own. What this book shows, however, is that Dorothy and her daughters were far from fine, that having 'made it' once, she had to do it all over again to feed them and herself, but right from the bottom this time and as a single parent with a working single parent's guilt and fears. What it also shows is that she did make it, and more, she paved the way for other showbiz females to make it.

Ghosted showbusiness autobiographies are ten-a-penny, but Dorothy wrote this book herself, and that shows in every sentence. On every page you will recognise her and the members of her family just as you do when she performs her one-woman shows, because what she has shown us is that they're just like us – we knew them already. That's the secret of her shows: the superb cast of relatives, the aunties in particular, are people we feel we know, because we do – there are at least two of my aunties in there for a start and I could prove it! Dorothy Paul didn't come from some higher stratum of society, nor does she inhabit one now, yet she has emerged with the affection of the public when many others would've been greeted with disappointment for stepping out of the character we thought they had. What Dorothy did to feed her children was the only thing she knew, but in making this new career over recent years, she has let us see that she is a woman like any other, who makes mistakes and suffers from them, acknowledging that for some reason she has always chosen the hard route and, in doing so, has earned the kind of affection that other stars have to strive for from behind the glitter. There's no sham there, Dorothy is as she is, and though often the public wants its idols to appear as distant figures swathed in glamour and mystery – and believe me, with some it's just as well they stay that way – what Dorothy's public welcomes without envy is that she has made it – again – and they understand from their own family experiences that her ability to survive is rooted in her background.

Dorothy's father was the eternal boy, great fun but as Dorothy said to me once he was never really husband or father material. Dorothy's mother Mae wanted better for her children than the poor background she grew up in, though like children everywhere they didn't think they were poor, because everyone was in the same boat. When I look back to my own similar background I pictured Mae paying for her daughters' lessons in singing, dancing and piano and I can't help admiring her. She managed to keep finding the wherewithal to give her children skills she knew could provide them with a better future. And I also know that as she persevered she would've drawn comments from other women about having ideas above her station, wasting good money on daft things like that when her family, like all the others round about, had little enough to survive on. So if you feel a little resentment as you read these pages you'll wonder what dreams and talents Mae herself had that she was never allowed to follow either. More than anything you'll wish you could've known her in life as you do through her daughter's memories.

And that, of course, was what enabled Dorothy to travel the road she did, from star to young wife of a high-flying provider, to widowed mother of two small children, through real poverty and back to star again. She did it through sheer hard work and determination, and because there was no choice, it was all she knew, and also because that was how she was brought up to react to bad breaks in life, you just got on with it. But there's another dimension to what Dorothy has achieved in recent years. She's always been a looker, she still is today, even without the sticky-oot dresses, back-combed hair and stilettoes, and in the eyes of the public, though more importantly, in the eyes of the male showbusiness wheelers and dealers, she had only one niche – as a good-looking singer, a soprano. Women weren't allowed to be funny, though ordinary women everywhere have always known this to be nonsense – what were those women-only backcourt performances, the clabbers, but women being funny to entertain each other? They weren't allowed to do it on stage or screen though, unless they were exceptionally ugly or had some kind of grotesquery, of course, like Gracie Clark's singing voice in later years that she shrewdly turned into comedy. So when Dorothy Paul, glamorous soprano, wanted to perform a one-woman show being funny, therefore, there were no financial backers beating a path to her door. And anyway – a one-woman show? What was that about? Her response was to take her courage in both hands and finance it herself, and she proved them all wrong. Not only was the public prepared to let her step out of her allotted role, but they were prepared to pay money to laugh with and at a woman, a good-looking woman at that, one who wasn't peculiar in some way.

Lots of people now give her credit for pulling it off against the odds, but there is considerably less recognition of the fact that she opened the way for other Scotswomen performers to do what she fought to do, she enabled them to follow on without facing the obstacles she did. Look around you today at women performers who have their own shows or who act in shows not just as foils to the comic talents of the men around, but getting laughs by themselves, and you realise that it never happened before Dorothy Paul made it acceptable. They're there today because she paved the way for them, and now that she has broken the mould so successfully, it's in the nature of things, perhaps, that all too few acknowledge that. We Scots are slow at what Dorothy's mother called 'pushing yourself forward', in case this might bring about the dreaded 'showing up' – words that haunt me to this day! – but it is right that we give credit where it's due, and the story of what Dorothy Paul achieved for herself and for the female performers who have followed down the path she made, deserves respect.

Read her book and you will see a snapshot of a time that has passed, and sadly much of the good has been swept away with the bad. If you were brought up in that era there are parts that will remind you so powerfully of now vanished people and events in your own life that you will laugh and cry at the same time, but by the end you will have more respect for 'hur aff the telly' than you had, because she still carries the stamp of where and who she came from, with neither need nor wish to forget. When she was working on this book Dorothy went into exile, and one day she phoned me to say she was giving up – it's a stage that happens to every writer on every book and always will, you just have to remember that and get past it. 'I mean to say,' she protested, 'I canny be arsed. Nobody will be interested in all that stuff.' Happily she was persuaded that she was wrong and to get back to work, for what her book does is breathe life into our memories and prove that they weren't entirely sentimental. It also gives confirmation of the worth of people like Dorothy and her family; they really were like that . . .

Meg Henderson

1

There is nothing so far removed from us as to be beyond our reach or so hidden that we cannot discover it.

DESCARTES

*T*he whole course of my life and my career changed one bleak January morning in 1991 while I was sitting at the untidy desk in my bedroom. The desk was piled high with bills, odd bits of paper, theatre programmes, more bills and a contract waiting to be signed. I looked around me and wondered yet again why I had chosen the blue floral wallpaper; the blue roses were oppressive and they didn't even look like real roses. I wished I'd gone the few pounds extra and bought the Sandersons. Hey ho, it was all I could afford at the time – hardly the ambience for a time-served depressive.

I straightened out the Equity contract. Michael Boyd, the Artistic Director of the Tron Theatre in Glasgow and a man I much respected, had asked me to appear in the rerun of a play he had produced the previous year. I had been quite well reviewed, and this was three months' work in prospect. I had my Biro poised over the contract, where it said 'Artiste Sign Here', when the most extraordinary thing happened. I heard a voice. There was no one else in the room, but I heard a voice loud and clear. So clear, in fact, that I said, 'What?'

There was no answer. The voice had spoken and it wasn't going to speak again. I could see it in the paper: 'Dorothy Paul taken away in a strait-jacket. A serious breakdown. The reason, she claims, was "the blue floral wallpaper".'

I had two choices: either I went straight to the doctor to seek help – perhaps psychotherapy – or I took it as a sign and phoned Michael.

Dorothy

What had the voice said? 'Billing', that was all, just 'Billing'. I shifted some of the paperwork, found the phone, dialled his number and got through to him straightaway. 'Hello, Michael.'

'Dorothy, what can I do for you?'

'I was wondering, Michael – what's the billing for this show?' I didn't mention the disembodied voice. Well, you don't, do you?

'I was afraid you'd ask that.'

'Oh, yes,' I replied weakly.

'Well, you see, the other actor wants top billing over the title.'

The other actor was a fair-sized 'name', but no higher in the echelon than myself. 'Whatever happened to alphabetical order, Michael?'

'The agent's demanding it.' This meant that the actor was demanding it.

'That doesn't seem fair, Michael.'

I was going to have a fight on my hands. Actors who are on a level with one another rarely demand top billing unless their name is guaranteed to put 'bums on seats' more than the next. In this instance, we were pretty evenly matched. This personage was 'coming it', as they say in Dennistoun; pushing their luck.

'You're probably right,' said Michael. 'Leave it with me and I'll see what I can do.'

Petty though it may seem, after much to-ing and fro-ing, and the actor's refusal to budge on the 'billing' stakes, I backed out, returned the contract and found myself looking forward to a year with no gainful employment in the diary. Something would turn up, and I had my wee drama classes and a lodger. We were not exactly heading for that mythical place called 'the grubber' just yet.

On a cold morning in February of that same year, I found myself yet again sitting at the untidy desk in the Hillhead flat. I had moved there in 1986 from a beautiful flat in Kirklee because of one of my hasty, ill-advised decisions in the midst of one of my 'I'm chucking the business' phases when I had lost my confidence. For 18 months I had financed and worked at a business I knew nothing about, making architectural models. Sufficient to say it had failed miserably. I blame no one but myself. I was imprudent, I lost every bit of my savings and

I still berate myself for putting my family at risk. The only bit of humour that came out of it was when the saleroom men came to cart away the equipment. One of them took a close look at me and said, 'Has anyone ever told you you're a ringer for Faith Brown, hen?'

I replied, 'No, they usually tell me I look like Dorothy Paul.'

He peered at me again and said, 'Naw, naw, hen, you're nothing like her and ah've seen her up close.' To add insult to injury, he gave me a nudge and added, 'Here, hen . . . I bet you wish you had her money, eh?'

It takes a long time to retrace your steps from the wrong road. I had to sell my Kirklee flat and move. In my situation many folk would have moved to a smaller place, but my thinking was that if I had a large flat I could always let a room. When my back has been to the wall, letting a room has always kept the wolf from the door. The new flat had been owned by an artist and there was a studio with a little dais at the window. Having had some experience of teaching drama, I decided that I could set up a studio, and let one of the other rooms. It was three stairs up, with a lovely view, so all in all I enjoyed my time there. I had some charming students from age six to sixty and I still hear from some of them.

So there I was, sitting at the desk with no voice to advise me. I was beginning to wonder why I had listened to the bloody voice in the first place. However, it proved to be a blessing, because if I had not heard it and acted on it, the next bit of the story would never have unfolded.

I decided that a wee bit of hustle was in order. I lifted the phone and dialled Michael's number. When he answered, I realised I'd done one of my hasty things. I didn't have a plan. Was he even speaking to me after the 'billing' débâcle?

'Hello, Michael.'

'Dorothy.'

He was still speaking to me. Words started to come out of my mouth. 'Had an idea, Michael . . .' What the hell was the idea? '. . . eh . . . was wondering if you could find a space for me in Mayfest?' Before he could reply, I dashed on with the first thing that came into my head. 'I know you'll have your programme fixed, but I wondered if there might be the possibility of a late-night kind of thing. You know

. . . songs, a monologue or two . . . that kind of thing . . .' My voice tailed off.

'There are no spaces at all, Dorothy, the Tron's booked solid for that time. I'm very sorry.' Well, at least I'd tried. Then he said, 'I'm looking at the book here and I have a week free in June. Write a one-woman show.' That's what he said. Just like that, 'Write a one-woman show.'

I couldn't believe it. I tried to sound cool. 'Oh, yes . . . mmm . . . Now there's an idea.'

'It's time you were doing something like that.'

My thoughts were racing. Of course I had to say yes. As usual I was rushing into something without sufficient thought. 'What kind of thing do you visualise, Michael?'

'I don't know, that's up to you.' Then he came out with, 'Write about yourself – your life, your experiences, there must be masses of material there. Some of it has to be good for a laugh.'

I wondered if he were mocking me. Well, maybe just a little, in a nice kind of way. I heard myself say, 'Okay, I'll give it a go.'

'Great, I'll pencil you in for that week commencing the 12th of June. Bye.'

I put the phone down. I was shaking with excitement about the idea; a one-woman show. I raised my hands to heaven and shouted, 'Thank you, God!' Was it a commission? Should I have asked for some money up front? I didn't want to push it, I'd manage. I had no serious income but that was a mere detail.

Now the first thing to do when faced with a blank piece of paper is clean out your cupboards. I made a career out of them, then went on to spring-clean the house, occasionally giving some thought to the script. The next thing to do is make cushions. All this displacement activity lasted for 8 weeks. I had been given 16 weeks to write the show and now I only had 8. My eldest daughter happened to ask me how I was getting on with the script. I told her I'd made a few notes, but of course I'd been too busy cleaning and things. Her reaction was shock horror.

'What? You haven't written anything? Mum, the show is only eight weeks away . . . Oh, my God, we're going to get a showing-up.'

Dorothy

I liked her saying 'we'. This was my mother speaking loud and clear. Her biggest phobia was 'the showing-up', brought to shame, never to hold your head up again, the talk of the steamie, black affronted and, worst of all, to be found out. Panic set in. She was right, of course. Eight weeks to write a one-woman show. How long would it take? How long is a bit of string? The few words I'd put down on paper about my life in show business didn't seem all that funny. If I was going to get away with a one-woman show, it had to have a few laughs in it. What was it Michael had said? 'Tell the story of your life, that must be good for a laugh.' Had he said that? That was certainly the gist of it. Oh really, Michael, very good, Michael, shit, Michael. It was all his fault.

My old boss in Kraft Cheese, where I worked from the age of 15 for three years, would call me into his office and ask me why I hadn't managed to balance my invoices that week. I would thrash around for excuses but in the end he'd say, 'Now, Dorothy, you said you could do it when you wrote in.' He was a kindly boss, Mr Haining, and he would send me away back to my desk, my typewriter and my electric adding machine, after a good 'talking to' and with a more responsible attitude to my work. I may have earned only 32/6d a week at that job but oh they were carefree days. How often during a play, when I couldn't learn the lines or someone was waiting for a cue and I was paraphrasing all over the place, had his words come back to me. I have always had an awful dread of being found out for the incompetent that I perceive myself to be. The old self-doubt. It's in the genes, the 'don't draw attention to yourself' kind of early childhood, the 'don't you give me a showing-up' background.

Back to the blank sheet of paper and a bit of focus. What was it Elaine C. Smith used to say when we were in the dressing-room making up for our roles in *The Steamie*? She said, 'Dorothy, tell us that one about Nellie Sutherland and the Pole Act.'

That was Nellie the theatrical agent, and when the Pole Act was pleading with her for work, she said, 'There's not a lot of call for Pole Acts these days, dear.'

The man went down on his knees. 'Nellie, I have to pay the rent, my children are starving. How about a weekend in the New Theatre in Paisley?'

Nellie replied, 'I'm sorry, dear, your pole's too big for Paisley.'

That's a good one, write it down. I wonder whatever happened to that man? Never mind wondering about him, get on with the script. Write funny lines. I felt about as funny as a scream for help.

Get back to my own life in the East End of Glasgow. I could only think about the bad things. What is comedy anyway, but tragedy with hindsight? I'd phone my pal Dave, an art teacher in Dumfries. Although I'd met him later in life, he had the same background as me, having been brought up just along the road near the Lady Well and Tennent's brewery. We'd both gone to Whitehill Senior Secondary but I'd been five years ahead of him. When you get Dave started, he has a treasure trove of stories about his childhood. We'd made a similar journey, so he sparked off memories in me. We were on the phone for about two hours and I made notes. He told me about the local drunks, fights outside pubs, sadistic schoolteachers, aunties, uncles. He told me about the time he asked, 'Dad, what's a homosexual?'

His dad had answered, 'A man who wears suede shoes, son.'

At the end of it he said, 'God, hen . . . I've depressed the hell out of myself going back down that road.' Nevertheless, to me it was all funny. Why? Because it was his story, not mine. It is a true saying that 'Comedy is a serious business.' I started on a road down the corridors of memory and opened doors, some of them marked 'Not to be opened again.' It was the only way.

2

Who wrote 'Happy Birthday', and is he or she still collecting the royalties?

D.P.

I have never understood my mother's earache cure. Some of her other homespun remedies I've used on my own children to good effect, for instance the hot salt in an old sock, the salt preferably being heated over a coal fire, then poured into an old sock rather than a new one. I guarantee the inflammation in the throat will be reduced the next day. Another one is the sugar-and-soap poultice. Mix sugar and carbolic soap in equal parts, apply it to a boil or a poisoned digit, bandage the wound and you find the inflammation gone by the morning. I remember waking up on many nights with the earache. My mother would make a bit of toast, put it in a sock, tie it round my head and say, 'That'll draw it out,' and go back to bed. The toast would be cold within seconds, the crumbs that escaped through the sock causing severe itching. That so-called cure never worked.

Childhood memories are fragments of light in the darkness. We seem to have a selection process that chooses the ones we wish to recall. One dark night, when I was about three and a half, I was hauled from my cot in the front bedroom where I slept with my sister. A flurry of hands zipped me up into a bottle-green hand-knitted siren suit and carried me into the lobby. Big people were sitting on chairs lining the walls, or on the floor, cups of tea and biscuits on the rectangular plate with orange flowers were being passed round the neighbours. Faces smiled and hands went out to me. Everyone was squashed into the small space. This was the night in March 1941 when the Germans blitzed Clydebank. There was the noise of distant explosions and the screeching of sirens. We lived in a low-down house at 108 Cardross Street, Dennistoun, and according to the ARP, the safest place in a tenement was the centre of a ground-floor flat. Just then there was the scream of something descending, an ominous silence, then an explosion. One of the German pilots must have decided to offload his last bomb on us. The house shook and the front windows shattered; everyone was terrified. Granny and two of my mother's sisters lived down the hill from us, which was where the noise of the blast had come from. My mother was screaming, 'Oh, ma mammy, ma mammy.' She would have been out the door if she hadn't been stopped. Eventually the all-clear siren was sounded and everyone went to investigate the damage. People in the street ran from their houses, turned right into Eveline Street, where Granny and the aunties lived, and looked down into Dunchattan Street where the bomb had dropped. I was carried in my father's arms. Thankfully the buildings hadn't had a direct hit. The bomb had landed in the middle of the street. The top floor of one of the houses was on fire but miraculously no one was killed.

We all dashed into Granny's house. She was sitting in her rocking-chair by the black range in the kitchen of her two-apartment house, covered from head to toe in black soot. She was unrecognisable. A black statue, rooted to the spot in a state of severe shock. 'Eeh, 'ar 'ria – that were a big 'un.' It would take more than a Jerry bomb and a fall of soot to kill off that old Lancashire lass.

After they had hosed Granny down, put her house into a semblance of order and got her off to bed, probably with a medicinal glass out of her gill bottle, we went back up the road to our own house. My mother yelled from the front bedroom when she found that the windows had imploded and my cot was full of shattered glass. She ran through to the kitchen in a state of extreme shock. 'My God, I could have lost my mother and ma wean in the one night.'

Some time later I found myself on a long, solemn tram-car ride to Clydebank. It was a sunny spring day. I can see myself between my parents, holding their hands. As far as the eye could see there was rubble, just building rubble. Where there had been rows of houses with shadows in between and living people going about their business, there was devastation and the sunlight glinting on the few possessions that had been left in one piece. People's clothes, handmade things, household objects, ornaments, pots and pans, a clock. All laid out reverently where they had been found.

'Look, Mummy, a fur coat. Mummy, it's a fur coat. Go and get it.'

I can clearly remember saying that. Wasn't she always talking about fur coats? She tightened the grip on my hand and said, 'No, hen.' I looked up at my parents. Tears were streaming from their eyes. My father, whose hat was never off his head, even in the house, was holding it against his chest. He had worked in Clydebank. I feel sure now that there was no mawkish curiosity in that visit. I believe they were there to pay their respects to the dead and to grieve.

As I write this, I am sitting by the seashore in El Cotillo in Fuerto Ventura, where I am enjoying a short holiday. In one of the apartments behind me there's an extended family of Germans, celebrating a child's birthday. They have a cake with candles burning, and they're singing 'Happy Birthday' in their own language, to a slightly different tune from the one we know. The grandparents, perhaps a few years older than I am, will remember the war as well as I do. I wonder if the name 'Clydebank' would mean anything to them? Surely they must have heard of it: one of Britain's big hopes of winning the war, with its shipbuilding and munitions factories. Would they remember that on that night, thousands of civilians were killed? Probably not. If they were asked what they remembered of the war, the first name on their lips might be Dresden.

The sun was truly up on my awareness when, in the middle of the war, Uncle George was in the navy and Uncle Robert was in the army; the sky was filled with anti-aircraft barrage balloons; there was the blackout, and in the dark folk were forever bumping into baffle-walls on the pavements outside the tenements; Lord Haw-Haw was on the radio, spewing out his anti-British propaganda and depressing everyone – and my mother decided she wanted a house with a bathroom.

Her eye lighted on a big flat, a four-room and kitchen and bathroom at the bottom of Whitehill Street with the big-room window looking onto Duke Street. It had belonged to a dentist. My mother and Auntie Lizzie dragged me and my cousin Isabel up to see the new house. She was 'away with it'.

'What do you think, Lizzie? Beautiful, isn't it?'

'Oh, aye, it's lovely.'

'Of course, I'll have to lay my hands on £50 key money.'

This apparently was some kind of bribe for the factor.

With her usual use of inversion she went on, 'He died, the dentist.'

'Did he?'

'Dropped dead in the middle of a patient.'

'Is that no terrible? Young?'

'No, old. Of course, before him, a big heart specialist had his consulting rooms here.' These factors seemed to add to the attraction of the flat; if it had been good enough for a big doctor and a dentist, it was certainly good enough for us. She was jumping about all over the place. 'But come here 'til I show you the bathroom. Look at that! Hot and cold running water, comes off a back boiler in the kitchen. You can come and have a bath anytime you want, Lizzie. It'll save you going to Whitevale.' Whitevale being the local public baths, swimming-pool and wash-house, which was known as the steamie. Steamies were built at the end of the last century when most of the population of a big city had cold-water flats with outside toilets.

In our previous cold-water flat at 108 Cardross Street, with the black sink in the kitchen and the brass swan-necked tap, it was a wee wash-down every day with a face-cloth at the sink and a visit to the baths once a week. Privacy was at a premium so this move was life-changing. The bathroom was quite a novelty but it was small, with a skylight onto the landing. There were bars on the skylight which my father and brother used to climb up to the ledge above the door where the front-door key was kept. There never seemed to be more than two keys, the one my mother kept in her bag and the one above the door.

Now we were in the room where the deceased dentist had snuffed it over some poor unsuspecting patient. It was probably a difficult extraction, because the dentists in those days seemed to do more of them than fillings. His surgery was painted hospital green. In the centre of the room stood the dentist's chair and in a corner was a box full of false teeth.

'Don't you touch them, somebody'll come for them,' my mother called out to Isabel and me as we started to investigate the macabre collection.

'He's dead, too, isn't he?' was Auntie Lizzie's next non-sequitur.

'Who?'

'The big heart specialist.'

My mother replied, 'Oh, aye.' To Auntie Lizzie's disappointment, my mother was unable to furnish her with details of his demise.

'Did oor Dorrie no attend him at one time?'

'I think she did.'

'Didnae do her much good.'

'Aye, but oor Dorrie's condition's chronic. Look you two, I told you not to touch those teeth – and don't put them near your mouth.'

No one ever did come for the box of teeth. My father took them down to the Barras and got a good price for them because they were new. In those days before the National Health Service, it was quite common for folk to purchase their false teeth at the Barras. Of course they were nearly always second-hand. Where they came from doesn't bear thinking of; sufficient to say that the source of these commodities also supplied second-hand spectacles. The previous owners would not be going for a new set, nor would they be needing another eye test.

My mother's delusions of grandeur were being fulfilled, and this house had her name on it. We were leaving a lovely little two-room and kitchen, with a leafy garden at the back and a small but efficient communal wash-house attached to the house, good neighbours, a friendly community, other relatives nearby and not forgetting Miss Marshall's wee corner shop. Miss Marshall was a sweet, enigmatic woman of indeterminate age of whom it was said that she had had a 'disappointment'; a euphemism for being cast aside by some cad. Her enigmatic quality came from the fact that she wore a wig; it didn't fit her well at all. Maybe she'd got it at the Barras.

My sister never forgave my mother for leaving the wee house, but Mother was determined and she managed to close her eyes to the drawbacks, not least the fact that the house was infested with mice. We never seemed to get rid of them. This was probably due to its being situated over shops that sold food. My mother and I were forever table-jumping. At the sight of a mouse she would grab me and jump onto the kitchen table while my father would run about, quite ineffectually, chasing it with a brush. I have a mouse phobia to this day. Only recently I had to get my neighbour out of his bed late at night to remove a 'dead' mouse that my cat had brought in. If he had been unavailable, I would have had no hesitation in calling the police to do the job.

The front rooms were so close to the main street that if you stood at the window, the folk in the smoky upper decks of the tram-cars could have a lip-reading conversation with you. Some would wave and some would make rude signs. Dirt and grime poured into the rooms from the busy, noisy street and the house was cold because of the size of the rooms, which we could ill afford to heat. Most of the living was done in the kitchen, huddling round the kitchen range trying to get a bit of warmth from one of my mother's banked-up fires. She would put on two or three bits of coal then bank it up with two shovels full of dross and vegetable peelings. It kept the fire in and heated the water, but there was no real heat from it. My father used to wait until she left the room, then get the poker and agitate it to get a wee flame going – a wee 'lou' as he called it.

The fact that my mother had taken on a large, cold, rodent-infested house was a minor problem compared to the state of the back court. The entrance to this communal area was through the 'dunny'; I assume that was short for dungeon. It was situated a third of the way up the first set of stairs. Into the dunny and down the stairs was an outside toilet for the use of the shopkeepers and their staff. Past that you were into the back court. Being the corner of the tenement building, it was dark, murky and sooty from years of neglect. The area was bordered by a high dyke against which was a line of auxiliary buildings in various states of disrepair. There were the middens where anarchy reigned, with the smelly detritus of people's lives spilling over; black plastic bags hadn't been invented. Next to that was a functioning communal wash-house, then there was an abandoned wash-house and, last but not least, another outside toilet. The door had been removed, the chipped, stained lavatory pan or toilet bowl as we call it now was lying on its side in the middle of the back court, long since disconnected from the uncapped waste pipe. This was the cause of a quite disgusting episode.

Dorothy

A little boy called up to his mother's kitchen window, 'Mammy, Mammy, look, there' jobby water coming out the pipe!' The child had got it right. Raw sewage was pouring out of the waste pipe and into the back where he was playing. It was a 'send for the factor' case. Disaster area though it was, we still played there, and when the 'authorities' built an air-raid shelter right in the middle of it, that was another place to play in. No one ever used it for its proper purpose; it was dark and dank and smelt of plaster that had never dried.

3

'Everyone carries a shadow,' says Jung, 'and the less it is embodied in the individual's conscious life, the blacker and denser it is. If an inferiority is conscious, one always has a chance to correct it. But if it is repressed and isolated from consciousness, it never gets corrected.'

JOLANDI JACOBS, *THE PSYCHOLOGY OF C.G. JUNG*

*A*t the age of four, the tonsillectomy window was approaching. It was always advisable to remove a child's tonsils before they went to school; get it out of the way. Before I was born, it was common for the specialist to come to the house and perform the operation on the kitchen table. I was a modern child and was taken up to Yorkhill Hospital for the job. Tonsils were 'wheeched out' whether it was necessary or not. A doctor friend of mine told me that during his training, a specialist had remarked, 'It's a poor throat you cannae see a fiver in.' Obviously this was the fee they charged. I don't think my mother knew the function of tonsils to absorb infection. A mother in those days would always be afraid of her child's throat closing up, as happened often with diphtheria, a disease which was endemic in Glasgow and claimed the lives of many children. Get them up to Yorkhill, get them taken out and no more worries.

There I was in a cot, wearing only a wee short 'simmit', with a little boy who was playing with an appendage to his anatomy, a thing I'd never seen before and something I didn't like the look of. A big nurse wearing a large hankie on her head saw what he was doing and smacked his hand. She called another nurse over, pointed to the little boy and said 'Chickenpox,' then walked away. There seemed to be hundreds of cots, with two children in each, all waiting in a queue to enter a big bright room. Finally it was my turn. I was placed on a table, feeling very cold, and a big man approached me with a tea-strainer, dropped some awful stuff on it and I found myself unable to breathe air. Then I was back in a cot in the ward and the big nurse was slapping my face. When I complained to my mother about it, she just said that the nurse was wakening me up. Most folk I know who went through the same experience around the same time only remember the ice-cream and jelly afterwards, to soothe the raw throat. I just remember the horror of it.

Back at home I was mollycoddled for a few days and I loved it. One day my mother called Auntie Lizzie to my bedside, pointed to me and asked, 'What do you make of that, Lizzie?' Auntie Lizzie replied, 'Chickenpox.' I was furious and said, 'I'm Dorothy. It was the wee boy in the cot who was called Chickenpox.'

We'd settled in the new house in Whitehill Street, where I was alone with my mother all day; my father, my big sister and brother were at work. My cousin Isabel and I were taken once a week to the Sunshine School of Dancing where we were learning the 'time step' to the tune of 'Ma, I Miss Your Apple Pie', a song that didn't survive the war. My mother was threatening to take me away from the lessons because I couldn't dance without sticking my tongue out. At the time it didn't worry me, because there was a wee girl there who kept nipping me. I hated her. I was at the age when I thought the whole world revolved around me, and when it came to the display at the Lyric Theatre in Sauchiehall Street, I got my first laugh on stage. The reason for this was that I was in a line of blue fairies next to the little bum-pincher. I was tall for my age, she was short, and her mother had made her tutu too long. We must have looked like Mutt and Jeff in ballet frocks. When we made our entrance, the audience fell about laughing. 'They're laughing at me,' I thought. I was humiliated.

One day there was a knock on the front door. My mother answered it and I heard a man say, 'I believe you have a daughter of school age,' or words to that effect. It was the School Board Officer with peaked cap and briefcase.

My mother replied meekly, 'Yes.' She was always meek in the face of authority – School Board Officers, wee doctors, big doctors, lawyers, teachers, even the factor and the wee society man who collected the insurance money.

The man produced a document from his case and declared, 'She will attend Alexandra Parade Primary School on the first of September.'

I wasn't prepared for this. I pinned myself against the wall next to the door, out of sight of the man, and whispered to my mother, 'Tell him you don't have a wee girl.' I was panic-stricken.

Then my mother betrayed me. 'Yes, I'll make sure she gets there.'

The man got her signature on the document and I was condemned to education.

The day arrived and she left me in a classroom full of noisy children. I found myself at a desk beside a pretty little girl who introduced herself as June Kelly. I was aware of boys in the room but they seemed to be a blur of arms and legs, flailing around noisily. The only feeling of safety I had was in the presence of that little girl, who smiled sweetly at me.

The noise subsided slightly when a tall person took her place behind the biggest desk, which faced us, banged a pointer on the blackboard and shouted something in a foreign language. This new language, I realised later, was 'posh'. I'd never seen or heard anyone like her before. Apart from the graceful and agile Miss McLellan at the dancing school, I had mostly come across wee fat women – wee corseted women, with soft bosoms and smiling faces and wraparound aprons. (Of course there was the wee thin woman up the stairs from us, who didn't have that rounded look and who always smelt of medicine. 'Aye, that's right, hen – medicine,' my mother would repeat my words to Auntie Lizzie and wink.)

This woman in front of us in the classroom did not belong to the world as I knew it. If I were asked to describe her now, I would say she had a face like a hatchet and eyes like cold steel, her hair an indeterminate shade of beige, and that she wore a print smock over something grey to match the grey lisle stockings and sensible polished shoes. The overall effect was nondescript. Miss Brown was one of God's unclaimed treasures; she would be returned to him marked 'Package unopened', an unwed haddock, a single fish. She didn't like us. We were the hoi polloi, the offspring of workmen and steamie women, 'common'. Perhaps she had been turned down for a post in a girls' private school in the West End. She was too good for us and she knew it; she would let us know it too. My mother would have crumbled in front of her and would have described her as 'very superior' but not a real lady like the ones who came to give improving talks to the Mothers' Union in the church. Those were real ladies from big houses in Great Western Road, near the Church of England cathedral, St Mary's. Those 'real ladies' would deign to come and visit our female congregation in the little mission church we attended in the Calton and tell them how to set a table for dinner, part with their secret recipes and give instruction as to how to make do and mend. My mother loved these visits from the 'quality'. It was a window into, as she called it, 'how the other half lived'. She would say, 'Of course, they're born to it, Lizzie.' Being born to it gave them the right to be superior.

'Be quate, children, where do you think you are? In a bear garden?'

A bear garden. What was that? I'd never heard of a garden with a bear in it. Was this the teddy-bears' picnic I'd heard of? I turned to my new-found friend and asked, 'What's a bear garden?'

Miss Brown caught me. 'Did you speak, girl?'

'Yes.'

'Yes, Miss Brown.'

'Yes, Miss Brown.' I cottoned on.

'Come out here, girl.'

I walked out to her big desk. From under the lid she produced a leather belt with the end cut into three narrow bits.

'Hold out your hand, girl.'

I held out my hand obediently and she brought the strap down on it with tremendous force. The humiliation was almost as bad as the pain. There was stunned silence in the class. This was what we could expect from Miss Brown. She must be a German, she belonged behind enemy lines, she was against us; she was power. I suppose I must have learned to read and write during the first year with her, but I shut down and have no recall of the rest of that year in school.

My mother must have collected me from school after that first day; I remember crying and telling her about the belting. She asked me the reason for it and I told her I was only talking. She said, 'See, that's you, always drawing attention to yourself.' My mother had condoned the woman's action, therefore I had to accept it without question. We never questioned in those days.

There was no warmth, no nurturing of the spirit from Miss Brown. We had to bob a curtsy to her every morning, say the Lord's Prayer, sing a little hymn and get on with learning the three Rs. Instead of projecting my thoughts into words, as I was wont to do, I started to live part of my life in my head, keeping a lot to myself. When we sang

> 'Jesus bids us shine with a pure clear light,
> Like a little candle burning in the night,
> In this world of darkness we must make it shine,
> You in your small corner and I in mine.'

I thought, that's where I am, in a wee corner with a candle. I liked that wee corner, I could visualise it and it gave me comfort. Keep it shining but keep it to yourself: that was the way to survive. Of course these are adult thoughts, but I believe that was my modus vivendi, my way of coping with harsh reality. I really wanted to be Rupert, from the annual I got for Christmas every year, and live in Nutwood, have magic adventures and go home at night to a wee bedroom with floral wallpaper and a floral coverlet, having had a good tea and the approval of my parents; or perhaps the little girl in the school reading book, who lived in a house with an upstairs and a downstairs, hollyhocks growing up the walls beside the pretty doorway, Daddy coming home at night with a paper under his arm, Mummy standing at the door wearing a clean pinny, a hot apple-pie in her hands and Spotty dog jumping up and down for joy. Wouldn't that have been lovely, instead of the confusion of Dad and the big brother having a boxing match in the kitchen, my sister trying to do an ironing in the midst of it, while my mother entertained her sisters in the big room with conversations like:

'Her floor collapsed.'

'Her kitchen floor?'

'No, her pelvic floor . . . hid tae have it all pulled up again . . . surgery,' with the hand movements representing the lifting of bowel, bladder and uterus.

The conversation that really had me confused was when my mother told the others that Mrs Macfarlane had a wooden chest. A woman with a wooden chest? How unusual. I visualised it as clinker-built, like the wooden boats you could take out for threepence on Hogganfield Loch, oary boats.

Someone once said that a child comes into the world and tries to make a cosmos out of chaos. Well, there was plenty of chaos to sort out in this household.

4

The mass of men lead lives of quiet desperation.

THOREAU

My mother struggled against the odds to provide her family with a healthy diet during the war. Actually she was struggling against my father's tea and sugar addiction. Had it been left to him he would have blown the rations in one day. If my mother went out and left my sister in charge of cooking a meal, I'd hear her say, 'The potatoes are in the hallstand, the mince is on top of the wardrobe, the tea is in the portmanteau where I keep the insurance policies on top of the bunker, and the sugar is in a shoebox under my bed. Don't tell your father, he'll only make tablet again, and if he mentions making doughnuts, don't let him. Remember the last time?'

The doughnut episode happened when my mother had gone out to visit Auntie Chrissie, whose daughter was going out with a foreign sailor she had met at the dancing. My mother was putting on her lipstick and telling Betty about her cousin's new boyfriend.

My sister asked, 'Is he a Petty Officer or something?'

My mother replied, 'Not at all, he's a Chantyrazzler.'

My sister accepted this title although it wasn't a rank she'd ever heard of. My mother went on, 'She's wantin' to get married to him, met him at the church social. That minister down there opens his doors to all the scruff of the day. I mean he's a nice fella – for a foreigner – but as I always say, if you don't know where he comes fae, you don't know who he's affae.' Having cast doubt on the poor sailor's pedigree, she continued, 'He says he comes from Canada but he talks French . . . something funny there, eh? I'm saying nothing but I'm thinking plenty – ye know what I mean?' I don't think my sister did know what she meant, but my mother was given to expressions like this. 'A nod is as good as a wink, eh? Anyway, Lizzie and me are away up to see Chrissie and he'll be there.'

'Who?'

My mother was exasperated. 'The Chantyrazzler, of course. He's going to be there with some stuff he's capauchled off the boat, ye see. So I'll take Chrissie up a wee tin of condensed milk and if the Chantyrazzler has his wee parcel with him, I'll maybe end up with a tin of salmon for the New Year unless your father gets his hands on it first.'

Auntie Lizzie and my mother came back laden to the gunwales with black market goodies: two tins of salmon, tins of fruit and catering-size powdered egg which they would be sharing with the rest of the sisters. They came up the road singing the boy's praises and saying how nice it would be for their niece to marry this felon. Mother arrived in the house to find my father, my sister and my brother all suffering minor burns to their faces and hands, which they had treated with calamine lotion.

She didn't have to ask, she just looked at my father.

'Eh, it was a wee accident with the chip pan, hen.'

'Who was making chips? Chips wasn't on the menu.'

Father got himself tied in knots thinking of how to put his next line. He started to make up a story as he went along. He was good at that. The judge was waiting and the counsel for the defence spoke.

'Ye see, hen, I was making doughnuts and all I did was put the doughnuts in the pan when lo and behold the pan exploded and my doughnuts poofed up to the ceiling.' He paused for breath and my mother came in.

'They poofed up to the ceiling?'

Encouraged, my father went on, pointing heavenwards, 'See that, hen, look up there – there's the proof of the poof on the roof.' The ceiling was dotted with horrible brown stuff, as were the walls. The whole business was getting out of hand, and getting more bizarre by the minute. His next line was a masterly stroke of invention. 'Ye see, hen, they're putting this new rising agent in the flour nowadays, ye jist don't know what you're eatin'. This stuff is called Salt Petre and it's an explosive, ye see.' He was working well. 'Now they should tell folk that so that they know what kind of temperature is critical, ye see. Ah think ah reached the critical and that caused the explosion.' He chanced his arm with his next line.

'Ah think you should report it to the Ministry of Food.' He rested his case.

Quick as a flash my mother retorted, 'Naw, ah'll report it to the Ministry of Defence. Ah'll tell them that ma man has invented a new weapon. Auld Churchill will be delighted. All he needs is a frying pan, six big poofs and he'll have the Hun on the run.'

The whole story was related to me by my sister much later. I had been sound asleep in bed during the pyrotechnics.

Everything we ate was grown in Britain; we were at war and ships were unable to get through from other countries, therefore our staple diet was carrots, leeks, parsley for soup made with a ham shank (my mother once made soup from a sheep's head and unfortunately told us – none of us would eat it). There was mince, pork, leg beef for making beef tea when someone was ill, potatoes, turnip and pulses. Eggs and butter were big treats. There was nothing exotic in the diet but it is said that we were healthier in those days and fewer people died of heart attacks. If anyone had an ear infection, my mother would send out to the chemist and get a small bottle of olive oil, the toast cure having been abandoned by then. She warmed the oil in a teaspoon over boiling water and dropped it into the affected ear. If someone had suggested that she cook with it, she'd have laughed in their face. She did always manage to produce beautiful sponge cakes. Instead of butter or margarine, she used liquid paraffin. It sounds awful but the cakes were delicious.

Before the war my mother and father had been at the pictures when Mr Chamberlain was on the Pathé Pictorial News telling the nation that since his negotiations with Mr Hitler had been unsuccessful, he had ruled out the possibility of our going to war with Germany, his famous 'I'm holding a piece of paper in my hand' speech.

My father's reaction to the great statesmen was, 'Ah don't trust any of these buggers, hen. If ah wis you, ah'd stockpile tins of food, because that Hitler wan is building up tae something.'

He then went down the Barras and came back with 24 tins of

pineapple chunks and said, 'Put these away, hen. When this war starts, you'll no be able to lay yer hands on these. You mark ma words.'

He was right. The war started soon after that, but my father had eaten all the pineapple chunks before Hitler invaded Poland.

The biggest woman in the world moved into the three-room and kitchen flat next door to us: Mrs Stevenson or Big Stevie as she was called. We were all amazed at the size of this woman. My mother and her sisters were hardly sylphs, in fact they were prone to be overweight, but this woman was enormous. My father was heard to remark, 'My God, I've never seen a wumman that size before, she's 25 stone if she's a day. Ah've never seen so many women in wan lump.'

The comedian Harry Gordon, in one of his sketches, said of his character, 'The big woman at the church bazaar, she had so many chins, you thought she was peering over a plate of pancakes.' He was describing Stevie. It seemed to take her days to get up the stairs. Sometimes I would find myself behind her; she'd stop to let me pass and I would hear her laboured grunts and groans. I would be terrified, imagining she was a great monster chasing me. Then she would really frighten me by pausing for breath and saying in a low, scratchy voice, echoing through the close, 'Ah'll cut off your head and sew on a button.'

She always said that – the woman was monstrous. When I rang the bell to get into my house she'd call up, 'Yer mammy's away wi' the sodgers.' It was always a great relief to see my mother opening the door.

Stevie had a small, thin husband called Hercules. We didn't know anything about the classical myth of Hercules; according to the dictionary, 'an ancient hero noted for his great strength, courage and the performance of 12 immense labours', whatever they were. Had we known, we would have thought the name Hercules more suited to Stevie; certainly by the look of her, anyway. We just thought Hercules was a funny name. He was never actually called Hercules. This small, energetic man's name was pronounced 'Herkless', or 'wee Herk', or when Stevie was annoyed she would shout, and her voice would resound throughout the whole building, 'Her . . . kliss!' Then you would hear the wee man's feet running to where his mistress called.

My mother always said that Stevie was a good neighbour and certainly she spent quite a lot of time in the woman's company. Stevie told a good story and was quite dramatic in her delivery. Always interested in subjects medical, my mother would hang on her every word. Stevie would relate how they discovered her condition – I think it was called elephantitis. Anyway, that's what my father called it.

'Aye, Mae, efter ma third, ah blew up like a balloon.'

My mother would feed her lines with, 'Oh, my God, Stevie, is that no terrible. Ye've had a terrible time of it.'

'Oh, aye, ah've hid a time of it.'

She would then grab hold of one of the lumps of fat which were distributed about her body and say, 'See that. That's glandular – everything ah eat goes doon tae ma ankles.'

I'd hear my mother say to her sister, 'See Stevie – she scunners me and fascinates me at the same time.' She didn't fascinate me, she just scunnered and terrified me.

The story goes that Stevie envied my mother her four-room and kitchen and was always alluding to the notion that it was too big for my mother. Certainly the kitchen was small and dark and too small for us all to sit round the banked-up fire of a winter's evening. We rarely used the big room. At that time I was 6, my sister was 16, and the big brother was almost 18, and did my mother not become pregnant at the age of 39 – this wee woman, who looked a good bit older than her age, with my father 'not playing the game', as it was called, on the work front, and a big house to clean. This was the right time for Stevie to get her 'neb' in and she persuaded my mother to exchange houses. I don't remember the move, but we found ourselves in the three-room and kitchen next door. We realised later the reason why Stevie wanted the bigger house. She wanted to take in lodgers, and she did. Her house was filled with men working away from home. Stevie must have 'wachled' about that wee kitchen dishing up breakfasts and dinners while wee Herk did all the running about.

My father and his best pal, Uncle Harry, Auntie Lizzie's husband, entered a new phase of 'homers': the removal of the old black ranges in folk's kitchens and the installation of the interior grate. This new abomination was all the rage because it had a back-boiler that heated the water; it cleaned with a wipe, instead of someone spending half a day cleaning the range with the black lead polish called Zebo; and it used less coal. The man who invented these dreadful fireplaces must be in hell, because nowadays he is still accused by people like myself who have bought old flats and had to pull them out and reinstate an old fireplace in character with the house. To buy a flat with an old range still *in situ* is a flat 'to die for'. But at that time, it was a new career for the do-it-yourself man like my dad. Of course my mother and her five sisters all wanted one. These grates came in a tile of mottled beige. They always reminded me of potted hough.

Something went horribly wrong when my father installed our interior grate in the kitchen. He and Uncle Harry hauled out the old range but they went too far, and left a gaping hole in the wall which let us see into the next tenement flat. There was a terrible to-do when Uncle Harry's big dog Rover made a dive into the woman's house next door. Fortunately she didn't have a fire on at the time. She had her grate built up with pup bricks but the hole was above them so part of her wall above her fire was missing. My mother 'went her mile' as they said.

Father had all kinds of excuses. 'Ah well, ye see, hen, it's the bridges on the chimney are broken and they've pulled down the wall with them. It was gonnae happen anyway, hen, honest. We couldnae foresee the problem. The main thing is the lintel is still intact, so it'll be awright. The hoose'll no faw doon.'

My mother wasn't interested in the mechanics of the problem, it was the 'showing-up' it gave her that she was worried about. 'When are you going to finish the job?'

'Aye, well, ye see we're waiting to "come by" the pups.' The 'come by' was the taking possession of the bricks after they had conveniently fallen off a lorry.

'That doesn't suit me,' said my mother, 'that woman next door can see into my house.'

The unfortunate woman into whose house we could look didn't seem to be the main problem. After the initial fracas about the hole in the wall, she was very civil about the inconvenience. We just moved the kitchen furniture to one end of the room and tried not to stare into her house through the hole in the wall. When the woman was cooking on her new electric cooker, my father would say, 'That wumman's man's getting a big plate of stew the night. How come we're only getting a slice o' gammon?' My mother would give him the high sign to shut his mouth. Yet another showing-up. If anyone raised their voice in anger she would make faces and say, 'Sshhh . . . do you want everyone to know our business?'

The pup bricks eventually arrived and the job was done. Uncle Harry elected to plaster the damaged walls both in our house and next door's. Plastering was one of Uncle Harry's skills – in fact, like my dad, he could turn his hand to anything.

Then there was the decorating. Wallpaper was in short supply during the war, as was paint. Dulux hadn't been invented and there were no B&Qs, so it was distemper. The colour range of distemper was limited: a custard yellow and a bright pink. Someone came up with the idea of combining the two colours in the form of stippling. Nowadays you hear people say, 'Oh, we're ragrolling the walls,' in those days it was stippling. My father loved that job. He was often asked by aunties and neighbours to come and stipple their walls. He'd get a pail of custard-yellow paint and that was the base coat, then he would get hold of a pair of old holey knickers and dip them into the pail of pink paint. The pattern that emerged on the walls was determined by the distribution of holes in the knickers. Often he would get carried away and paint a mural on the wall, thus giving vent to his artistic inclinations. A woman was heard to say, 'This big bloke came up tae stipple ma walls. Ah wis oot and when ah come hame he'd painted hills and a waterfall above ma new interior. Ah jist says, hey you, this is ma hoose no the pristine chapel.'

The yellow and pink distemper must have come in job lots because every house I went into had the same décor as ours.

The house was ready for the new arrival. I knew nothing of this forthcoming event, although I used to hear my dad say to my brother, who was his apprentice at the time, 'Wait 'til wee Malkie comes.' Who was this wee Malkie they were always talking about?

One Sunday morning I was awakened by my Aunt Isa rushing into the bedroom where my sister and I slept. She was almost fainting and I thought something terrible had happened. My sister of course knew the story, but hadn't told me about it. Auntie was shouting, 'It's wee Malkie . . . it's wee Malkie!'

Wee Malkie?

My aunt led me by the hand into the kitchen, where there was a midwife sitting on a chair by the new interior grate, washing a small but very long baby. The nurse smiled at me and beckoned me over to see this new wee boy. I fell in love with him immediately. I turned to the bed recess and there was my mother, smiling proudly. I ran to her and she hugged me. That was a joyous day. He wasn't called Malkie, he was called Robert after my uncle who was in the army and my grandfather.

5

The most beautiful thing we can experience is the mysterious. It is the source of all true art and science.

ALBERT EINSTEIN

My father was out of work. Doctor Wilson, father's doctor, paid a few visits to the house. I was aware of tension in the family but as far as I was concerned, there was no sign of illness. If anyone enquired, my mother was heard to say, 'He's just different from the rest of us. That's what Dr Wilson says.' There was no further explanation, certainly not in my hearing, and my mother seemed satisfied with the 'press release' she handed out. No one was prepared to gainsay her.

Towards the end of his life, when my father was not only different but impossible and positively anti-social in his behaviour, I enquired into his medical records. Doctor Wilson, by then retired, sent me a very nice letter saying that my father had suffered from a nervous breakdown. This explained a lot; why he never held down a job for any length of time, his wandering off without our knowing where he was, his trips to the Renton in Dunbartonshire (with me tagging along) to where his granny had lived and had recently died – the granny whom he had frequently run away from his childhood home to be with when life had become too harsh.

'A nervous breakdown' was a condition that was never discussed in those days, along with other subjects. Illnesses of a psychiatric nature were swept under the carpet. Puberty was described as 'altering', the menopause was 'the change', a miscarriage was said to be, in hushed tones, a 'mis'. Menstruation was a taboo subject not even explained to girls who were going through it; goodness knows how boys coped with their hormonal changes. Sex was never mentioned. Anyway, women in those days didn't have time for sex, they were too busy having weans.

My father's 'difference' was to cause me and my siblings a great deal of social embarrassment, although don't everyone's parents cause embarrassment at some stage or another? In my case, everyone else's father 'held down a good job', whereas my father was in the house playing the musical saw or fixing wirelesses or reading American comics. He wanted to be in Nutwood too, but he was a daddy. When he was in work, the household was peaceful; when he wasn't, he always kept himself busy. Fixing wirelesses was a great pastime for him. Unfortunately, this was not acceptable to my mother because he would set up a table in the big room, and have it littered with valves, condensers, wires. Eventually my mother would get fed up with the mess and throw the lot in the midden. You'd hear my father complain volubly.

'Whit did ye throw that oot fur? A wumman's waiting fur that. Oh, my God, where's ma good soldering bolt? I'll need tae run doon the Barras and get another one – and ma solder, whit hiv ye done wi' ma solder? Aw, where the hell's ma flux?'

He obviously needed this kind of focus to help him in his recovery but it wasn't allowed. I heard unfamiliar words floating around, like 'the Parish'; this seemed to be a place akin to the famous 'grubber'. Parish boots were threatened: it would be a showing-up for children to wear these. I was the only child around at the time, baby Robert was too small to wear boots, so I would be the one wearing them. I imagined them to be heavy boots with steel toecaps and 'segs' hammered into the soles and, since they were meant for workmen, they would be far too big for me. There were plenty of jobs going during the war for a time-served electrician and my father was forced to get out there and get one, and he did. That was apart from all the other jobs he did around and about the district. A wee boy would come to the door and ask, 'My mother says would Mr Pollock come to our house and do a wee job for her in the toilet?'

With a new mouth to feed, it was essential that the wages came in on a regular basis. He worked at Renfrew Aerodrome for a while, and the Clydebank shipyards. One of his favourite stories came from the yards. He had an apprentice with him on a job and one day when they sat down to have their lunch the boy exclaimed, 'Aw, naw, ah've forgot ma pieces.' His sandwiches had been left behind at home.

My father asked, 'Where did you leave them, son?'

The boy replied, 'On the kitchen mantelpiece.'

'That's a shame, son, and here's me goat six big pieces the wife made me. Salmon pieces – she goat the salmon fae some Chantyrazzler aff the boats.'

The boy was drooling. 'Aye, right enough, they look great so they dae.'

'Have you goat a knife there, son?'

'Aye, here ye are,' he said, offering his penknife expectantly.

'Well, son, ah've goat a bit o' string here and ah'm gonnae cut ye a bit.'

Dejectedly the boy said, 'Whit dae ah want wi' a bit o' string?'

Father said, 'You tie that roon yer finger, son, and ye'll no forget yer pieces in the morning.'

He also for a time had a job with Glasgow Corporation, wiring up people's houses for electricity. Only 50 years ago houses were still lit by gas. He would describe the wonder of the new technological age.

'Ah goes intae this wee wumman's hoose an' ah wires up the place an' pits the bulbs in. Ah says tae her, "Right, missus, turn on yer auld gas mantle," an' the wee wumman turns on the auld flame and her hoose's aw kinna yellow lookin'. Then ah says tae her, "Right, missus, sit doon there" an' she sits in her chair and ah says, "Wait 'til ye see this." Ah switches on the electric light an' dae ye know whit she says? She says, "My God, wid ye look at ma hoose – it's filthy!" Is that no great?'

Another night he came home with some object hidden under his jacket.

'Wait 'til ye see this, hen.' This was what was called a 'lucky'. From under his jacket he produced an ornate vase.

'I wis wiring up a big toff's hoose up the West End an' ah was in the attic and this wis jist lying in a corner gathering dust. See that, hen, it's a genuine Wedgwood vase. See it's signed at the bottom, C.V. Wedgwood.'

My mother raised her eyes to heaven and said, 'My God, ye'll get the jail.' The expression 'you'll go to the jail' was never used in our house, you always 'got the jail'.

'Naw, bit whit dae ye think of it, hen? Lovely, intit? It's an objay dartay, hen.'

Mother's reply was, 'Ah'm no struck. It's just something else to lie up and down the house and anyway it's awful old-fashioned.'

'Jist you wait and see what ah'm gonnae do with it, hen.'

Father took this beautiful Wedgwood vase, he bored a hole in the bottom of it, wired it up and made a lamp out of it. My mother was quite pleased and bought a shade to put on it. This, of course, completely ruined the look and the value of the piece.

I realise now that my father and I shared a common fault: a low boredom threshold. This was probably why he didn't hold a job for any length of time. He simply got fed up with routine. There was always a new and more exciting challenge just around the corner. Whilst I have the ability to structure my work, he was at the mercy of whatever came along. If he had a job that he enjoyed, he saw it through to the finish. If it was boring, he abandoned it halfway through. These jobs were what my mother called his 'unfinished symphonies'. One accusation that was levelled at him by a relative was, 'Aye, Sam, you're very clever but you don't apply yourself to anything.' When people made these statements I would weep for my father and wish that he'd had greater inner strength. He always seemed to be put down but never really given any guidance. To this very day if I feel like a taking a day off or just want to laze about, I am sharply reminded of the old work ethic and can hear my mother's voice: 'You'll come to nothing and end up like your father.' A dreadful impeachment of a man; however, from her point of view, a man was expected to keep his family fed and clothed. In those days men brought home the bread and women kept house: that was how it was. I know I have inherited many traits from him – the ability to tell a story, an appreciation of the arts – yet it is his inability to stick at what he had set out to do that has haunted me throughout my life.

My mother always seemed 'trachled', what with the new baby, the other four in the family, washing, cleaning, trying to make a quarter pound of mince cut thin go five ways, then her sister-in-law and her new baby came to stay with us. It was a busy house and my mother was at the hub of it. She was never very well and when she complained about her health we just thought that she was moaning. Yet she would never see her 60th birthday. My sister did a lot of the babysitting to let my mother get out, and her own life was hard enough, working six days a week in the C&A millinery department. Her half-day on a Tuesday was spent ironing for the family. Neither my father nor my big brother was expected to contribute to the house cleaning. If Mother was ill, one of her sisters would come in and clean. When my sister married, I took on her chores.

Whether it was part of his illness, I don't know, but Father didn't seem to worry about anything. When things got too hot in the house he would go AWOL and face the consequences on his return. It didn't seem to bother him that my mother would shout at him. 'God, wumman, you could start a row in an empty hoose' – that's all he would say and go into the big room to tinker with one of his wireless sets, or he would say to me, 'Get your coat on, hen. There's a good picture on in the Parade, a dancing and singing picture. Slip out and don't let your mother see you.' I knew this would lead to a row later but I never could resist a dancing and singing picture. Afterwards my father and I would tap-dance down the road to face the music. He really was a good tap-dancer. Sometimes he would carry me on his shoulders, whistle 'Pop Goes the Weasel' and do a little skip which made me laugh. We'd never know if, when we got home, it would be the silent treatment or the 'you'll make that wean as irresponsible as yourself' treatment. It was usually the latter; my mother was up front with her emotions.

One behavioural aspect my mother never had to worry about was the evil 'drink'. My father was rarely in a pub. In those days women often used to stand outside factories and wait for their men to come out and when they did, the wives would grab the pay packet from them before they could go and drink it. Sometimes he'd talk about going to the pub to see someone about a 'wee job' and boast about drinking two milk stouts. He felt this was the right thing to say. My father would never have raised a hand to my mother, he wouldn't have dared. Looking back, I suppose my father didn't have the responsible attitude to marriage that my mother had; he was the eternal boy who just wouldn't be tamed.

Dorothy

On many occasions my father took me with him on the 'wee jobs' and this enabled me to observe other households apart from our own. There was a single-end in Bridgeton where a young woman lived alone with her new baby; her husband was in the war. The house was beautiful but tiny. Everything was in its place and there was an atmosphere of organisation and discipline. Her sister was with her that day and they were both slim and beautifully dressed. They looked like girls out of the *Woman's Own* magazine. They even had make-up on. What impressed me most about this young woman's organisational skills was that she could obviously not afford a cot, so she had pulled out the top drawer of a chest and made a bed for the baby in the drawer, which sat on a scrubbed white table. She had made a little palace out of this one room and her happiness spilled over onto me.

Another house we went to was a bungalow with a garden. I played in the garden while my father was working in the house. I discovered lupins. Dad said, 'They're wee foxes' gloves, hen.' Ever after that I called lupins foxgloves.

My father had a friend called Laurence Kirbie who lived in a room and kitchen in Eveline Street. He had known Laurence since he had served his time with him and they always had a laugh together.

My mother would say, 'I hope you didn't take the wean up to that character's house.' That character, as she called him, always greeted us warmly. At the weekends his attire was a silk dressing-gown; he'd have a glass in his hand and a cigarette in the other. His lady – she wasn't his wife – would appear from the bedroom, also in a dressing-gown and looking very glamorous. I sensed there was something different about this relationship because 'the lady' always had a strange little smile on her face. She slinked around the small living-room cum kitchen and draped herself on the arm of Laurence's chair. Laurence would offer my father some of his 'medicine' but my father always refused and asked for a strong cup of tea. That was his tipple. In fact it embarrassed me when he was working in someone's house and before he was invited he would say to the woman, 'I'd like some tea. A nice strong cup, ma'am.' I wished that he'd wait until the woman had offered it.

Larry Kirbie and my father would reminisce about their boyhood and it was always a happy visit. On our return home I'd hear my mother say something disparaging about a 'bidey in'. My father would say that the woman was very nice. My mother would retort, 'And so she should be very nice, it's aw she's got to do.'

There was a man who had a small shop near us in Sword Street. He dealt in fabrics and occasionally he managed to find some bales of material which people would queue up for, of course. The cry would go out amongst the little girls, 'Mr King's got ribbons.' We'd all dash round to the shop and watch him cut off strips of silky fabric with pinking-shears for a penny a time. My stock soared with my friends when my dad got the job of wiring up his shop. Years later I was in the Sword Street warehouse choosing some fabric when I was invited up to Mr King's posh office. I had tea with him and was proud when he told me how my father had wired up his first shop. Now, of course, Remnant Kings is a family-run empire.

Another request at the door was a woman who enquired, 'Is this the man who flushes your panels?'

'Yes,' my mother replied.

'Could he come up and do ma loaby doors?'

I never understood the panel-flushing business. My father would take a perfectly good door made of natural wood with lovely panelling and he would flush it with hardboard, then he would paint and grain it to make it look like real wood. He could do all the patterns, which again gave vent to his artistic talents. He would say to the woman, 'Right, missus, I can dae ye burr walnut or pyranna pine. Please yourself, ah've goat the tools. Wid ye prefer an oak? Ah kin dae that as well.' The woman would make her choice and Father would varnish the hardboard then run a comb-like tool up and down the wood to create the grain. Eventually people got fed up with the grained doors and just went for the '50s style of flat painted wood.

My big brother was 'called up' and went into the Merchant Navy. My mother was bereft. 'Oh, Lizzie, I've got one son in the war and another in the pram.' God knows the stress mothers went through in those days. I can't imagine what her days must have been like. Fortunately she wouldn't have to wait too long, as the war was nearly ending.

The household was fraught with anxiety during this time and

anxiety didn't suit my father. He seemed to worry about things to a certain level then he would reach his cut-out point. He was a tall, thin man who smoked too much, was teetotal, and lived until he was 84. Genetics probably come into the equation but I somehow think his attitude to life accounted, to some extent, for his longevity. He also had wider interests than my mother. Going out with my father was always an adventure. We visited the Museum and Art Galleries in Kelvingrove.

'Now you see that building, hen. The architect that designed that wanted it to face the other way roon. But the builders built it back tae front, ye see. When this man Simpson, the architect, saw whit the builders had done wi' his plans, he was that disappointed he committed suicide. Threw hi'sel' in the Kelvin.'

It was a well-known apocryphal story but I believed it and thought my dad was very knowledgeable. We'd walk round the art galleries and Father would explain the paintings to me. There was a wee story for each one. One of the pictures called *The Tinker's Camp*, which is now housed in the Burrell, had in the forefront an old tinker. My father said, 'See that, hen? Whit dae ye think is wrong with that picture?' I puzzled but couldn't come up with the answer. 'Well, I'll tell ye, hen. See the old man's feet? The artist has painted them young. Those feet don't belong to an old man.' He was absolutely right. I've posed that question to my own children.

In his uneducated way he would discuss the paintings and, whether he was right or wrong, he taught me to look and trained my eyes to appreciate. He loved the pictures so much that I believe he taught himself about art. In the '50s, when Dali's painting *St John of the Cross* was purchased for the city, Father and I went to see it. 'See that, hen? That's awful hard tae paint that. The way Jesus is looking down on the world. Foreshortening that's called. Anybody can paint a man standing up but it takes skill tae paint a man lookin' doon.' He had the right words and I understood what he meant.

In search of silence and peace he'd take me down to Uncle Archie's in the Renton. Uncle Archie would make a pot of strong tea and they'd sit and blether. Then we would stroll along the banks of the Leven and my father would tell me about his childhood. How beautiful his mother was, Annie, a girl from Islay, and how his father made life hard for her. Only later did I hear that my father was born out of wedlock and that he always felt resented by his father. His mother made up for this lack of love from his other parent. My father at the end of his life made me promise that at all costs he would be buried with his mother. I kept that promise, but in so doing he had to be buried with the father he hated as well.

He told me stories about his boyhood adventures and he'd imitate one of his schoolteachers in her rendition of poems, doing all the actions:

> The wind one morning sprang up from sleep,
> 'Now for a frolic, now for a leap,
> Now for a madcap galloping chase,
> I'll cause a commotion in every place.'

That would get a laugh and he'd parody 'Young Lochinvar':

> 'Haste ye, haste ye,' the maiden cried,
> 'Don't stand there and blether,
> If ma faither sees ye here,
> Your bluid will stain the heather.'

'Tell me another one, Daddy.'

> The boy stood on the burning deck,
> His feet were covered in blisters,
> He had not troosers to put on,
> And so he wore his sister's.

He had a fund of these parodies and together with his gestures they had me in kinks. Sometimes they'd degenerate into little songs such as:

> Oh Mrs Goagilee
> Come tae bed alang wi' me
> Ah'll gie ye a cup o' tea
> Tae keep yer belly warm.

Dorothy

We once passed a garden where raspberries were growing and had ripened. He helped me through a hole in the fence and we stole some. I'd never tasted them before. Even now I never taste a raspberry but I remember how delicious was that illicit fruit.

6

Hope is itself a species of happiness, and, perhaps, the chief happiness that this world affords.

SAMUEL JOHNSON

My brother's ship had been torpedoed. Then he was taken prisoner. My mother was out of her mind.

Towards the end of the war, men were coming home, not only walking wounded, but those psychologically damaged for the rest of their lives. You'd hear expressions like 'He's awful bad with his nerves' or 'He's no the boy he was.'

One night, when I was six, my sister was babysitting me and the wee brother. My mother and father were out at the Pattisons, their bi-weekly Saturday visit. There was a great noise of banging at the front door. My sister answered it, and as she was standing in the hall she was shouting, 'Our Jack's back from the war.' There was my brother, just 19. All the neighbours came in and they shook him by the hand. Somebody ran down the road in the blackout to get our parents. When they came home, my father stood back as they entered the house so that my mother could approach him first. It was very quiet. She just stood there and looked at him and kept repeating, 'Oh, my son . . . oh, my son.'

I didn't know at the time, but 25 years earlier my mother's brother had gone to the First World War. They had the same name, were the same age and our Jack and my uncle looked very alike. But Uncle Jack had been killed in the trenches by mustard gas.

Our neighbour Stevie said, 'I've got rations in there, I'll go and get them.' All the neighbours chipped in and we had a celebration with scarce food.

Dorothy

After that my brother stayed in a lot. Slept a lot. He occasionally took a wee bad turn. He received an honourable discharge from the Merchant Navy.

I will never forget my father coming home one day in a terrible state. He tried hard but he couldn't stop the tears. My mother asked, 'What's wrong with you?'

'Oh, Mae, ah've jist seen a terrible thing. I heard aboot a warrant sale in somebody's hoose in the Gallowgate and ah'd never been tae wan, an' ah'd been told there was a good wireless for sale. So ah goes up tae this hoose and Mae, ye widnae believe it, it wis a young woman and her two weans that wis being thrown oot because she couldnae pay her rent. Mae, ye've never seen anything like it. Aw her stuff was taken off her. Ah tried tae stop them, Mae, but they wouldnae listen tae me. Oh, my God, they're terrible things they warrant sales. The wee lassie wis greetin' and so were her weans – ah'll never forget it as long as ah live. Ah couldnae dae anything for her, so ah jist gave her ten shillings and ah gret aw the way up the road.'

My father wasn't well for days after that.

He was yet again on the lookout for an interesting occupation when one night he was on the top deck of a tram-car travelling east along Alexandra Parade from the town. He was reading the *Evening Citizen* small ads section, where the Glasgow Corporation were advertising for certain kinds of pipe lengths – something like three inches in diameter. They needed a large quantity. When the tram-car stopped opposite Wills' cigarette factory, my father looked down on the north side of the road and there in a yard owned by the Glasgow Corporation was a large quantity of what seemed to be the kind of piping for which another department of the Corporation was looking. The next day he went up to the yard, looked round, and sure enough they were exactly the right size. He approached the supervisor and asked him what was happening to the pipes. He told my father that they were just scrap and they would eventually be disposed of. Dad made him an offer, 'Ah could take them aff yer hands, bring up a lorry and take them away.'

Obviously the man could see a few pounds for himself in this deal. 'Call it 50 quid and you can take the lot.'

Father rushed home and made the mistake of asking my mother for the money. Her reply was, 'If I had £50, I'd have a policeman watching it.' He told her what he needed the money for and she nearly hit the roof. 'Do you mean you're going to buy pipes off the Corporation and then sell them back to the Corporation?'

Father said, 'Aye, hen, no one'll be any the wiser.'

'Are you kidding? You'll get the jail.'

My father assured her that he wouldn't do anything further about the transaction but he did. Somehow or other he got hold of the money and someone with a lorry. He took the pipes straight down to the other section of the Glasgow Corporation, did the deal, and came home with £300. I suppose it was a slightly dubious business deal, but my mother saw it as a grand felony. She kept the money under her mattress for weeks, ready to give it back if the police came to the door. She went on about it so much that my father feared she might be right, and they had many sleepless nights over it. Eventually, when nothing happened and the Fraud Squad failed to appear, she took a wee trip up to a woman in James Orr Street who was selling an Indian lamb fur coat. It was the most frivolous purchase she'd ever made in her life, and although she enjoyed wearing it, she felt it had come from crime. I never understood why she loved that coat so much. It was a square-cut wartime style and as she walked down the road in it, she looked like a wee fur box.

My father purchased a motorbike with his share of the money, an old Ariel. One day he arrived at my school with it and I was thrilled when in front of my pals, he told me to hop on the back and gave me a lift home. 'Come on, hen, I'll give you a wee run doon tae the Renton.' He obviously wanted to show it off to Uncle Archie.

We had many runs on the bike but eventually the machine gave up and he never got another. The story goes that the insurance was still in place and, in order to recoup his investment, he took the bike up to the Sugarolly Mountains, now called Easterhouse, and set fire to it. The bike was burning away good style when a policeman wandered up to him, catching him in the act. My father stuttered and stammered about how it had caught fire accidentally. The policeman was sympathetic and ran off to get a pail of water. While my father was fanning the flames with his bunnet, the policeman was trying to put the fire out.

7

A happy childhood often spoils the chance of an interesting adult.

ROBERTSON DAVIES

The war in Europe was coming to an end. Apart from news broadcasts of Allied victories and the liberation of France, the word was going round that the Germans were eating black bread. 'Black bread, they're eating black bread.' This was the word on the street and it conjured up a terrible deprivation.

As a child I had no memory of eating bananas, but if anyone asked me what was my favourite fruit I always said 'Bananas.' I'd seen the coloured posters of them in the Co-operative in Sword Street, along with pictures of packets of cornflakes and Stork margarine. None of these items were on sale between 1939 and 1945. In the school playground the word was passed around that a girl had a banana. We all crowded round her while she ate it. This was a huge event. She offered some of her pals a bit of the skin; I managed to get a bit, too, but it tasted awful. I wondered what all the fuss was about.

Eventually the big day came. The war in Europe was over. There were bonfires and dancing in the streets. Of course the war with Japan was still raging. I don't remember much about Nagasaki or Hiroshima, only that it brought the war to a conclusion. The nuclear age had begun. My generation and their children have lived their lives with the threat of that holocaust hanging over their heads. I do remember overhearing a conversation between my parents and the Pattisons when they were discussing the testing of the atom bomb. My mother said, 'Well, Mary, what worries me about it is that the whole world could cave in and then where would we be?' I was horrified. If the world caved in, my little brother would die. I hugged him and cried until finally I fell asleep.

With the end of the war we started rebuilding our lives. We would have street lighting again; we could take down the big curtains that kept the light from being seen by the Jerries; baffle walls and the air-raid shelters were removed; father had a new job wiring up new houses and I had a new teacher, Miss Picken.

I believe that under the cloak of the blackout some alien beings from a strange planet landed on earth. They called themselves primary schoolteachers and took up positions in Alexandra Parade school for the sole purpose of making my life a misery. Miss Picken was like nothing I had ever seen on Planet Earth. She was a Desperate Dan lookalike with a chin like a sink, a full-blown moustache and designer stubble. She always wore a kilt. She might even have tossed the caber at weekends. She was big in the SNP, in fact, rumour later had it that she single-handedly lifted the Stone of Destiny from Westminster Abbey. She was heavily corseted; this was obvious because of a stray corset-bone that stuck through her jumper. She went in, she went out, and when it came to her top half she went out and forgot to come back in. She always spoke as if she were in pain, with a kind of whine in the voice. Perhaps, like Miss Marshall, she'd had a 'disappointment' and if she had, it certainly showed in the sour expression. The snow was always blowing in her face.

'Right now, boys and girls, hands together and heads bowed. Our Father . . .' As she was invoking the power of the Divinity she was lovingly fingering her big belt, and as sure as God was in heaven I was going to do something that day that would get me three strokes of that belt.

I would look round and find another fiend observing me: Jessie McCardley. Oh, how I hated her. She had two front teeth missing and fangs at each side of the space. Her glasses had a sticky plaster over one lens. She was built like an ox. We used to call her 'Pansy Potter the strong man's daughter'. She frightened the living daylights out of me. Then she gave me the sign. She'd hold up her right hand which she made into a fist, she'd point at me, then hold up four fingers. This meant she was going to get me and batter me at four o'clock. I often wonder what happened to that girl. She's probably taken early retirement from the SAS by now. I have not given her real name for security purposes. She may be still around with her aggressive tendencies. I would do a runner after school, but she always managed to catch up with me and kick me between Ingleby Drive and Armadale Street.

Well, that was two rotten things I had to look forward to. The only blessing I had was in the friendship with my wee pals: Rita Watson, Nancy McKay and Sheila McInnes. I spent many happy hours with them climbing dykes in back courts, dressing up, and playing at shops and post offices. The Dennistoun Palais was at the end of Roselea Drive and there was a bit of spare ground beside it which in the summer was a mass of ox-eye daisies. Sometimes the side door of the Palais was open so we could look in and see the dancers and listen to the big band playing the latest tunes. Nancy McKay lived over shops in Duke Street but her back court was elevated and was a smooth tarmacadamed area, nice and clean. One day we set up a little house made of old sheets and blankets; we were playing at houses with our dolls when some bad boys came in the 'back' and started to rough us up. Much to our dismay they pulled down our house, threw our dolls about and then, when they could think of nothing else nasty to do, one of them said, 'Come on, we'll pull their balls.' We couldn't think what they meant. Before they could carry out their threat and get a big surprise, somebody from an upstairs window answered our screams for help. 'Away and leave these wee lassies alone or I'll come amongst you!' They didn't answer back, they just ran away.

Tenement 'dunnies' were places that always held terror for us. They were dark places between the closes and the backcourts. Every one of them was different. I think the architects designed them that way to frighten the weans. A girl told us that there was a 'dunnie' in Garthland Drive that had false teeth growing up the wall. False teeth growing up the wall? This was terrifying but intriguing. We were hyped up with excitement as we walked along the Drive. Sometimes we'd stop on the way and decide that we didn't want to see this dreadful thing, but the girl drove us on by accusing us of being 'fearties'. We finally arrived at the close, entered the dunnie and gingerly approached the macabre sight. There they were, growing up the corner of the wall. Great gnashing false teeth. One quick look was enough – we all screamed and ran away. The suggestion had been implanted in our minds and what we saw was what we believed was there. It was actually fungus growing up the wall.

The school trip was imminent. Miss Picken sat on the front desk facing the class. This was the position she took up when she wanted to be chatty. That was a sight to frighten the Germans. Her Directoire knickers, the kind that came down to the knee, were exposed. In the winter they were interlock and came in three shades: grey, greyish pink and fawn (we call that taupe nowadays). We always knew when summer had arrived; Miss Picken would treat us to a sight of her silk Directoires. She would start her little talk by clearing out her sinuses and that was enough to put you off your school dinners. Then she'd stick her hankie up the knickers. I had a pocket in my knickers but I always kept my digestive biscuit there. That was my play piece.

'Now, boys and girls,' she whined, 'we're coming to the highlight of the school year. The school trip.' It wasn't a highlight for me.

'This year we'll be taking the tram-car to Rouken Glen Park. If the weather is inclement, we'll be camping out in the BB hut in Possilpark. Either way I think it'll be quite a jolly day. Now, what have we to remember to bring with us?'

Edward the Elephant, a boy who had done something dreadful in his pants one day in the drill hall when I was partnering him in the Roger de Coverley, put up his hand. 'Please, Miss, wur pieces.'

'Edward, I do wish you'd learn to speak properly. It's not "wur pieces". It's our sendwidges . . . saaaaangwidges. What else have we to remember?'

Everyone was frightened to make a suggestion.

'Well, of course, as I always say, dunderheads have no memory. Now where did I put my hankie?'

One little boy put his hand up and innocently offered, 'Please, Miss . . . eh . . . eh . . . it's up yer kilt.'

None was meant but offence was taken.

'Willie McKechnie! Come out here and stand with your face in that corner. I will not tolerate such language. There will be no language in my classroom.'

This was a very confusing statement. Surely language was what this ten-year ordeal was all about?

'I'll deal with you, boy, after the bible reading.' To add to all this, wee William wet his pants and had to be sent out.

'Every year I remind you children and every year someone arrives at the tram-car without their "tinnie". You must bring your tinnie. What are you going to drink your hot soup out of if you don't bring your tinnie?' The school trip was beginning to hold no joy for us. 'And let me make one thing perfectly clear. On this trip there will be no behaviour.' What did that mean? 'So what are we not going to bring with us this year, Edward?'

'Please, Miss . . . eh . . .eh . . .'

'Speak up, boy, and don't stutter.' A remark guaranteed to make the boy stumble over his words.

'Please, Miss . . . eh . . . ah cannae remember.'

'Yes you do, Edward. You did a bad thing with it.'

'Please, Miss . . . ah remember, Miss . . . eh, ma bow anna arra.'

'That is correct: your bow annanarra. I mean your bow and arrow.'

'Please, Miss, kin ah bring ma peashooter?'

'You certainly cannot. Just bring your tinnie, you can't do much damage with that. Just remember, Edward, it's all down in the headmaster's big black book what you did last year. And baby Jesus saw you, too.'

By this time wee William had reappeared in the classroom and taken up his position with his face to the wall. Miss Picken caught sight of him doing the unmentionable thing that brought some comfort to a distressed little boy.

'William McKechnie! Keep your face to that wall and stop doing that. You'll go to the bad fire for that.' William was now laughed at by the rest of the class and he became a quivering little heap of humiliation. Miss Picken went back to her own desk and announced, 'Now, boys and girls, the text for today is from . . .' her hands were fervently clutching her bit of comfort; her belt. I think the text that day may have been 'Suffer the little children to come unto Me'.

It was a day of indifferent weather for the school trip. We all boarded the tram-car for the long journey across Glasgow to Rouken Glen

Park, our tinnies tied round our necks with string, and Jessie McCardley making the outset a misery for me with her nipping and surreptitious elbow-jabbing. During the sports events, she tripped me up in the egg and spoon race and put paid to my hope of winning a prize. 'The 'sangwidges' didn't survive the journey; they were soggy and warm and the milk was turned. I hated milk at the best of times. I felt sick on the way home, I had pains in my legs and was glad to stumble up the stairs crying for sympathy from my mother. 'Jessie McCardley stole my tinnie.'

There was no sympathy. She was all harassed. 'See . . . I don't know if I'm making soup or washin.' One of her favourite harassed phrases. 'Look at the state of you.'

Then there was a look of concern on her face. 'Your knees are all swollen.'

'My legs are sore again.'

'I've had enough of the sore legs, I'm taking you to Dr Brown right away. I know what he'll say: "It's just growing pains".'

I certainly was growing at a rate; I was the tallest in the class. The pains in the legs, however, turned out to be rheumatism. I spent all the summer holidays in bed with my legs wrapped in scratchy blankets, orders of Dr Brown. After a few weeks my mother half-carried me up to Alexandra Park for the sake of some sunshine and fresh air. I was hardly allowed to even walk around. We fed the ducks, which took all of five minutes, then we just sat and watched them. If I tried to climb the palings around the pond my mother would shout, 'Ah, ah, here comes the man.' If I wandered around the shrubs behind the park bench she'd shout, 'Ah, ah, here comes the man.' She could see the man, Auntie Lizzie could see the man, but I couldn't see the man.

When my mother told the doctor what she'd done, he chastised her for going against his orders, but I was well enough to go back to school in September 1946. I was glad to get out of the house.

Joy upon joy, Miss Haining, our new teacher, was someone who belonged to the human race. I started to enjoy school. I was no longer bullied, because I was 'not too well'. The downside was that because of the rheumatics I had to wear warm lisle stockings with suspenders attached to my liberty bodice, a complicated vest reinforced with tape and fleecy-lined. No one else had to wear lisle stockings and I envied the other girls with their top hose. My mother was afraid I'd take rheumatic fever, which was not unusual in those days: 'If you don't wear stockings you could end up with a murmur at your heart.'

She knew what she was about when it came to child-rearing, but she rarely gave adequate explanations for anything. I was never allowed to wear anything but good stout shoes. I asked her if I could wear sandals on good days like the other girls.

'No, your feet'll spread.'

'Can I wear wellingtons on wet days?'

'No, they'll sweat your feet.'

I could understand her reasons up to a point, but my father flummoxed me with his reason for not eating too much ice-cream. 'Ice-cream paralyses your stomach for four hours.' I don't think medical science knows about that one.

I came home from school one day to find Dad sitting by the banked-up fire and on the fire-guard he had written in chalk, 'This is a fire-guard.' He was going through one of his bad times again.

At the cinema after the war they showed film of the results of the atrocities in concentration camps in Germany. Before they came on screen, the manager of the cinema would make an announcement that children were to be taken into the foyer during these scenes. My father would say, 'Jist coorie doon and the man'll no see ye.' The sight of the emaciated people and the bodies being thrown into mass graves, ordinary people like ourselves, only naked, was too much for me; in some way I seemed to shut off, although I had nightmares about them later. What really made me 'coorie doon' was when they showed the Three Stooges. I couldn't bear to watch their cruelty to one another, especially when the bald one had sticky tape on his head and another Stooge pulled it off slowly. I had to close my eyes. What never failed to affect me, though, was the way people became inured to what they saw in the atrocity films, and how they would describe a thin person as 'a Belsen horror'.

The Park cinema, near my school, had a strange custom. There was an usher, a small thin man, neatly mustachioed, who wore maroon livery a couple of sizes too big for him, with a peaked cap heavily worked with gold braid. On his coat were enormous, sagging epaulettes also in gold with fringes. He was a cross between Hermann Goering and the Student Prince. After everyone was seated and before the programme started, he'd go round the cinema with what looked like a fly-spray and spray everyone with DDT, nowadays known to have carcinogenic properties. There we sat, while this man showered us with a dangerous chemical. On the other hand, the cinema at the top of Millerston Street, the Scotia, had no such routine and you always came out playing host to a flea. My father would say, 'See the Scotia – you're itchin' to get in and scratchin' to get out.'

The pictures figured largely in everyone's life. Two or three nights a week we went to the pictures. Everyone had their favourite genre: men and boys liked the cowboys and Indians; women liked the love stories, and many, including my mother, lived a vicarious romantic life through the pictures. A great pastime in our house was re-enacting scenes from films. For all my mother had her broad streak of practicality and gravitas, she enjoyed her wee bit of fantasy in her favourite film stars. They would temporarily carry her away from the hardships of her life. One night she came home from the pictures and stood at the kitchen door, her eyes shining as she quoted dramatically, 'To be the wife of Johann Strauss is not a little thing.' That was all, then she put the kettle on and made a cup of tea.

American films were what people wanted to see. A common cry, when looking up the paper to see what was on, was 'Oh no, I'm not going to see that. It's a British picture.' In those days British pictures were about English middle-class people whom we didn't want to know about. The exception was Laurence Olivier in *Wuthering Heights*. I can still sob at the scene when Cathy calls, 'Heathcliffe . . . Heathcliffe.'

The big brother was a great quoter of lines from the pictures. He was guaranteed to make women swoon with a line he made his own; 'How can I live by candlelight after I've seen the sun?' As we say in Glasgow, 'whit a stoater'. I used to be asked to do Bette Davis lines because I looked like her. I didn't want to look like Bette Davis: I saw myself as Lana Turner.

My big sister, who worked in the C&A, had a customer who frequently gave her complimentary seats for the Empress theatre on

Monday nights. I used to love it when she took me. There I was introduced to the Fraser Neil Players. Little did I know that ten years later I would be working for Fraser Neil. I saw *Smiling Through*, which I'd also seen on film with Jeanette McDonald and Nelson Eddy. The panto in the Empress really got me going; it was the way the Principal Boy in tights strode about the stage and jumped on and off a boat with sword in hand. I thought she was wonderful. I think the panto was *Dick Whittington*, never to be forgotten when I played the boy many years later because in it was the famous line when the Principal Girl, Alice, is searching for her love: 'Here we are, ten miles from London and still no sign of Dick.' I'll never know how we got away with that.

Sitting in the Empress Theatre at nine years of age I was thrilled with the spectacle. I turned to my sister and asked, 'How much will she get paid for that?'

My sister replied, 'About £8 a week.'

I was amazed that someone who was all dressed up and was dancing and singing on a stage would get £8 a week as well. After that, when I caw Cyd Charisse or my favourite, Vera Ellen, dancing on the big screen, I thought to myself, 'They're getting £8 a week!' It seemed an incredibly thrilling way to earn a living.

I totally identified with Margaret O'Brien. She was a little girl like me. She could cry at the drop of a hat – her weeping scenes were legendary. I sent a letter to Burbank, Hollywood, and got a signed photograph from her. I tried to cry just by thinking about it but it didn't work. I had to have a reason. Not long after that I had a reason not just to cry but to cry hysterically.

I was taken to see *The Wizard of Oz* and here was a girl called Dorothy. I became the character and went around quoting Judy Garland's lines. 'I don't think you're in Kansas now, D'rothy.' I got great fun out of playing the character and one day I found a little dog who was exactly like Toto. My cup was running over. I took the dog home. I might have expected the reaction; the bubble burst.

'I'll Toto ye, I'll give ye Toto. We're having no dogs in this house! I've enough with your father, and Granny's coming to stay here. So you can take Toto back to where he came from. Somebody'll be looking for him.'

I was in such a state that she agreed to keep him overnight. The next day I came home from school; no Toto. 'The dog ran away,' my mother lied. I was beside myself with grief. I ran out of the house and spent hours in and out of closes, down dunnies and back courts shouting, 'Toto . . . Toto.' There was no Tin Man, Scarecrow or Cowardly Lion to accompany me. All I got was folk sticking their heads out of the doors wondering what all the noise was about.

Mostly the replies were to the effect, 'Away and gie us peace.'

I never saw Toto again. When I returned home, in a state of misery, I got battered in a circle for staying out after dark.

8

Children have more need of models than of critics.

JOSEPH JOUBERT

*G*ranny was brought home to our house to die in the same bed recess where three years earlier my little brother had been born. She had everything wrong with her, not least old age; the old body was breaking down. At 74 she looked the way many 90-year-olds look today. She would die in the bosom of her family; that was the way of it. Her quality of life so diminished that she was allowed to go. There was no medical or chemical way of keeping her alive. Her husband, old Robert Gourlay, had died in 1936 at the age of 67; the year before I was born. He had what some people call a 'good death', propped up in bed, surrounded by his family while he held court. His last words were to his wife, 'Maria, send these young people away. They don't want to sit and watch an old man dying.' He died that night, having made his peace with everyone and with a good exit line. Of course Grandfather had been an actor.

He was born of an Irish family from Derry. His father and mother, Terence and Hannah, sailed over to Scotland, landing in Ardrossan around 1870. From there they walked with their children and all their belongings to Kilwinning, where they set up house in Dubbs Cottage. They moved around quite a bit after that and lived in Old Monkland, Cumbernauld, then back to Kilwinning, where my grandfather was born.

No one knows how or why my grandfather became an actor, but he toured England with a theatre company called the Latimer Players. During the course of the tour, being rather fond of a 'refreshment', he happened upon a hostelry in St Helens in Lancashire, where he met my grandmother, Maria Brown. The bold Robert must have thought he'd died and gone to heaven, as Maria was a publican's daughter.

Granny's father died and the pub was sold. By this time Robert seems to have given up on his theatrical career. Robert and Maria moved to Glasgow where they set up home in Barrack Street, Dennistoun. He was employed by the Glasgow Corporation as the driver of a horse-drawn tram-car but after a while was summarily dismissed, having been found drunk in charge of a horse and tram and endangering the lives of his passengers. The rest of his working life was spent as a storeman/clerk.

He must have got a grip of himself after that and settled down. During the week both he and Grandmother would work hard; he at his storeman duties and she taking in washing and mangling. In his spare time he seems to have been a compulsive performer. On a Saturday night he and Granny would both dress up in their finery and visit various pubs in the Gallowgate. He could be seen swaggering along the road in the Calton, near the Barras, and on passing a beggar he would turn to his wife and say, 'Maria, give that poor person thruppence.' Maria would reach into her moth-eaten reticule and part with some of her hard-earned money.

When they got home, in order to give him an audience, their children would be hauled from their beds and made to sit round the kitchen in the early hours of the morning while their father performed scenes from the melodramas in the Henry Irving style. He would recite monologues and sing sad songs with words such as:

> Poor poor poor Nellie Brown,
> We will never see her more,
> Gone's the sunshine of our home,
> Gone to a far far distant shore.

This evoked tears from his audience, which was the desired effect, and brought back memories of the two children who had died of the dreaded diphtheria.

Apart from Saturday nights, they lived a life of respectable poverty, their meals at times consisting of bread and dripping followed by broken biscuits. Now with the death of Grandmother, this family chapter was coming to a close.

Dorothy

Death was something that was faced with dignity. Granny was laid out in her coffin in our big room. The blinds were drawn to let everyone know there was a death in the house. Family and friends visited to view the corpse and say their farewells. People felt obliged to dig up the time-worn phrases:

'She's come right back to herself.'

'Aye, so she has. The years have dropped away.'

'Gone to a better place.'

Many cups of tea were handed round and a bottle of whisky was produced to give the men a 'wee hauf'.

My cousin Isabel and I would sneak into the room, fascinated by seeing Granny lying there, looking quite different from how she had before. We would touch her cold face and jump back with a shriek. Isabel had a good idea to cheer up Granny. She sang a song and did a tap-dance for her. My mother dragged us out of the room, horrified. We were fed up with all the solemnity.

Isabel and I enjoyed the funeral. Tables had been set up in the big room after Granny had been taken away by the men in the family. (Women never attended burials in those days.) Out came the steak pies, potatoes and peas. My cousin and I sat opposite one another, the minister said grace and we got wired into the food. This was a state occasion. I had been told to behave myself and I really meant to be good but during the meal I had occasion to say to my cousin, 'Would you pass me over the pea dish?' trying out a posh accent. She went into fits of laughter. 'You said the pea dish.' We giggled uncontrollably and were put out of the room to finish our meal in the kitchen.

Later we all sang Victorian parlour songs and when Isabel, with her beautiful soprano voice, sang 'I'll Walk Beside You', the floodgates opened and there wasn't a dry eye in the house. Oh, how I longed to sing like her. She had a naturally beautiful voice and her mother, Auntie Lizzie, sat proudly and received great compliments on having such a talented daughter. Auntie Lizzie had lost six children at birth and one at the age of five. Isabel was her much-loved surviving child. Her father, Uncle Harry, treated her like his little princess and made beautiful toys for her. We all loved this exceptional little girl, and that day she was able to articulate the family's sorrow.

9

Not ignorance, but ignorance of ignorance is the death
of knowledge.

ALFRED NORTH WHITEHEAD

*I*t always amazes me how you can look back and remember
moments in life that were pointers to the future. No one has total
recall, but I can list events in my childhood that correlate with how
my adulthood unfolded. Someone has said that this is called
'remembering the future'. It can be quite spooky.

My father had done some work for the comedian Sammy Murray,
who worked almost constantly in the Queen's Theatre behind the
Saltmarket, near Glasgow Cross. We received three complimentary
tickets for a panto in which he was appearing. It was a beautiful little
theatre and in those days people were allowed to smoke in the
auditorium. The smell of smoke, oranges, old coats and urine from
the one and only toilet at the back of the stalls pervaded the air.
Outside the theatre, someone sold chipped fruit to the audience as
they went in. My mother would never have bought it; she would have
bought her own chipped fruit in a shop, taken it home and washed it
before going to the theatre. I don't remember which pantomime they
were performing but the Principal Boy was Mabel Jackson, who
entered the stage when Sammy Murray was being berated by the
villain. Sammy, as Sara the Cook, was saying, 'Suh help ma God,
Baron, ah hivnae the money tae pey the rent.' The Principal Boy took
out his sword, pointed it at the Baron and declared, 'If it weren't for
your age, Baron, I'd thrash you within an inch of your life. Be off with
you. But never mind, Sara, there are always blue skies around the
corner.' And she'd burst into song.

That was the night I remember hearing my first joke and it was very racist. Nowadays it wouldn't be allowed. Sammy Murray and his comedy feed were dressed as Glasgow housewives, wearing wraparound overalls and turbans; they were leaning out of two windows on a stage flat denoting a tenement building. This was called having a 'hing', meaning hanging out the window for a blether. As the sketch progressed, the stage lighting dimmed to indicate twilight. Just then another member of the cast walked on, playing the part of an ARP officer. He said, 'Right, missus, close your curtains for the blackout. You don't want a wee chink at your windae.'

Sammy Murray replied, 'Oh aye, we dae – if ye see wan, send him in, we're aw desperate.'

At the finale Sammy Murray, who played the Dame, took his final bow as top of the bill. He pulled off his hat and his wig, which caused me great discomfort on his behalf, thinking it was his real hair. It was the custom in those days for males in drag to let the audience see the man underneath the character at the end of the show. Afterwards my parents took me backstage to meet Sammy. He shook hands with my mother and in his gruff voice said to her, 'Whit dae ye 'hink, hen? It's a helluva way tae make a livin', eh?' She often related this story, being absolutely thrilled by her brush with stardom.

While they were talking, I wandered out into the corridor and was enthralled to watch the dancing girls in their costumes, and other members of the cast. The corridor was empty when a beautiful woman dressed in a garment I'd never seen before, a brightly coloured satin kimono, came down the spiral staircase. Her black, wavy hair cascaded down past her shoulders and her face, although mask-like with stage make-up, was stunning. I must have been staring at her but she only glanced at me, our eyes making contact for a second. She didn't acknowledge me but simply glided on her way. That was the one and only time I saw Doris Droy, but I never forgot her. She and her husband, Frank Droy, did a singing act together and, as is the way in variety, she also did comedy with Sammy Murray. Her acting skills matched her lovely singing voice. Her husband was fond of a 'refreshment' and this kept them back from greater things. The great C.B. Cochrane had seen her and asked her to come and star in one of his big productions in London. She told him that unless she could work with Frank, she wasn't interested. C.B. Cochrane wasn't interested in Frank, so she never made the big time.

Having said that, Frank and Doris Droy were very highly paid artistes for that time. It was said that their wages were in the region of £100 a week, while Sammy Murray was earning £7 10s. After all, they lived in a middle-class area, Novar Drive in the West End, whereas Sammy lived just along the road in a single-end in the Gallowgate, and was much loved by people in the East End. The literati and glitterati of the time would deign to come down from the number one theatres of an afternoon to see how the poor people were entertained – there were three shows a day at the Queen's – and would dismiss the performances as 'populist theatre', not unlike the way they do nowadays. Sammy and Doris provided much-needed entertainment for people who could just afford the 2/- ticket, and enjoyed a bit of colour, music and comedy. When Sammy Murray died, he had one of the biggest funerals Glasgow has ever seen: he was a cult figure in his time.

Many years later I was working in a summer season in the Whitehall Theatre, Dundee, with a stand-up comic who had absolutely no discipline when it came to doing sketches. I wrote for him but he just couldn't get the hang of acting. The stage manager, Malcolm Morton, who has since become a good friend, said to me one night, 'You know, when you're on that stage working comedy, you're like Doris Droy reincarnated.' It was a wonderful compliment, and I told him of my one and only glimpse of her.

Recently I was given a tape of Doris Droy singing songs written by herself and her husband, one of her solos being 'Suicide Sal'. The marvellous thing about them is that she sang with an uncompromising Glasgow accent.

My cousin Isabel and I were sent to piano lessons. We didn't go to the same teacher. Dennistoun, in those days, seemed to have a high population of accomplished but disappointed spinsters left over from a more genteel era, who found themselves in reduced circumstances and were forced to take in the children of aspiring mothers to help them bridge the gap between Chopsticks and Chopin.

In a ground-floor flat in Armadale Street lived two sisters on whom

Hinge and Bracket could have styled themselves. Their mode of attire was locked into the Edwardian period and their windows were hung not with curtains but with coloured beads in pretty shades of blue and green. No doubt they caught the morning sun, as their flat faced east. However, when I arrived for my lesson after school, the room was dim, dusty and crowded with bric-a-brac. The old upright piano had candlesticks at each side – a beautiful piece of furniture which matched the horsehair chaise-longue. Now I would find the room utterly charming, but it was far away from what I was used to and children like familiarity.

I learned where FACE and EGBD and F came on the musical staves and on the piano but as with Miss Brown, this Miss whateverhernamewas employed the aversion therapy. If I put a finger wrong, down came the pencil with the metal tube extension on the knuckles. The black notes caused me quite a bit of pain. I didn't last long with her.

Isabel was doing well, so this prompted my mother to find another teacher in the form of Miss Gouldwell, a pretty young woman who didn't use the pencil. I thrived under her tuition but the damage had been done. The music was in my heart and in my head but it never really reached the fingers. I achieved grade IV but I was no child prodigy.

It was a busy wee life with school, church, and the Sunday School, run by a family of bakers called the McGraths, whose lives were dedicated to the church and who shared their resources with the poor folk who attended the little mission church in the Calton. The maiden ladies of the family, the Misses Miller, ran the Brownies, and Mrs McGrath was the Guide Mistress and Sunday School leader. They gave us parties and trips, and a Christmas present to every child in the Sunday School. We had a procession on Mothering Sunday where we all presented our mothers with a bunch of daffodils and a piece of simnel cake provided by the McGraths. They truly lived their Christianity, and many people of my age who attended St Cuthbert's will remember them fondly.

Our church hall was situated about half a mile from the church, above a shop at the corner of Gallowgate and Barrack Street. I remember the thrill of going up the wooden stairs and passing the tiny kitchen where Mrs Gresham, an old lady still wearing long black Edwardian dresses, would be boiling up the tea-urn and setting out the home-baking for the women's 'socials'. The evening would start with prayers, then a talk, and then the wee concert would start. All of the women had their own songs. My mother's song was 'The Hills of Donegal', which she sang in her deep contralto with much feeling. Last year I walked in the Donegal Hills (I more often than not holiday on my own) and at the top of my voice I sang her song; ending up, of course, in tears. But she had hardly travelled at all and had never seen what she was singing about. I sang just for her. I wonder if she heard me? I have discovered that sadness is a state that we have to move through sometimes. I don't fight it now. I take it along with my joys and see it as part of the learning process.

There was never any overt religious prejudice in our home. Auntie Lizzie was a Catholic, and the fact that she changed her religion when she married Uncle Harry wasn't a problem. In fact my mother and I often visited the 'Chapel', as they called it, with Auntie Lizzie and Isabel. We were with them one day around Easter when there was a service in which part of the ritual was kissing the feet of Christ. An effigy of the Saviour was lying on the floor at the altar, His feet towards the congregation. There was a procession of people passing by, and they bent to kiss His feet. When it came to Isabel's turn to join the procession, I made to go with her, thinking it was a wonderful and emotional thing to do. As I got up, my mother whispered sharply, 'Sit where you are.'

I said, 'But Mum, I want to kiss Jesus's feet . . .'

'Sit where you are.' She meant it and her tone of voice rooted me to the spot. I was hugely disappointed. I felt I had missed out on a moving experience, not to mention a touch of the theatrical.

One of the cousins was engaged to a Catholic girl. Both families were uncomfortable about the union and one Thursday the auntie who was the mother of the prospective bridegroom held the floor.

'Aye, he brought her up last week – nice enough lassie, goes to the university. So ah says, whit's your name again? She says, Teresa Reilly.'

There was a sharp intake of breath all round.

'Ah says, oh aye. And did you go to the same school as oor John? She says, no. So ah says, whit school did you go to again? She says, the Immaculate Conception.'

There were great sighs from the others and much shifting in chairs. Auntie carried on, 'So ah says,' here she paused to deliver the *coup de grace*. 'well, he's no turning.'

My cousin married the lovely girl in a 'hidden wedding', held in the Sacristy out of sight of the altar. At the reception, my cousin laughed when my father said to him, 'Aye, son, that's you a Calathumpian noo.' During the evening the bride's old granny sat with an inscrutable expression on her face, clutching a bottle of holy water she had brought from Lourdes. As the Protestants danced by, she sprinkled them with the holy liquid.

All the memories of my upbringing in the church are happy ones. There was a gentility about it which was lacking in the greyness of everyday life. In this community my mother and I could surmount our dull surroundings. There was not much colour in life in those days, the colour came from the people who inhabited it. Although we didn't realise it at the time, my father was the most colourful of all. I loved that little church. It was spiritual refreshment to me and my mother, as walking in the Scottish hills is to me now. My father, who was born with a natural immunity to religion, called us 'hauf and half'; neither Catholics nor Protestants.

When the minister would visit our house, my mother would try to keep my father out of the way. It never worked: he always seemed to be around at these times and felt it beholden on him to get his fourpenceworth in. The minister would be seated with a cup of tea in hand, my mother would be darting around handing out sponge-cake, when Father would draw himself up to his full height and, in a declamatory fashion, give forth with his views.

'Well, ye see, meenister, I am a man of peace.' We were all about to get a showing-up. 'You cannae deny that religion has been the cause of all the wars throughout history.'

My mother would get behind the minister's chair and make signs for my father to shut up, but to no avail. He had the ball at his feet and he was winning with it.

'Ye see, I predict that in the future there'll no be any religions, mankind will come to its senses.' At this point he would interpolate one of his favourite platitudes, which had nothing to do with anything: 'Aye, the king will come the cadger's way.'

The minister would smile benignly and Father, taking this for encouragement, would continue down a bizarre road. 'Ye see, when man achieves the speed of light, and that's in the foreseeable future, we'll make contact with other life-forms in other dimensions. These'll be folk like ourselves, only they'll be more advanced than we are and these beings will learn us how to live right . . . they'll learn us where we're going wrong . . . they'll . . .' As he paused to take breath and think of his next line, my mother would dash in with a bit of homemade shortbread and change the subject.

When the minister left, she would say, 'Do you try to black affront me? That's you and your American comics.' She didn't mean Bob Hope or Jack Benny, she was referring to Captain Marvel and Buck Rogers. In my father's mind, speculation on the mysteries of the future was as valid as the mystical rites of the church. The conversation always ended with his criticism of the clergy. 'Ah widnae mind a joab like his. Never gets his hauns dirty.'

On Saturday nights Father and I made our way along to the top of Abercromby Street on Duke Street; this junction was called Bellgrove. There was a second-hand bookshop where we bought the American comics. On the way back home we popped into the Rendezvous Café and got ice-cream and a bottle of ginger to make ice drinks, the treat of the week. I always remember seeing in one of the comics a story which involved the fourth dimension. I asked my father what the fourth dimension was. Never fazed by any question, he launched in. 'Well, ye see, hen, that was Einstein. He was the man who thought up the theory of relativity.'

'What's relativity, Daddy?'

'Well, ah'll explain that, hen.' He then demonstrated with his hand going back and forwards. 'Ye know how we go back and furrit . . . back and furrit?'

'Back and forward?'

'Aye, back and furrit – well, with relativity ye go back and furrit at the speed of light, ye see, 'til ye reach the fourth dimension.'

'What's the fourth dimension, Daddy?'

'Aye, well, that's where your relativity comes into play. You go back and furrit at the speed of light 'til you reach the fourth dimension and then . . . you go up, doon and sideyweys.'

How about that for an explanation of Einstein's E=MC2?

I hated the Brownies until I was made a Sixer, then I could boss the smaller ones. At one point I even joined the Band of Hope in Rutherford Church. If you stood up and said the motto, 'I promise on my honour to abstain from alcoholic liquor as a beverage and to help others to do the same', you got a pie and a cup of tea. That seemed a fair exchange. As I was only ten at the time, the promise wasn't really a problem.

I started to read the Sunday papers and found the divorce columns in the *News of the World* quite fascinating. In those days every divorce was reported with all the 'seamy' evidence. Such and such a person divorced such and such a person with somebody cited as co-respondent. It seemed the only way to get a divorce was by adultery. The case always ended up with the phrase 'intimacy took place'.

'Mum, what does intimacy took place mean?'

Mother replied, 'Away through the room and stay there.'

'But, Mum . . .'

'Away ye go and don't let me see your face 'til teatime.'

What had I done? I heard her saying to my father, 'My God, you wouldn't be up to her. See, that's you. We're just going to get the *Sunday Post* from now on.'

Then my father said, 'Ye cannae have the wean staying in the room aw afternoon. I'll take her doon the Barras for a wee walk.' The magic words 'the Barras'. 'Right, hen, get your coat on – we're gawn oot.' Another one of my educational tours.

I'd hear my mother shout down the stairs after us, 'That wean had better no come home here with a flea.' She always pronounced it a 'flay', perhaps something to do with her part-Irish background.

My father knew several stalls in the Barras where treasures could be found: Wedgwood vases, a cylindrical record-player with one record of a man singing, slightly speeded up, 'Oh, Mr Captain, stop the ship I want to get off and walk', which was always a source of amusement until my mother put it in the midden. A whole cross-section of Glasgow visited the Barras and still does; the street-criers were 'turns' in themselves. The fruit-seller, 'Erra perra perrs, cherries furra Herries, flooers furra hooers.' Dad would pick up old wireless sets and valves, more stuff for my mother to throw out. One day he bought a painting by E.A. Walton for 2/3d. It was a beautiful scene of an old fisherman sitting by a boathouse. He rushed home with it and was bitterly disappointed when my mother didn't like it.

'But, hen, there's E.A. Walton in the Art Galleries.'

'Well, I'm not wanting one in here. We've no room for it. I've got my mother's brass mirror, the picture of Capetown and Table Mountain and the wee Dutch boy and girl' – this was a dreadful depiction of a little boy and girl in Dutch national dress and wearing wooden clogs, executed in the medium of different kinds of silver paper – 'It'll only be another dust gatherer.'

She had no time to appreciate the works of art; her sole purpose in life was to keep body and soul together, to feed and clothe us, to keep her head above water whilst half-drowning under the burden of a family; she did her best as she saw it. He sold his E.A. Walton to someone for 2/6d and they sold it later for thousands of pounds. After he died, I found among his things a pastiche of the painting he had done in watercolour, with a cheap frame round it. It is a lively wee painting and I treasure it.

We had two social orders, they were the church and the Co-operative. Every night there was something to attend in our local Co-operative Hall, situated next to the Orient Cinema on the Gallowgate. On a Monday night there was Scottish country dancing. I always thought there was something very sensible looking about the people who attended. They were hearty and healthy and wore the kilt – the women as well. Their legs seemed to come to a point in their hand-knitted kiltie socks and the fine lace-up pumps. There were lots of Morags and Hamishes. On a Tuesday night it was the League of Health and Beauty for healthy young women. This organisation, I think, had its origins in Hitler's Germany, but it was the precursor of the keep-fit and aerobics classes we attend now. Wednesday nights were cookery classes for housewives on tight rations, with an enthusiastic teacher who could make six nourishing meals out of a pig's cheek, not to mention how she got carried away and told them how she'd used a hot rice-pudding as a poultice, which she slapped on her husband's chest and cured his cough in no time. Thursdays were taken up with some activity for healthy young men. Then, on Friday night, the children came into their own at the Co-operative Choir practice led by Mr Inwood.

My cousin Isabel and I joined the choir. I loved to sing but could never match up to my cousin's beautiful singing voice. My mother used to encourage me to 'stick in' at the piano so that I could accompany her. However, I saw the choir, which I believe was a good one, as an outlet for my closet soprano. We learned harmonies and some lovely Scottish songs and, of course, the tried and tested 'Nymphs and Shepherds Come Away'. It was a great thrill to sing in 'concert' with others. We even made a showing at the Paisley Festival. I competed in the soloist class with 'Ye Fauns and Ye Dryads' and 'Oh, Can Ye Sew Cushions'. As a performer I have played the Paisley Town Hall many times and I never stand on that stage without remembering my first appearance there as a child, shivering with nerves, so much so that my kilt looked as though it had a life of its own. I had left the house with my mother's supportive words ringing in my ear: 'Now, don't forget to stand right forward or the man'll no be able to hear you, and sing out, because when you're nervous ye cannae hear ye behind a tram-car ticket. And don't stand like a half-shut knife or it'll no come out. If you don't stand right, you'll lose points.' Girded with these encouraging words I came last, having forgotten what I was doing with sewing my cushions. All my life when I was nervous singing, I would make up words to songs as I went along, sometimes with disastrous results. My self-perception on that stage in Paisley Town Hall was of a quivering, hump-backed nonentity.

The reason for the hump was that at the age of ten and a half I was what they called in those days 'well developed'. In this department I was ahead of my peers, but it was not something I was proud of – in fact, I was ashamed. Everyone said I was big for my size. I'd hear my mother say to the aunties, whilst cupping her hands in front of her bosom, 'She's big in the top storey' or 'She's way ahead of herself upstairs.' The 'showing' – or should I say 'showing-up'? – I gave myself at the Paisley Festival only reinforced my mother's advice to 'stick in at the piano'. It was the old gag about the lassie who went for an audition and told the impresario that she could sing and she could juggle. The man asked her to sing, and when she was finished he said, 'For Christ's sake, juggle.'

Yet my happiest moments were sitting at the piano in the big room, getting out the *Family Song Album* and belting out with my own accompaniment 'Carry Me Back To Old Virginny' or 'I Dreamt I Dwelt in Marble Halls'. These times took me into a realm of rest, far from the family hassle. I felt sure I had something to offer the world of music.

My career in the Co-operative Choir came to an ignominious finish one night when Mr Inwood was finding it hard to keep order. We were all getting to the stage where we were interested in members of the opposite sex and that night there was much furtive hand-holding and giggling. Mr Inwood picked me out as the worst offender; I can't think why. He moved me from the altos to the sopranos so that I could be beside my well-behaved cousin and she could keep an eye on me.

A few weeks before, I had blotted my copybook when my cousin had suggested me for a solo in the forthcoming choir concert. He looked at the accompanist, Miss Crawford, a heavily made-up spinster with badly dyed blonde hair, who seemed to be in thrall of Mr Inwood. They both laughed at the idea of Dorothy singing a solo. I was asked to come out of the choir and sing a test piece for him to hear. He chose a Gaelic song, the opening words of which were 'Eetle a doovil Eetle a doho ro' – a song I had never taken to. After a few false starts I started to cry. Mr Inwood had no sympathy with tears and asked me what was wrong. I told him I thought 'Eetle a doovil' sounded a bit daft. He went into a big number.

'Oh, really, a bit daft? Do you hear that, Miss Crawford?' Miss Crawford held up her hands to heaven. Inwood continued, 'Well, you learn something different every day, don't you, Miss Crawford?' She smiled her agreement. 'So you think "Eetle a doovil" is a bit daft? Only Sir Hugh Robertson of the Glasgow Orpheus Choir has chosen "Eetle a doovil" to be included in his programme of songs when the King comes to visit Glasgow next February – and this girl thinks it's a bit daft?' He went on and on. 'Only Sir Hugh Robertson has included "Eetle a doovil" in his new songbook *A Gaelic Hooley Round the Old Campfire* and this girl thinks it's a bit daft.' By this time I could have killed my cousin for suggesting me for a solo.

'Well now, girl, how would you like to favour us with a rendition?'

I hesitated, then I came out with, 'I'd like to sing "Danny Boy".'

He was very nearly apoplectic. He screamed, '"Danny Boy"! "Danny Boy"! How dare you! Where do you think you are? In some free-for-all in a public house in Maryhill? This is the Co-operative Choir you're in, and don't you forget it! I'll give you "Danny Boy"! Away back to your seat.'

I shuffled back to my place in the sopranos. I was determined to keep my nose clean and I did for a couple of weeks. On this fateful night, however, he told us to get out our pieces for 'The Isle of Mull is of Isles the Fairest' and turned to Miss Crawford – a self-confessed martyr to the vagaries of the Corporation tram-cars, who came all the way from Rutherglen to accompany us – and asked her to play the first verse *pp*, which meant double piano (very softly). Had he only said it once, everything would have been fine, but he repeated it and I was still in a hyper state. '*Pp*, Miss Crawford, yes – *pp*.'

That did it. I leaned towards my cousin and said, as I thought sotto voce, 'He said, "*pp* Miss Crawford".'

The shit hit the fan.

'Come out here, Dorothy Pollock, and bring your pieces! Come on, bring out your music and leave it on my table. I've had enough of you and your carry-ons. I'm not taking any more of your disruption.'

I was flabbergasted but I did as I was told. I gathered up my music, including 'Eetle a doovil', and laid it down on his table in front of everyone.

'Now leave my choir, and don't come back!'

There was a sharp intake of breath from the bleachers. Then I embarked on the longest walk of my life, from Mr Inwood's table across the entire choir. When I finally arrived at the door and was about to make my exit, he added, 'You'll be no loss to this choir, I can assure you.'

With that I found myself outside the practice room, with my faithful cousin by my side. She had handed in her music, too, and left with me. I really appreciated that gesture because I don't know how I could have walked up that road home without her. She 'oxtered' me up Sword Street, across the Bellfield Bridge, on to Duke Street. All the while I was inconsolable; sobbing quietly but constantly. When I arrived at the close mouth of 2 Whitehill Street, I let out a yell of pent-up pain. The awful agony of a rejected soprano. It wouldn't be the last rejection I would have to endure in life, but oh, how it hurt.

In an attempt to console me, my cousin said, 'I think you're a lovely singer.'

This only made me worse and I let out another cry from the heart. My father heard this one and rushed out the door and down the stairs, thinking I had been attacked. He was shouting, 'Where is he? Where is he?'

When all was explained he carried me up the stairs and into the kitchen, where my mother and Auntie Lizzie were having a cup of tea. As I was incoherent with grief and humiliation, Isabel told the story. My mother's reaction was, 'See, that's her. I might have known.' Then she raised her hands and eyes to heaven in an effort to invoke the power of the Deity. 'God in heaven, what am I to do with this girl?' was her prayer. Then to Auntie Lizzie, 'She'll drive me to an early grave with her shenanigans. God, Lizzie, I've heard of lassies being sent to the home for bad girls, I've heard of boys being sent to borstal, but who in the city of Glasgow ever had a daughter that's been thrown out of the Co-operative Choir?'

Auntie Lizzie brought a note of sanity to this heavy emotional scene with an interesting suggestion: 'Look – my Isabel's joining a concert party that's run by some telephone engineers in Hillhead. Ah'll see if I can join Dorothy as well.' Things were starting to look up again. My singing career looked as though it was being rescued from the toilet.

10

Fashions, after all, are only induced epidemics.

GEORGE BERNARD SHAW

*M*y sister's wedding was imminent. She chose to be married in the Church of Scotland attended by her prospective husband's family. The reception would not be held in the Co-operative Hall; she favoured a function suite called the Windsor, which was tucked away behind a shop in Bridgeton Cross. The hall, the 'purvey' and photographer were all inclusive. Preparations were in hand. Our cousin Edith, my mother's eldest sister's daughter, would be the chief bridesmaid and I was the second bridesmaid. No doubt my sister felt she had to give me my 'place'. For this I was very grateful; contrary to my mother's teaching, I would be able to draw attention to myself. Not exactly a starring role but an important member of the supporting cast. Edith made her own dress for the wedding, duck-egg blue with a 'sprig'. Her headdress resembled a Roman laurel-leaf crown. She also made my dress, which was in pale pink taffeta with a full gathered skirt. I was delighted with this but I didn't like the headdress suggested for me, a small, tiara-style frill of the same material. It seemed too plain, although my sister tried to explain that it was a classic, timeless style. She, being in the millinery department of the C&A, was an expert on these matters. I wasn't persuaded. I wanted to wear the same affair that Carmellia wore at her sister's wedding, a rosette style resembling a show-jumping prize. Carmellia was the daughter of one of my mother's acquaintances. Carmellia had beauty and talent – she had a solo dance at one of Miss McLellan's dance displays, which riled me since my mother had indeed taken me away from the dancing school; she had Shirley

Temple curls with enough hair for two folk, and the face of an angel – a face I was always tempted to punch. My mother tried to please me by asking for the loan of Carmellia's headdress. Carmellia's mother was very willing to lend it to me for the wedding and my mother asked her up for afternoon tea.

I was in the back court with my pals and had a great game going, taking turns at 'dreep the dyke' and balancing on the wall of death, which meant walking along the wall, ten feet up, between the tenement end and the wash-house roof. My mother called down to me from the kitchen window, 'Come up and get ready! Carmellia and her mummy'll be here in a minute. Come up and get some of the glaur off you.'

I reluctantly went up to the house and my mother let me in. 'State of you . . . you're a sight. What's that you've got on?'

I replied, 'It's Auntie Dorrie's old frock and I hate it. Mrs Morrow says I look like a wee wumman cut down.' Unfortunately because of my height, I was heiress to all the young aunties' old frocks.

'Aye, well, Mrs Morrow's just too pass remarkable. She misses nothing that one. Go and get washed and change into something, you're like a bag tied in the middle. And don't leave a tide-mark round your neck and comb that hair. Carmellia and her mummy'll be all style.'

I went to the kitchen window and shouted down to my pals, 'I'll be out in a wee while – don't go down the claypit without me.'

My mother heard me. 'You're going down no claypit. Carmellia's no used to claypits and middens. She lives in a bungalow with all her orders.'

I pondered this. 'Why don't we live in a bungalow with all our orders?'

'Because your daddy doesnae have a good job high up in the meat market with a good pay and wholesale mince.'

'What's wholesale mince?'

'Same as ordinary mince and plenty of it through the black market, and she doesn't have to queue up for it. She gets her mince brought home to her in a motor car.'

'Why don't we have a motor car?'

'Because your daddy didn't come into money.'

'Did Carmellia's daddy come into money?'

'Aye, after the grandfather died of a bad throat – and that's no wonder because he poured two hotels and a grocer's shop over it and still left enough to set his two sons up in business. Two farms and a shop that supplies the best ham and eggs to the Yanks at Prestwick aerodrome. I thought I told you to comb that hair.'

I was fascinated by all this information. This kind of thing was usually given in hushed tones to the aunties in the big room under the heading 'big people's business'. There was a wee resentment coming out here.

'Why can't I have curls like Carmellia?'

My mother was busy putting out the good china and the sandwiches. 'Because when the good Lord was giving out curls you were at the back of the queue.' This conjured up a strange and unjust picture.

'Was Carmellia at the front of the queue?'

'Aye, just like her mother. If there's anything going on she's up at four in the morning. If a parachute landed in her garden during the night, she'd have three frocks made out of it by eight o'clock.'

The doorbell rang.

'That's them.'

Carmellia arrived, wearing the coveted headdress, her golden curls dancing around it. I thought it was the most beautiful thing I'd ever seen in my life.

I opened the conversation by pointing at the coveted object. 'I've to get that.'

The beautiful Carmellia replied, 'You've only to get a shot of it.'

'I know that, I know that.' I wanted to pull it off her head but had to restrain myself or the 'ball would be on the slates' and I'd never get it.

My mother had to sit and listen to Carmellia's mother yacking on about her daughter's wedding, which had been in the Marlborough; a very posh function suite. 'It was £5 a head,' she boasted (this was in 1947). My mother blushed furiously when I asked if they had had wholesale mince. Eventually, the business of the headdress was discussed and Carmellia was persuaded to part with it. Instinct told me not to try it on just yet. Carmellia's mother said, 'Oh, come on.

Let's see it on you.' I refused. My mother suggested that we wait until the dress was finished and we would try it on then. She also assured the woman that we would be very careful with it and return it soon after the wedding.

After they had gone, I couldn't wait to try it on. It didn't suit me. It needed Carmellia's voluminous hair to balance the rosette style and I was no Shirley Temple. I had the Bette Davis looks which called for a simple, unobtrusive style. In Carmellia's headdress I resembled a prize donkey. I still wanted to wear it, and suggested that if I let my hair grow a bit longer my mother could curl it overnight with rags to achieve the ringlets. Her reaction was unkind. 'My God, that's all you're short of. Bliddy ringlets roon that wee farthing face of yours, and that tuppence worth of hair.'

I would never suit curls; even when I turned a bit good-looking in my twenties, curls never suited me. I started to cry. 'Don't start the greetin',' my mother shouted, and my sister joined in, quite rightly: 'Whose day is this anyway?'

Mother said, 'Everybody'll be lookin' at the bride, not at you.'

I, of course, didn't believe this. My tears were in full flow, and I was only quietened down when my sister said that if I didn't stop, she wouldn't allow me to be a bridesmaid at all. That did the trick. I went along with Edith's design and everyone was kind and told me I looked 'very nice'. Isabel thought I was beautiful.

My sister was a lovely bride in a white sweetheart-neck satin dress and white camellias in her hair. Her supervisor in C&A had made it for her and gave her the veil as a wedding present. The wedding was wonderful, except that the photographer employed by the Windsor arrived drunk and the group photograph was out of focus. Apart from that, it was a memorable day.

11

I've been on a constant diet for the last two decades. I've lost a total of 789 pounds. By all accounts I should be hanging from a charm bracelet.

ERMA BOMBECK

Somehow or other, my mother seldom embraced the company of my father's family, although we did have some contact with them. They were tall, good-looking people, Father being the eldest. He had four sisters, two of whom played tennis, which none of my mother's family did. His brother, big Jake, whom I adored, was only two years older than my big brother. In the company of the Pollock aunties and uncles I always felt the world was a sunnier place. Their conversations were bright and interesting; my mother called them 'airy fairy' blethers. I assume this meant that they were far removed from the mundane and domestic subjects which were predominant among my mother's sisters: health, operations, the woman up the road, the price of fish, etc. There was little space for light and air to enter: theirs was an enclosed order.

As mother's sisters approached the punishing menopause that all of them most certainly suffered, they would discuss the symptoms. I remember one auntie opening a conversation with, 'Do you know I've had cauld water running up and doon ma back aw day.' Yet again an auntie was baffling medical science.

My sister remembers when the family were invited to Granny Pollock's house for Sunday dinner. The table was big enough for a large gathering, the china was beautiful and the vegetables were served separately in dishes. Obviously my grandmother had 'standards'. I never heard my mother say a bad word about the

Dorothy

Pollocks; in fact, in a generous mood my mother would say that Granny Pollock was a ladybody. She had come from the island of Islay to go into service in Glasgow when she was a girl. My mother would say, 'She always set a lovely table' – one of the criteria of respectability. She died before I was born – in fact it was said that my father never got over her death.

We lost touch with the family, probably because the matriarchal influence was such that my mother's sisters and their offspring took precedence. I have since met my cousins through their coming to see my show, and they are delightful people. My father said that Granny was 'fey'. I've been told that at times I'm a bit psychic, so perhaps I've had intuitions about the roads I should take – unfortunately, I haven't always been wise in my choices.

My mother's sisters were busy wee women, joined at the hip in a mutual support system that kept them buoyant. I had two lovely uncles, both trained in Cochrane's grocers, who eventually owned their own shops. The sisters-in-law were warmly invited into the compact group; what distanced them slightly was the fact that they were a bit better off than the others. Having said that, my mother and Uncle Robert's wife were brought close when her one and only child was born, my dear cousin Eleanor.

Aunt Isa had her little girl in the Royal Maternity Hospital, and at that time there was an outbreak of gastro-enteritis in the wards. My aunt had two friends whose babies died in the epidemic. She herself returned home with a very sick child. The doctor called to see them and announced that Uncle Robert should be recalled from duty on compassionate grounds, as the child was not expected to live. Aunt Isa sent for my mother, who took her and the baby into her house and took over the nursing. Baby Eleanor reached a critical stage late one night; she went into convulsions with a high temperature. My mother bathed the child alternately in warm and cool water, then wrapped her and held her close all night. She said, 'Isa, if we get this child through the night, she'll see the rest of her life.' The power of my mother's healing and their prayers saw the wee girl through. She grew up to be the light of her parents' life, and to have two children of her own. Uncle Robert came home on leave to find his wife and child thriving.

Auntie Sarah, the eldest of my mother's sisters and said to be the cleverest, married a handsome Lancashire man, who came home from the First World War shell-shocked and palsied. He was kept in his room for the rest of his life. Apart from the shakiness there was nothing much wrong with him, and any time he dared to put his nose out of his bedroom to speak to me, he was charming. During the Second World War, when I was just five years old, Auntie Sarah asked my mother if she would send me along to stay with her for company; her son Robert and her daughter Edith were in the forces. Auntie Sarah was always boiling something to extract the juice; some days it would be blackcurrants to make pureé, other times it would be beetroot. I hated the smell that permeated the small flat. She never had any contact with poor Uncle Sid. She would put his food on a tray on the floor, knock on the door, and when the door opened a hand would come through and lift the tray into the room. The man was held prisoner. Many years later he escaped, opened a reasonably successful fruit and vegetable shop, but died three years later. Perhaps the stresses of the world on the outside were too much for him. Auntie Sarah had two very bright children who did well in life and had successful careers. Her son went to university to study French and German and ended up as Deputy Director of Education. Cousin Edith attended the famous Skerrie's College and became a first-class stenographer. She did resent the fact that she was not allowed to go to university, and that being a shorthand typist seemed good enough for her because she was female. In those days only 25 per cent of students at Glasgow University were girls. When Auntie Sarah 'walked off the park' during the menopause and took to her bed, Edith became one of the world's 'carers'. Auntie Sarah, not having taken too much out of herself, lived until she was 90, whilst her daughter, who held down a stressful job as secretary to a specialist in the Royal Infirmary, only enjoyed two years of her retirement and died aged 64.

Auntie Lizzie could be good fun although prone to 'tired turns'. I believe that she, in common with my mother, suffered from depression but could rise above it. Her husband, Uncle Harry, was a wonderful wee man; he and my father were a double act. Auntie Lizzie's tragedy, as I've mentioned, was losing six children at birth and one beautiful wee girl who died at the age of five of gastro-enteritis. One day Isabel took me to the Catholic cemetery in Dalmarnock to see her sister's grave. There was a little headstone which Uncle Harry had carved himself out of a marble table-top, inscribed 'In Memory of Marie'. Auntie Lizzie had good reason for a lifelong depression.

After my mother came Auntie Nellie, baptised Mary Ellen. When you visited her, she always tasted your tea before she gave it to you. I never liked that habit but I suppose she was only making sure it wasn't too hot. She had two daughters and a son. The girls, Irene and Jean, were childhood playmates and Jean became my cycling and hostelling companion.

Auntie Agnes, the only surviving sister today and the hardest working of them all, was widowed young. Her husband had taken a small refreshment and, 'under the influence', was riding on the platform of a tram-car when he let go of the pole as the car rounded a corner. He crashed to the ground, fracturing his skull, and was dead on arrival at the Royal Infirmary. She brought up three children on her own and earned a hard living by making children's jerkins and trousers out of her customers' old coats. At one time she had a shop. She is now 83 and still works for the community where she lives in Inverkeithing. She is a beautiful old lady with hardly a wrinkle and a neat little figure; she still worries about 'the diet'. She would pass for a woman of 65, even though in her mid-forties she suffered from an under-active thyroid gland which went undetected for many years. She would have died had it not been for modern medicine.

Only recently Auntie Agnes told me about my mother and father's courtship. The two sisters were walking along the road, Father was walking ahead of them when my mother turned to Auntie Agnes and said, 'Look at him, Agnes. He's like a young god.' I was most surprised to hear this, because as long as I knew them there was disharmony and I couldn't imagine my mother being as lyrical as that. She wanted him to be sensible, responsible and hard-working and he wanted to be accepted as he was: a free spirit.

Auntie Vera, my Uncle George's wife, was a much-loved and cosseted woman. Their two daughters were great friends of mine in childhood. They had the privilege of attending a private school; my mother called it 'fee paying'. They went into 'the professions'; one a lawyer and the other a schoolteacher. Their great claim to fame, and one my mother always boasted about, was the fact that Moira married the man whose brother was Robert McLeish, author of *The Gorbals Story*.

What can I say about my mother's youngest sister, Dorrie, after whom I am named? She came into the world angry and left the same way. She was her own worst enemy and caused her sisters much heartache. She suffered from a genetic heart defect – my mother described it as 'damaged walls', whatever that meant. Her illnesses perhaps contributed to her difficult nature. She had two very big heart operations, the second performed in London by the famous heart surgeon Mr Yacoub. My mother used to say, 'Aye, well, we've got to understand oor Dorrie. She's not a well woman. She could go at any time.' She survived until she was 74. No one ever thought she would see 40. My mother was devoted to all of them.

There's always someone who suffers when a new phase of industry takes hold. With the advent of the National Health Service, dental mechanics enjoyed an upsurge in business when Aneurin Bevan announced in the House of Commons that there would be free dentures for all, but the wee man who had the second-hand teeth stall at the Barras found his business going to the wall. The same went for his second-hand spectacles; new glasses were free on the NHS. Some young women, who had perfectly good teeth but who had admired the piano-key type 'choppers' of the Hollywood film stars, demanded that all their teeth be taken out and a new set of dentures put in. My mother and her five sisters went first in the queue for the latest fad. 'If we're getting them for nothing, Lizzie, I want a new set of wallies.'

I've often heard people with 'falsers' say that they had lovely teeth but their gums were bad. Of course no one flossed in those days. I was lucky that my mother was very conscious of my appearance; my bottom teeth were over my top set so, thanks to the NHS, I got the services of a first-class orthodontist who straightened them out with a brace, otherwise I would have ended up like my own gag: with a chin like a sink.

All the sisters applied for the new spectacles and of course they favoured the Dame Edna Everage type, 'flyaways' studded with fake diamonds. They were thrilled with them.

Life was changing radically. Christian Dior brought out the 'New Look' with voluminous skirts, swagger jackets and hemlines dropping to 'ballet length'. We all queued up at the C&A January sales for the affordable version of this wonderful new fashion. The clothes were gorgeous and as we stood there in the winter frost I saw a lovely red coat in the window.

'Oh, Mummy, please can I get a red coat? Can I get that red coat? Oh, please, please can I get a red coat?'

'No,' she was adamant, 'you can't get a red coat, you'll only draw attention to yourself.'

The coat my mother bought me was a dream. It was turquoise blue with black buttons and a little hat to match. I thought I was great. Hairstyles went from sweeps to sausage curls, which took ages to achieve, to a new style called the 'bubble cut'. We couldn't afford to go to the hairdresser but fortunately there was a man along the road in Barrack Street, called That Wullie King, who did perms in his own home at night. He was a gas-fitter during the day but he led a double life, and either he had the perming equipment or he adapted his plumbing tools, anyway he was able to perform this service for women. No doubt he got home around five in the afternoon, had his tea and did the quick turnabout from manual worker to Mr Teasy Weasy. I never had the pleasure of one of his hair-dos but the sisters were regular clients. They would trek along to his house at six o'clock in the evening, returning at one o'clock in the morning with their faces all red, dying for a cup of tea and two aspirins. Every time the aunties came back from That Wullie King's they vowed they would never return.

'Ah'm never going back to That Wullie King ever again. It's a bloody torture chamber he's got there.' This remark conjured up all sorts of horrors.

Another would say, 'Ah know . . . he pulls the heid aff ye.'

'Aw that bother for a wee curl.'

As far as I could see, there was no evidence of a curl. The effect achieved was more like an imitation of a lavatory brush. They looked as though Wullie King had given them a cut and blow-torch. It was a kind of straight frizz, giving them a perpetually startled appearance. Many hairdressers, even these days, after giving someone a perm that would keep an appearance-conscious woman under house arrest for six weeks, will say, 'Don't worry, it'll settle down.' Of course it never does. In the case of the Wullie King experience, two weeks later the perm resembled ripped-out knitting. There were no shampoos in those days that would help revivify dried-out hair, nor did we have conditioners. The only conditioner we knew about was a Bob Martin's for the dog. Skin care hadn't been invented as far as we were concerned; the only skin care available was Gentian Violet for ringworm.

My mother and her five sisters entered the new decade of the 1950s with a confidence given them by new teeth, new glasses, the New Look from the lower end of the market and the bubble cut which hadn't quite come off. All the latest fads were discussed at the Thursday high tea and fancies night. The high tea was a lettuce leaf, half a tomato and a slice of gammon through which you could see the pattern of the plate. The main attraction was my mother's home-baking, so popular that not a morsel was left for the rest of us. Father and Uncle Harry were relegated to the kitchen, where they either played cards or put up shelves or, as happened on one occasion, boxed in the sink because my mother wanted hers boxed in the way Joan Crawford had had hers done in one of her films. At the end of the affair, Uncle Harry's dog Rover was missing, only to be heard whining from behind the new fixture. The whole business had to be taken apart to let the poor animal out.

Until this time all the aunties had worn corsets. These were quite complicated contraptions that started under the bust and came down to the thigh. They were constructed with whalebones placed at regular intervals to hold in the excess fat. They gave a solid look to the figure, except when a whalebone managed to break free and stuck out in a point, which distorted the line of a dress. The new 'roll-ons' promised to give a smooth look. These were white rubber tubes with air holes, and suspenders attached. Father and Uncle Harry were told on no account to come into the big room where the trying on of roll-ons was in progress. Father couldn't find the sugar and, having forgotten about the no-entry rule, walked in on them. There were screams and shouts and Father hastily made an exit. 'Christ, Harry,' he said when he reached the safety of the kitchen, 'that was a sight tae frighten the Germans. They're rolling aboot there like sausages bursting oot their skins.' The trouble with these garments was that in trying to put them on you had to be a bit of a contortionist, and sometimes you had to lie on the floor to get the purchase to haul them up.

After the war, slowly but surely, we started to be influenced by the USA. Anything American was desirable. Many young women had married Americans and would send us over women's magazines which were much more interesting than ours. We had *Woman* and *Woman's Own* and *The People's Friend*. In those days they were big on articles on how to keep your man happy. 'If you want to keep your man at the fireside, make yourself look attractive for him coming home from work. Wear a clean apron, have the dinner hot in the oven – husbands like to come home to the aroma of something cooking – and children bathed and ready for bed. Visit the hairdresser once a week and apply a subtle make-up.' There were knitting patterns for two-ply wool which would take six months to complete whilst sitting at the fireside with your husband. He would be depicted in the typical happy family group reading his paper and smoking his pipe. The children would be playing snakes and ladders at their parents' feet. I never saw any families like that anywhere. Articles for the younger mother would deal with 'natural feeding'. The breast word was never mentioned, but books with graphic descriptions of the natural method could be obtained at the baby clinic: for mothers' eyes only.

The American magazines showed pretty women in gingham dresses, with their hair in ponytails, cooking in modern kitchens equipped with the latest washing machines and refrigerators. They were a long way from the old kitchen cabinet and the wringer that we had. They had leisure time to play tennis and indulge in other interesting outdoor activities because of their labour-saving devices. Perhaps the sisters imagined themselves as tennis-playing glamour girls wearing gingham, but if they did, they would have to lose the weight and so were seduced by the American magazines into, not *Woman's Own* 'reducing diet for ladies', but what our transatlantic cousins called 'slimming'. Over a plate of glistening cakes you'd hear one of them say, 'Well, God knows ah've tried but ah cannae shift it, and I don't know what ah'm doing wrong.' They tried every diet – the banana diet, the egg diet – but nothing worked. The only diet they were not prepared to try was the 'stopping the fork going to the mouth' diet. As they were putting on the weight, the roll-ons were inclined to roll up the body, causing red indentation weals which were only relieved when they removed the roll-ons and had a good scratch.

Help was at hand in the form of wee Uncle George, Dorrie's husband. He was in the way of 'coming by' commodities which hadn't quite reached the shops. My mother used to say that wee George was 'up tae aw the dodges'. Glass nylons – sheer and very shiny – were a much-prized commodity that Uncle George managed to come by. He brought a consignment up to the house and had the aunties all excited about them. 'Of course they're seconds,' he declared. He wasn't kidding. There were no feet in them.

One night he came up to the house with a box of black and white capsules. They were called black bombers. These were given out to patients at the discretion of the doctor, and somehow wee George had managed to get hold of them. They must have come in a shipload, because many women in Glasgow were taking them. They were slimming pills, Dexedrine, known nowadays as 'speed'. The only word the sisters heard was 'slimming'. They ate them like Smarties. For about five days they were running about with eyes popping out of their heads, cleaning their houses, cleaning the stairs and closes, washing and ironing clothes without even stopping for sleep. These pills were magic. Before the weight could get a chance to fall away, they had to stop taking them because of sheer exhaustion. When they stopped, they came down with a thump. The depression set in and of course the only way to cure that was to eat. They were back where they started: wee fat women spilling out of their roll-ons.

12

When we remember that we are all mad, the mysteries disappear and life stands explained.

MARK TWAIN

*A*nother woman who withdrew from society in her mid-50s like Auntie Sarah was our next-door neighbour, big Stevie. She retreated to the bed recess in the kitchen and from then on all business was conducted from her recumbent position via the energetic wee Hercules. Stevie took a notion to move house yet again. She'd heard about a low-down house that was being vacated in Roselea Drive.

'Herkliss – ye'll need tae get me tae see that hoose, Herkliss.'

The careworn Hercules replied, 'How the hell am ah gonnae dae that, Maw?'

Stevie could walk if she wanted to, but she had decided to play it 'infirm'. 'Tell the doacter ah need a stretcher.'

'Who's gonnae carry the stretcher, Maw?'

'Don't be so stupit, Herkliss. There'll be two ambulance men wi' it of course.'

This seemed an impossible task, but somehow or other Hercules managed to persuade the doctor that it should be done, and two poor, unsuspecting ambulance men were commissioned for the job of carrying Stevie from her house, down the stairs, out of the close, up Whitehill Street and round the corner to Roselea Drive to view the prospective dwelling. They wrapped her in three red blankets and with great danger to life and limb (theirs) managed to get her there. Goodness knows what the incumbent tenants thought of this circus. After looking around the house, peering into the cupboards, testing the bed in the kitchen recess, in front of everyone she declared, 'Ah don't fancy it. Take me back tae ma ain hoose.'

No reason was given for her dislike of the flat: Stevie had spoken.

The ambulance men, much to their chagrin, returned the big woman to her bed recess in the house next door to ours, where she stayed until she was carried down the stairs to the hearse by the funeral undertakers (one of them ending up in the Royal with a hernia).

Another time she looked at Hercules and stated, 'God, Herkliss, ah'm fed up starin' at these four walls. Ah'm helluva lonely, Herkliss.'

Hercules said, 'But, Maw . . . ye've goat me.'

Her reply to that was, 'Away tae hell. Gawn doon the Gallowgate and get me a wee budgie tae keep me company, Herkliss.'

'Aye, awright, Maw.' Hercules did as he was told and returned with a budgie, green in colour, in a smart cage.

'Aw, Herkliss, is that no lovely – a wee green wan. Dis it talk, Herkliss?'

'Aw, Maw, you've goat tae learn it tae talk.'

Stevie addressed the budgie affectionately, 'Aw, who's a cheeky boy? We'll call it wee Cheeky, Herkliss. Away doon the Gallowgate and get some accoutrements fur its cage. Get it a wee bath, a swing and a mirror.' Herkliss came back with toys for the budgie and a set of beads on a string. 'Whit hiv ye bought the beads fur, Herkliss? Whit the hell's the budgie tae dae wi' the beads?'

Herkliss smiled and said, 'Aye, well, ye see, Maw, the wumman in the pet shop said that if it's a wee Catholic budgie it can say its rosary, and if it's a Protestant budgie, it can dae its sums.' He was pleased with his wee joke.

After a few weeks Stevie noticed something was wrong with the little bird. 'Herkliss, that wee budgie's limpin', Herkliss. Away doon the Gallowgate to that vet and see whit's wrang wi' it.' Off he went down to the vet with wee Cheeky. He returned with an empty cage.

'Whit the hell's happened tae ma wee Cheeky, Herkliss?'

'Ah, well, Maw, the vet said that wee Cheeky hid broken its leg.'

'Broken its leg? That's your fault for letting it swing on that pulley.'

'And the vet said he wid have to put a plaster on it, and ah says you widnae like that.'

'Bloody sure and ah widnae, Herkliss. Whoever heard of a budgie wi' a stookie on its leg?'

'That's whit ah thought, Maw, so . . .' he paused.

'So whit, Herkliss?'

'He gave Cheeky a wee injection.'

'A wee injection? Dis that mean ma wee Cheeky has passed away?'

'Aye, Maw – he's deid.'

Stevie was beside herself with grief. Everyone who came into the house got the story of her dear departed Cheeky. Eventually, one day when she was all 'cried out', she said to Hercules, 'Herkliss, away doon the Gallowgate and get me another budgie.'

Hercules was delighted to put an end to all this emotion. 'Ah'll go right away, Maw.'

As he was getting on his coat, Stevie shouted to him going out the door, 'Oh, Herkliss, get a blue wan this time. The Catholic wans urny very good talkers.'

We had a very disparate group of neighbours. Young and old, respectable and slightly less so. There was an old couple directly above us who often asked me into their house for a cup of tea and a biscuit, especially when I came home from school and my mother was out. They were what I would have described as bordering on the decrepit, moving around very slowly, and yet on a Saturday night at 6.30 p.m. there was a programme on the wireless called *Here We Come Dancing*. It was a programme of Scottish country dancing music; very jolly and lively. At this time our ceiling would creak and heave as the two old folk upstairs danced to the music. We never understood how they managed it.

There was a lady two stairs up who quietly drank herself into oblivion. She kept herself to herself, but one day I was going up to the top floor to deliver the wash-house key when she came out of the door. She called me over. 'I had a wee girl like you once.' She started to cry and I didn't know what to do. I let her cuddle me for a wee while then I needed to escape. When I told my mother she said, 'Poor wee soul. We don't know the half of it, an' there's no help for her.'

Many years before, when my mother and father stayed in their first single apartment in Comely Bank Street, Mother met a neighbour who was to become a lifelong friend, Auntie Esther. She lived in the one-apartment flat downstairs and was newly widowed with a little girl. When my mother recounted this story, she was apt to make it one of her bravura performances.

'Esther came up to me after they laid him out. There she was, a young widow and wee Cathy to rear herself. She said to me, "Oh, Mae, why was he taken so young?" I said to her, "Esther, Alastair came all the way from the Highlands to be a policeman in Glasgow, and he couldnae thrive in the city. Look at the way he walked, Esther, with his knees lifted high at every step. Do ye no see, Esther, he was used to walking in the heather?"'

This spurious explanation seemed to have satisfied Esther. It wasn't the illness that had taken him, but the fact that he missed his native turf. Mother continued: 'Then she said to me, "Oh, Mae, I couldnae stay in that hoose wi' the coffin and him lying there." I said, "Esther, you and wee Cathy will come and sleep wi' me until the funeral. My Sam will go down and sleep wi' the coffin, he'll no mind."'

Years later, my father told me, 'She made me go down and sleep in the same room for four nights wi' that bliddy corpse. There he wis, in the middle of the room, toasted breid, and me in the bed recess. Ah couldnae let them see ah was feart, could ah? But ah wis.'

Just at the end of the war, I had come home one day to find my mother and some of the neighbours out on the stairhead (this was the landing between two flats). They were all worked up into a state of high dudgeon. My mother was leading the band, with my young brother in her arms.

'Well, that's a right ticket that's moved in up the stairs. Did you see her hanging out the window on to Duke Street, shouting down to her pal? It's just not the thing in Whitehill Street.'

The women nodded their agreement. Another neighbour joined in, 'It's a disgrace, so it is. I mean, whit do we pay our rates for?'

My mother continued, 'Her pal was shouting up at her, "Haw, Senga".'

Mrs Forsyth turned to the others and enlightened them, 'That's Agnes backwards.'

My mother went on, '"Haw, Senga, ah'm scunnered so ah am," this is what she's shouting. She says, "Come oan hurry up and get ready, the Barrowland's full of Canadians," that's what she said and her a married woman with two children and her man no demobbed yet.'

Murmurings of 'That's terrible so it is.'

Someone joined in: 'I was wakened up in the middle of the night with a noise outside my door and I goes to see who it is and she's there with her pal and a big Canadian causing a rumpus, with a lot of drink taken. That was them back from the Barrowland ballroom at that time of night.' Sharp intake of breath. 'If you're up at that time of night, you're up to no good.'

My mother became aware of me standing listening to all this, 'Away wi' you into the kitchen and take off those shoes and don't scrape the linoleum.' I listened in from behind the door, naturally.

'She was chewing chewing-gum and wearing glass nylons.' OOOOHH. By then I couldn't make out which voice was which.

'Did you hear about the fur coat?'

'No.' This would be a juicy one.

'Yes, flank musquash. Her and her pal were laughin' away. The pal says, "Whit did ye do for that?" She says, "Whit do you think? I took the hem up." Killin' themselves, so they were.'

The 'ticket', I don't remember her real name, was the scandal of the close if not the district. My mother said, 'That wan up the stairs – she does what she likes.' To do what you liked wasn't allowed. Women were supposed to do what was expected of them. Respectability was all. Anything short of that was intolerable. She was ostracised by the women and she didn't care. As far as I see, she didn't have to care, she had her passport out of the ordinary because she was beautiful, a film star with exceptional good looks. She was Hedy Lamarr or Lana Turner; she had had a taste of drudgery and it wasn't for her. The woman who lived up the stairs aspired to nowhere further than a holiday in Rothesay or Dunoon, but the 'ticket's' plans were in place. She would be missing when her husband came back from the war.

Some time later, on one of the sisters' Thursday nights, I heard my mother 'laying it off': 'I hear there's going to be a d.i.v.o.r.c.e.' She couldn't bring herself to say the word. She pointed upstairs. 'Big

Chuck . . . Canadian. No bad, eh? New daddy for the weans – no bad, eh?'

Then one hot summer's day the women were all outside in the back court, some hanging out their washing, some beating the carpets, and children were playing, when suddenly the 'ticket' appeared at her window. Someone caught sight of her and said to the others, 'She's at the window. Look . . . look the hair's all dyed.' Everyone looked up at the window as she stuck her beautiful head out and called to her two sons who were playing in the back, 'Haw, Kevin and Derek . . . Come up and get ready for Canada.'

We never heard of her again.

13

Humour plays close to the big, hot fire which is the truth, and the reader feels the heat.

E.B. WHITE

My mother was taken into hospital with acute gall-bladder trouble. At one point after the operation her heart failed, and the report line was sent out for her. This was the equivalent of someone being taken into intensive care and the relatives being summoned by phone. Few people had telephones in those days, so two policemen were sent to your door to ask you to go to the hospital. Their visit meant that death could be imminent. We were all around her bed. Her eyes were glassy with morphine but all she worried about was her family. Her first words to my father were, 'You'll have to keep working or these weans'll end up in the poor house,' and to me she said, 'Keep up your practice.' Even in her extremity the work ethic was strong.

The ground was crumbling beneath my feet. I was losing my mother and I realised how ineffectual my father would be if he had to take over the running of the house and the rearing of my little brother and me. As it was I had the family purse with ten shillings in it, and had to shop and cook the meals. I was already cleaning the house and looking after my wee brother. My sister, who was married and staying with her mother-in-law, stepped in to help. At one stage I was taken to Auntie Lizzie's house and looked after there; my little brother was with someone else. We were a fragmented family and it felt awful. My mother recovered, and after a long stay in hospital was sent to a convalescent home. She came home a month before my qualifying exam. Instead of studying, I took the rheumatics again and was put to bed between the blankets, only being allowed up to attend the exam. On reflection, I believe I was so distressed by her illness that my own illness was psychosomatic. I just wanted my mother to look after me, to prove that she was really well again. The result of my falling apart was to achieve an S2 in the 'qually'. It didn't cross anyone's mind to appeal on my behalf. All my pals achieved an S1 and were in much higher classes. This meant our paths didn't cross as they had done in primary school, and eventually we lost touch. In my late teens I used to have recurring dreams about being at the university and art school. When I woke, I would be in tears with the realisation that I had left school at 15 without so much as a third-year leaving certificate.

This lack of certification has haunted me all my life. I would eventually see my children with excellent degrees in engineering and architecture, and this gave me tremendous joy, but *I* wanted to be clever too. *I* wanted knowledge and education for its own sake. The university doors were closed to me; I had let the opportunity pass me by. In those days you didn't get a second chance.

My mother was never strong after her illness but she still pushed herself to keep up her standards. Father had to be bolstered up since he had fallen away at the thought of losing her; everyone demanded her time, her attention and her flagging energy.

As if she didn't have a big enough workload in her everyday life, when it came to holidays she always added to it. Around March or April she and Auntie Lizzie would go to one of the favoured holiday resorts – Rothesay, Dunoon or Saltcoats – and 'get a house'. They would find a place to rent for a fortnight in the summer, usually a room and kitchen with an outside toilet for the first fortnight in July. They would say to the woman who was letting that it was only for four people, but it didn't work out like that. When the time came for us all to troop down with our cases, buckets and spades for my wee brother, and her good frying pan, she would say, 'I'm just going to ask Dorrie down for a week, she's not been that well.' With Dorrie's two wild boys, we ended up sleeping three to a bed. Then another auntie would arrive with children 'just for the day', and end up staying for a few days. This would involve bodies strewn about the floor, massive washings, cooking and making beds. My mother could never say no to her sisters. My father didn't usually come on these holidays, knowing it would only end up in grief. (My father didn't like other people's children. If they misbehaved, he would accidentally-on-purpose stand on their toes to inflict pain.) Dorrie, who had definitely outstayed her welcome, was enjoying her break so much that she pleaded with my mother to let her and her children stay on. My mother said, 'Oh, all right. Give me 3/6d and you can stay another day.' Her 3/6d went into the catering kitty and was the daily rate for an auntie and her two children.

One of the best holidays was when Isabel and I were 14 and we went with Auntie Lizzie, Uncle Harry and my mother to Dunoon. We had some 'camp followers' that year as well, but the house was a villa with a garden and there was plenty of space. The Dunoon Council ran a 'Go As You Please' competition every day in the Town Hall. We went every day and every day either Isabel or I won the prize: two tickets for the late-night dancing. The other contestants had very diverse talents. There were tap-dancers, yodellers, a harmonica player who started off his medley cheerily with 'It's A Long Way To Tipperary' and ended gloomily with The Last Post; there was even a wee lassie who was double-jointed and could bend backwards to pick up a pin off the stage with her eyelashes. When we appeared, the other contestants were almost always hostile because we had a sure-fire winner of a song, 'This Is My Lovely Day' from a musical called *Bless the Bride*. It was a toss-up to see who would sing it. If Isabel did, she won, and if I did, I got the prize. We couldn't fail with that song, especially if we 'went up at the end', hitting the top note. It was guaranteed to bring the house down. We were allowed to go to the late-night dancing accompanied by our mothers. They could hardly refuse as we had won the tickets.

Another holiday we had in our teens was in Rothesay. The accommodation was cramped but there was always lots to do in Rothesay. For the children there was Uncle Phil's Punch and Judy on the prom, with his son playing the accordion for community singing and toddlers who could sing nursery rhymes. Uncle Phil, wearing a fez, would invite the small children up on to a little box to sing a solo. My wee brother was persuaded to get up and sing the only song he knew; a rather gory cowboy song called 'There's Blood On The

Saddle'. This always took the trick with the audience, as he sang it very seriously whilst miming playing a guitar. Uncle Phil and his son's Punch and Judy show was an institution in Rothesay and much appreciated by holidaymakers. They gave two shows a day and people thronged to take their children. There were bus runs to lovely beaches and, most popular of all, there were the Rothesay Entertainers in the little round Victorian theatre on the Prom called the Winter Gardens. Isabel and I would stand for hours outside the stage-door waiting for the stars to come out.

The headliners in the summer seasons in those days were Clark and Murray, a husband-and-wife team whose comedy would stand the test of time today. Little did I know that in the future I would work with them and learn my trade the hard way. One night after a performance, Gracie Clark announced that Renee Houston was in the audience – an East End of Glasgow actress of international renown, who was famous for a comedy double-act on stage with her husband, Donald Stewart. They were big stars in those days, and after the death of her beloved husband she went on to be a film star. Her most famous role was in *A Town Like Alice*. That night she was called onto the stage and everyone was thrilled when she made her speech.

'I've been in the business for 32 years, and I can honestly say that I've never enjoyed a show so much as this one I've seen tonight.'

Perhaps a little over the top, but it pleased the cast and audience alike. Renee Houston was someone I was to work with, too, and I remember her as one of the most generous people I've ever known.

Auntie Lizzie, true to her word, got me 'joined' into the Hillhead telephone engineers' concert party. We attended several rehearsals in the Post Office telephones premises. We were tutored in the opening chorus, a little routine including, of course, the song 'I Want To Say Hello'. Isabel and I took part in some of the sketches, playing wee Glesga women. We did shows in old folk's homes and geriatric hospitals. We had captive audiences. We accompanied each other, singing our solos and duets; Isabel, now studying singing, had a lovely repertoire of songs whilst I got my programme from the *Family Song Album*. One night we were entertaining some old folk who were bedridden. In the midst of one of my songs – an inappropriate choice,

Dorothy

'The Heart Bowed Down By Weight of Woe' – an old man called me over to his bedside and took my hand. He didn't speak so I carried on singing. At the end of it he had tears in his eyes. I said that I hoped I hadn't made him sad. He struggled for breath and replied in a croaky voice, 'Naw, hen, ah jist wanted you to shut up. Ah'm trying tae sleep.'

It's a wonder I didn't just give up my big ideas about the singing and dancing pictures; it certainly wasn't because I had a lot of confidence: I didn't. Nor was it because of any serious rivalry with Isabel. If there was an competitiveness it was between Auntie Lizzie and my mother. My mother would goad me on to practise with, 'Get in there and do an hour at that piano. Isabel's got "In a Monastery Garden" off by heart and you haven't even got halfway through "The Robin's Return".'

My piano teacher, Miss Gouldwell, was also a singing teacher and she took quite an interest in me. Her sitting-room where she taught was beautiful, with colours that were the height of fashion; eggshell green walls and a maroon suite. Walking into this room was like entering a jewel box. It was, to me, absolutely conducive to the art of music. Her upright piano was in tune the way ours wasn't, and the room was always warm and welcoming. She would ask me how I was doing at school and was genuinely interested in my progress. I told her about being in a concert party and one day she asked me to sing for her. The next time my mother attended one of my piano lessons, which she often did, Miss Gouldwell suggested that I take singing lessons too. My mother said she would think about it. However, going down the road afterwards, she burst into tears and told me that she just couldn't afford the fees. When I told my teacher that we wouldn't be taking her up on her offer, she asked me why. I was embarrassed but had to tell her the truth. She made an offer my mother couldn't refuse: she would teach me singing and piano for the same fee. When I was 14 the piano was abandoned, as by then the singing lessons had become paramount.

Isabel and I moved on to another concert party. We called ourselves The Gaels. It was run by a charming couple, Mr and Mrs Arneil, whose son played the piano very well, although at that time he was a singing boy wonder. They were of the spiritualist persuasion, Mr Arneil being a spiritualist medium. I got a message, no pun intended, to appear at a church in Hamilton; their usual soloist was off with a cold and could I take her place for the Sunday evening service? Throughout the years I've met spiritualist mediums who have impressed me very much, but the lady who was giving the messages that night was one of the less gifted. She was a stout woman with blonde 'Dolly Dimple' curls tied with a blue bow, and during the second hymn she started to go into her trance state. She wobbled about, emitted strange sounds, and frightened me to bits. She started to talk to invisible people beside her and chose some members of the congregation to receive the messages.

'The lady in the red hat.'

'Yes?'

'Your grandmother is pleased with your choice of new wallpaper. She thinks it looks like a beautiful garden.' The lady in the red hat was grateful for her loved one's approval.

'The gentleman sitting at the back with the green tie. There's a message for you from your brother in the spirit world: he is very happy and you've not to worry.'

To a lady in a brown coat she imparted, 'Uncle Willie is glad that you still keep his cap on the hallstand.'

It crossed my immature but impressionable mind that if these spirits had breached the impenetrable veil between this world and the after-life, could they not impart information of more import? All the messages that were coming across were so trivial and mundane. What gave me the shivers was when she told a lady in the front row that the spirit of her grandmother was sitting beside her in the empty seat. The thought of a ghost only a yard or two away caused my voice to shake when eventually I stood up and sang 'If I can help somebody as I pass along, then my living will not be in vain', yet another winner from the *Family Song Album*.

My singing was improving but my progress at school was not. I had never got over the fact that I was in a lower class than my primary school peers. I was in what was called a 'commercial year', which meant that I learned shorthand and typing, sewing and cookery, while the pals were ahead of me doing Latin and French or German, along with English and the dreaded mathematics. I just couldn't get a handle on mathematics. In those days, without a pass mark in this particular subject, you had no chance of a higher education. Of course, the first day in that class got off to a bad start. We were all sitting there waiting for the teacher to arrive when who should walk in the door but Tojo the Japanese war criminal. I thought he had been hanged but no, he had outwitted the Allies, escaped, and was now holding down a position as a maths teacher in Whitehill Senior Secondary. The other thing that put me off was the fact that when he said x+y=xy (I think), he made a 'sloosh' sound. Poor man, it's easy to blame him for the fact that I just didn't have that kind of brain. They say that understanding the mathematical progressions of the piano go along with learning maths. Well, I wasn't wonderful in either department.

I also didn't fare well in the first-year history class. Our teacher was a ringer for John Christie, the mass murderer. He had great staring eyes and wore sandals, even in the winter. He positively drooled over blood and gore and managed to spread Anne Boleyn's beheading over two periods. He left teaching not long after that and 'found God'. Thereafter he could be found outside Lewis's Polytechnic in Argyle Street on a Saturday, preaching of the hellfire and damnation in store for all the folk who had only gone there to buy a new outfit. I spoke to an old school friend who told me that our history teacher had wanted to start a new religion. As he put it, 'He ended up going around the streets of Glasgow making a cult of himself.'

The one teacher in Whitehill School whom I really took to was Miss Cameron, the French teacher. She was flamboyant and young and I loved her teaching – with the result that I am able to communicate quite well in French. Only last year I discovered her address and invited her to my one-woman show. She accepted graciously and came to see me backstage, thanking me for the night's entertainment. I thanked her for introducing me to the French language, and also for her inspiration. She was delighted to hear this, but confessed, 'Dorothy – I don't remember you at Whitehill.' Why would she have remembered me? The main thing is that I had remembered her and profited from her teaching: there are few 'greats' in any walk of life.

Dorothy

I had made a bad start at secondary school, and I think I just switched off from the whole business. I felt like a second-rate citizen and left at Christmas in 1952, having learned to type, sew a little, and cook. There has been no evidence of my having any aptitude for the latter, although the little bit of typing was to stand me in good stead. I was ashamed that I couldn't keep up with my friends, and had even given up my big ideas about appearing in the singing and dancing pictures. I believed that if you wanted to earn £8 a week, you needed your Highers. Who would pay a numpty that kind of money?

14

The heavens are still; no sound.
Where then shall God be found?
Seek not the distant skies;
In man's own heart he lies.
SHAO TNG, 11TH CENTURY

I got a job at the C&A. As a junior in the shop I spent six months humphing coats and cleaning mirrors with newspaper and methylated spirits. Little did I know that I was there at the same time as Vera Weisfeld, who created the What Every Woman Wants chain and is now a multi-millionaire. I have met her subsequently and we've recalled the days when we were juniors in our different departments. Some wag overheard our conversation and said, 'Here, Dorothy, maybe you went into the wrong business. Look where you might have been if you'd stuck with the C&A!'

I didn't stick with the C&A because by then I had learned to 'go' a bike and was entering into the most wonderful and wholesome phase of my entire life. I joined the CTC, Cyclists' Touring Club, and started hostelling. I had to get a job that would give me Saturday afternoons off.

My sister-in-law 'spoke for me', and I started in the Kraft Cheese Company, whose offices and warehouse were up by the canal at Port Dundas in Glasgow. I loved the job and made many friends there; many of the girls have since come to see my show. There was a complete cross-section of young Glasgow womanhood in that office. We were mostly invoice typists and all had our own desks, typewriters and adding machines. Mr Haining had an office with glass walls so that he could see what we were doing.

Since further education was not an option open to me and feminism was not in our language, I was seduced by the prospect of a small and satisfying life and a big handsome prince, time-served, who would carry me off to a two-room and kitchen with white walls and contemporary furniture. I was in a dreamy state, with one foot in adulthood and the other still in the Rupert-book existence. There weren't enough hours in the week to enjoy myself.

Working hours were nine to five, with an hour and a half for lunch. Our working remit was to total the invoices, reconcile, type them up and send them out. We could talk while we worked and sometimes we sang the latest hits. If someone's invoices didn't reconcile, we'd put our heads together and work them out. At lunchtime we'd sit over a hot pie or two from Angus's shop down the road; we must have had good immune systems because old Angus was not exactly strong in the hygiene department. We were a mixture of types, ages and religions and we all got on well, discussing everything within our understanding and exchanging ideas about engagement rings. We had colourful characters like Etta, who one day jumped up and screamed, 'Aw naw, it's Friday and ah'm eatin' a pie!' She paused momentarily until she had squared the argument within herself, 'Disnae matter, ah jist forgot. Ah'll go tae confession on Saturday.'

We had sharing sessions about boyfriends, but if anyone was sexually active outside of marriage they would never have mentioned it. It just wasn't done. Rehearsals weren't allowed in those days. The most interesting discussions were when the newly married girls dropped little tit-bits of their married lives. We'd drool over someone mentioning going to bed the previous night. Just saying the words 'When we went to bed' was enough to have us on the edge of our seats. No information was forthcoming about what happened then, but our imaginations ran riot. Oh the joy of playing wee houses, having lovely children and an adoring husband bringing home an unopened pay packet! Could life hold more? Never to make the mistakes your parents made. To have the perfect marriage and a world ordered the way you wanted it to be; no one else had achieved this perfect state but we would.

Now and again there would be a spate of engagements. We'd go to a party in the girls' houses and take a present of a pair of tea-towels or a pot-holder. I couldn't envisage a better life than this; a good job among interesting girls, all the pies you could eat, and a pay packet every week with 32/6d in it. Sometimes we'd have lunchtime concerts and this would give me a chance to sing. 'One Fine Day' from *Madame Butterfly* was always requested. I became the little geisha girl who had been deserted by Lieutenant Pinkerton: someday he would come back. I would be filled with emotion which would be transmitted to the others. 'They Call Me Mimi', from *La Bohème*, was another winner with the pals.

Life was exciting except when a boyfriend chucked you and you spent most of the day in the toilet, weeping, while your pals stood outside counselling you with words of wisdom straight from the office girls' book of platitudes: 'There's more fish in the sea than ever came out of it.'

'But I lo......ved him.'

'D'ye fancy going to the Palais tonight?'

Eventually you would be persuaded and next day you'd come into the office with a gleam in your eye.

'Did you get a lumber?'

'Yes' – and away you were again.

As a child, the dunny in the close was a frightening place, but when you were older it had its uses: for snogging sessions when your boyfriend took you home. At one time I was going out with a dental mechanic, and as he kissed me goodnight, I fainted. The boy was terrified because he thought I had died. It would take more than the kiss of a dental mechanic to make me die of bliss. He carried me up to my house, my mother opened the door, and he carried me into the kitchen and laid me on the floor. By this time I was coming round. My father asked him what had happened and the innocent boy said, 'I only kissed her goodnight.'

My father landed him a punch on the nose. 'A dental mechanic? A bloody sex mechanic! Away and leave ma daughter alone from now on.'

The young man was put out the house with his nose swollen and bleeding, saying to himself, 'What did I do wrong?'

It was my custom to cycle to work and back every day, leave my bike in the warehouse, and change in the ladies into my office gear.

Dorothy

One day I overheard one of the warehousemen ask another, 'Whose's that bike?'

'Oh, that's big Dorothy's bike.'

Big Dorothy? Who was that? Were they talking about me? Surely not. That was my first indication that I was overweight; puppy-fat, my mother called it. Could this have something to do with Angus's pies? It was the start of a diet that was to last the rest of my life.

As well as having a dream of a job, there was something on every night. Monday in the summer I was out training on the bike. This involved rushing home for tea then meeting the club at Renfrew Cross and racing down to the roundabout at Greenock and back. I never actually won any races, although I was a member of the 'hard riders' as well as the tourers. I was pretty average, and I think I only joined the racers because there were terrific-looking big boys in it. I had given up the old upright Raleigh with six gears that I started with, and now had an Italian bike which I'd got out of the paper, an Olmo that you could lift with your pinkie it was so light. It had a fixed wheel – serious stuff. I sometimes regretted this bit of flash when going up the Duke's Pass from Aberfoyle, when all the other tourers were going up the gears. Once started on a fixed wheel it would have been a disgrace and a showing-up to go back to gears. Another showing-up was to get off your bike and walk when ascending even the steepest gradient. Why did I always choose the hard road?

I enjoyed the club night when the members would get together to discuss the next weekend's run. We'd chat and drink coffee or tea and then, treat of treats, some older members would show the slides of his holiday in the Western Highlands. The narrative would go something like: 'Ho, ho, now here's my good lady wife attempting to climb Stac Polly.' The younger ones would be arranging dates for the pictures while the good lady wife was struggling up the mountain. Other evenings in the week would be taken up with the pictures and the dancing.

Come what may, I had to do an hour's singing practice every evening; it was just a way of life and had to be done. Miss Gouldwell took me to my first opera, *Faust*, which was performed by the

Glasgow Grand Opera Society. I was enthralled by it. I'd given up the idea of dancing and singing pictures in favour of being an operatic diva, which didn't really equate with my ambition to be married and live a life of domestic bliss. I think I was confused.

Every weekend I would meet with the other members of the CTC at 12.30 p.m. at Anniesland Cross, and we'd set off to some youth hostel which had been organised in advance by the president. Our saddle-bags were packed and we'd cycle perhaps to Inveraray in an afternoon, 75 miles, and arrive starving at the hostel. We'd put the sausage-rolls in the over (I did vary my diet sometimes) with the beans, then we'd wash, have our tea and get ready for the ceilidh which was held either in the common-room or the village hall.

There would be much hooching and yelping during the country dances and then we'd have the 'turns'. My cousin Jean and I were cycling and hostelling companions, and we were also members of the Cycling Hostelling Ensemble. We didn't exactly call ourselves a choir as there were only about seven of us. We practised every Wednesday night in the leader's house. Mrs Thomson was a very special lady, an enthusiastic cyclist, scooter-rider and hiker. On the nights we got together to practise, she would have prepared a wonderful tea which we would devour after having sung for two hours. We were the star turns of the ceilidh but often Mrs Thomson would have to search the grounds of the hostel to assemble her ensemble, as we would be strolling in the moonlight with some of the boys.

Our programme included beautiful Scottish songs such as 'Dream Angus' or 'The Isle of Mull', which of course I had learned in the Co-operative Choir days, but we always started off with 'I Love to Go A-wandering' with 'valdaree, valdara' and all that. I got to sing a solo, which was usually 'Danny Boy' or 'Comin' Through the Rye'. There was a Gaelic singer, Winifred Farquhar, who was 'big' in the Mod – mind you, she was big anywhere, another big square wumman with a leg at each corner. She sang the Gaelic songs, one of which sounded to us like 'ah hoorin, ah hoorin . . . broken down in Gourock'. Willie Reilly, who was one of the characters in the club, and at the age of 80 was still cycling up hill and down dale, used to say, 'Ah, here's Winifred at the hoorin ah hoorin again.'

Another character in the club was Fred Speed, whose name belied his abilities. We had all been struggling up a hill on a hot day when Fred suggested we stop at a cottage and ask the lady of the house for some water. He knocked at the door and a lady came out. Fred bowed and said, 'Could you provide us with a pail of water for some thirsty horses?' The woman went into her house and came back with a dirty old pail of undrinkable water, put it down on the step and shut the door on us. Everyone said, 'Oh, Fred, could you not just have asked for some water like anyone else?'

If we were cycling a long journey, we would stop for a 'drum up'. This involved getting out the Primus stoves and boiling water for the tea, which we drank out of a billy-can. The weather never put us off going away at weekends. We often cycled many miles with the rain squishing out of our cycling shoes with every downward pedal. The strange thing was that, from the time I started cycling in all weathers, I never had rheumatics again. Perhaps I'd grown out of them. One day my cousin and I were cycling up to Crianlarich on our own when we stopped outside the Tarbert Hotel on Loch Lomond. The rain was horizontal and we had stopped to adjust our saddle-bags. A posh lady came out of the hotel, took one look at us, and before she got into her car said, 'You poor things, you're absolutely dripping wet. Here's five shillings. Away you go into that hotel and get yourself some tea and sandwiches.' I felt a little like a beggar taking the posh woman's money, but my cousin had no such qualms. 'Come on, it's no often you get an offer like that.' It was the first time I'd been in a big hotel and I felt quite out of place in the salubrious surroundings, but we ate everything on the three-tiered cake-stand and set off on our way again.

I became aware of 'light' on a holiday up north with my cousin Jean. It was the first holiday I'd had away from 'maw, paw and the weans' doon the watter. We set off to tour Scotland, starting at Crianlarich; next stop was Glencoe, a place that always shrouds me in depression, perhaps because I'm a MacDonald. We were then heading up to Loch Lochy Hostel on Loch Ness. Jean was inclined to take lifts and this caused some arguments, because a dedicated cyclist stuck to the rules: no lifts. Apart from that, she was the ideal cycling companion. She went away on a lorry with her bike in the back, and I suddenly regretted my decision because a big black dog chased me after I got off the Ballachulish ferry. As I was going up a hill, I didn't have the speed to escape him. Just then two fellows on racing bikes came up behind me and chased the dog with their bicycle pumps: knights of the road saving a maiden in distress. They asked me where I was going and if I was on my own. I explained the situation and one of them said, 'Jist hang wur wheel, hen, we'll see ye up tae Fort William.' To hang a wheel meant that you would tuck yourself in behind the cyclist in front and they would act as a windbreak, a great advantage when there was a head wind. These boys were serious cyclists so I had to go at a rate of knots to keep up with them, but I did.

When we got to Fort William, we found a spot at the side of the road and shared the cyclists' communion: a drum-up. We were ships that passed in the night but the camaraderie of cycling hostellers was such that you need have no fear. I identified them by their gear, their bikes and their language. Over our meal we told stories of previous runs and experiences. We had a language all of our own. One of the boys told me a story of what every cyclist feared.

'Ye see, ah wis gawn up the Rest and Be Thankful when I took the "Knock". Ah fell aff ma bike and ah couldnae move. Ma legs wis paralysed and ah wis shakin' like a leaf. Jist as well ah saw a shepherd. Ah caws him ower and he could see that state ah wis in. He asked me if ah wis a diabetic; ah says naw, it's the Knock, the Knock. He goat the picture and gied me some chocolate and some of his pieces and tea oot his flask. If it hidnae been fur him, ah'd a been a gonner.'

What he was describing was a condition caused by cycling too many miles without food or drink: for some reason we called it the 'Knock'. We parted company, the boys going west and I heading north. We didn't meet again, but I've never forgotten those great lads.

When I arrived at the hotel I was starving as usual. We didn't have much money to last us the fortnight so we had to eat cheap, filling food. For tea that night it was semolina – about three platefuls. We journeyed on to Inverness, to Carbisdale Castle, which was a youth hostel then, and crossed over to the west coast. At one point, I nearly fell off my bike at a most amazing scene. A great mountain loomed up; it was called Siulvan. The angle we were approaching at made it look like a great cone. Beyond that was the sea where the sun shone through the clouds in beautiful rays, turning the Summer Isles to bright gold. I thought I was in heaven. I was aware that I was having a mystical and magical experience. I was light-headed and filled with an emotion I'd never felt before. The light I saw that day was the purest and brightest I'd ever seen. I got off the bike and ran up a hill to get a better view. I was overcome by the sight and simply cried out for the joy of it. My cousin got out the Primus stove and started to make semolina. I asked her why she was doing that and she said, 'I'm worried about you. I thought you were taking the "Knock" there.'

I learned early to appreciate the beauties of Scotland through being part of a terrific club. I have had a love affair with Scotland all my life and have never seen a place yet that can match it. We may not get the weather, but one day of good weather in Scotland is worth seven on any continental beach. Whenever I've had enough of the city, the work, the stress, I take to the hills to restore my spirit. It is a true saying that you may be depressed but if you walk up a big hill you will come down feeling a hundred times better. Some of my favourite lines by Sir Walter Scott sum up my feelings:

> Breathes there the man, with soul so dead,
> Who never to himself hath said,
> This is my own, my native land.

15

The dark, uneasy world of family life — where the
greatest can fail and the humblest succeed.

RANDALL JARRELL

One morning in the late summer of 1954 I received a notification to
attend an audition at a church hall in Albion Street, Glasgow. It
was sent to me by Archie McCulloch, a journalist at that time with the
Evening Citizen. The newspaper was running a talent competition. I was
rather intrigued and wondered how they had heard of me. It all became
apparent when I went to work and told the girls about it. Mrs
Thomson owned up to putting my name in for it, because it was such
a shame that I wasn't getting a chance to do something with 'a God-
given talent'. I thought it was a lovely thing to say and that she was a
great friend to have gone to the trouble of writing in on my behalf, but
I disagreed with the 'God-given talent' remark. I realised that my voice
had improved quite a bit as I had grown, and with thanks to my
wonderful teacher Miss Gouldwell, but once you get it into your head
at an early age that you are really not very good at something, it sticks
in the mind. For that very reason, I have always watched what I say to
youngsters when they ask for advice about their talent. It takes a lot of
persuasion to undo destructive criticism in the young psyche. If you do
something well, you are apt to think, 'Oh, there you are, I've got off
with it,' feeling a bit of a fraud. This lack of self-perception might have
been inherited or even learned behaviour, because as a family we were
apt to deride each other's achievements. We were very Scottish in our
attitude to success, an example being, 'You're at the top of the class,
are you? Well, we'll see how long you can stay there.' I had never really
worked up any confidence in my voice, although I enjoyed singing.

Dorothy

I turned up at the auditorium, which was being taken by the famous BBC broadcaster Howard M. Lockhart. My mother came along with me and we sat among hundreds of hopefuls of all ages in an ante-room. We were taken into the hall two at a time; I entered along with a girl crooner, who went first. She didn't have music with her so the accompanist, Harry Carmichael, had to 'busk', which he did very well. She sang some eminently forgettable song but I thought she had quite a good voice. The pianist was very kind and had a warm, encouraging smile, which I'm sure he had for everyone. I can see us sitting there, in the dusty atmosphere of that church hall, which had a very high ceiling, ideal for a soprano voice.

Howard M. Lockhart was obviously drained; he must have been sitting there for hours listening, watching and making notes as folk went through their paces. I felt very self-conscious because my mother had insisted that I wear short socks and a frock that was too young for me. She said, 'The man'll be more impressed if he thinks you're younger than you are.' I couldn't see the logic of this. I was a well-developed, big girl of 16 and felt stupid, but of course I did as my mother – however misguided – told me.

The girl in front of me finished her song. Mr Lockhart shuffled his papers and without looking up at her said, 'You've come a long way, my dear. Kilmarnock, is it?' My mother and I looked at one another and got the picture immediately. He didn't think much of her singing if that was all he could say. What would he say to me? I lived only a few tram-stops away, so it would be, 'Well, at least you've not got too far to travel.' If he said that, I'd know I was out of the running.

He called me over to his table, shook my hand and gave me a weak, tired smile, asking what I was going to sing and whether I had music. I said yes, I did have music and I was going to sing 'Vissi d'Arte' from *Tosca*. He sighed and shifted uncomfortably in his seat and said, 'I never think it's a good idea for children to sing major operatic arias.' The short socks had him fooled. 'Give Harry your music, my dear.' I gave the music to the pianist, who seemed a little bit more enthusiastic and nodded encouragement.

I felt I was off to a bad start. I turned to my mother, who was giving me the high signs that indicated 'Stand right forward and straighten your back.' Having got the feel of the room I didn't stand forward, I stood back to get the full resonance. At the start of the aria there are only two bell notes. The pianist played these confidently and I hit the first note square on. I knew that I had made a good start after all. My voice resounded through the hall and I took a wee dose of confidence and sang the aria quite well. When I was finished, I looked at Mr Lockhart, who was writing away furiously. He hit a full-stop, looked up and said, 'That was quite beautiful, my dear. Your voice has a maturity unusual in one so young. I am putting you straight through to the finals.' He gave me the date of the appearance and I was on a tram-car home before my feet hit the ground.

The Talent Competition was to be part of a television exhibition held in St Andrews Hall in Charing Cross; it is now the Mitchell Theatre since the halls burned down. As I remember, the exhibition was to get people interested in the concept of television and my father was fascinated by the new technology. 'Ah'll take a race up there and see whit it's aw aboot.' He bought himself a new hat, went along on the first day it opened and every day. He was able to touch the sets and discuss them with the experts. He came home full of talk about tubes, lines, valves and polarities. We all ignored him because we hadn't a clue what he was talking about.

The big night came, and thankfully I didn't have to wear the short socks. There had been 800 contestants altogether and now there were about 20 finalists, mostly singers and musicians. I chatted to some of the contestants. There was Marcia Dawn, a semi-professional from Kirkcaldy, who admitted that her real name was Bunty Gibson. She wore a pale pink pearlised nail varnish, which I'd never seen before, and a pink dress exactly the same colour. I thought she was beautiful. Another girl was Elizabeth O'Hare, a lyrical soprano who sang songs from the shows. She was quite tiny and I wondered how she could achieve such a wonderful sound with so small a frame. Elizabeth came from Possil and was married, with a new baby.

Among the adjudicators was Kathy Kay, Archie McCulloch's wife, who was a well-known singer in London and sang on Billy Cotton's Band Show, which was broadcast nationally on Sunday afternoons.

I remember she wore a striking mulberry-coloured silk suit and matching hat, reminiscent of Carmellia's headdress.

There were to be four winners and the atmosphere was very tense.

Dorothy

This was the culmination of the exhibition and we could all be seen on closed-circuit television. Imagine how my mother and father must have felt to see me singing in a medium almost unknown in those days. The found themselves a spot in the hall where they could see me on stage and on the television at the same time. I sang 'Vissi d'Arte' again and was given a great round of applause. I came off the stage and I could see that my parents were pleased. Mother said, 'Well, you may not have won but you did well, hen.' Not long after, we seemed to be leaving the hall. I don't remember why we weren't staying until the end, but I know we were almost on the street when a man with a clipboard dashed up to us and said, 'Bunty Gibson – don't go away, you've won!' We told him he had the wrong girl but he insisted, and we almost got into an argument. He finally admitted that perhaps he had the wrong name but I was definitely a winner and they wanted me to sing again. I still wasn't convinced. However, as we approached the stage, Archie McCulloch was scouring the hall for me and waffling to the audience until I turned up. At last he could see me and said to the audience, 'Well, here she is, the wee lassie with the big voice, all the way from Dennistoun.' I was hustled on stage and told to stand beside the other winners. They were Elizabeth O'Hare, a boy soprano and a young pianist who arranged music as well. Archie asked, 'Now, my dear, have you got another song you could sing for us?' I said 'Comin' Through the Rye'. He made some joke about this that got a smattering of laughter, then he turned to the pianist and said, 'Got the music there, Harry?' The pianist nodded 'Yes'. He hadn't, but he busked it with great skill. I sang and received tumultuous applause, which Archie milked for all it was worth. We then were presented with little silver cups which said 'Search for Talent 1954'. They were taken away again to have our names inscribed. Archie went on to tell the audience what the prize was, and I could hardly believe it.

He announced: 'These young people will go on a trip to London, where they will stay at the Coburg Court Hotel in Bayswater. They will see the sights in a chauffeur-driven limousine, and they will see a film in the new Cinerama. There will be a visit to the Elstree Studios, where they will meet Gregory Peck, who is at present making the film *Moby Dick*, and they will have an audition with the world-renowned impresario Jack Hylton at the Adelphi Theatre.'

Dorothy

The excitement was overwhelming. Dancing and singing pictures, here I come!

When the pals in the cycling club heard about it, Willie Reilly was heard to say, 'I hear oor Dorothy's going to be a film star.' The girls in Kraft Cheese were delighted and Mr Haining, without hesitation, gave me time off for the trip. My big brother's girlfriend, Maureen Genoe, who was to become his wife, was a model whose kind nature matched her beauty, and she lent me some of her lovely clothes. We all went down to London on the overnight sleeper, arriving at the Coburg Court Hotel early in the morning. We went into breakfast with the waiters running around after us and making us feel very special. The menu was amazing and the little boy singer who was with us asked for fish. The waiter took his order and the little boy said, 'Do you get chips with it?' This was at eight o'clock in the morning, but the waiter brought his chips with his kippers, which he couldn't eat because of all the bones. Archie was with us and a nice lady who acted as our chaperone. Everything that had been promised was fulfilled. The best of all was the trip to Elstree. We were shown round the sets and met Gregory Peck on a great half a ship; it was cut right down the middle to let the cameras in. Mr Peck couldn't have been nicer and we even had lunch in the canteen with him. The audition with Jack Hylton didn't go so well. I was half-expecting him to offer me a part in one of his big musicals, but all he said was, 'You have a lovely voice but you must go back to Scotland and get some experience before you come back to London.' I never did appear in London.

We went back home on the sleeper. Somehow or other I had an upset stomach, and when I got off the bus from the station and went up the stairs of 2 Whitehill Street, I was sick. It was worth it. Everyone wanted to know how I got on and I had many stories to tell. The photographs of the trip arrived by post and when I saw them I realised that I had a long way to go. I was a wee fat lassie bursting out of Maureen's beautiful clothes. I didn't look like someone who could earn £8 a week. The next day I was back at the Kraft Cheese.

Miss Gouldwell declared that she had taken me as far as she could, and it was now time for her to pass me on to her teacher, Hugh Love

Elliot. We went together to his studio in Lansdowne Crescent in the West End of Glasgow, where I was introduced and asked to sing for him. He agreed to take me on and I spent the next two years under his tutelage. He seemed slightly concerned that my voice had matured at such an early age; perhaps I'd peaked too early. However, I went from strength to strength and was now studying Mozart arias. I loved the elegance of Mozart and how his arias taught me control, although I still loved the great overblown dramatic arias of Puccini. I also enjoyed Michaela's arias from Carmen, 'Je Suis Titania' from *Mignon*, the Jewel Song from *Faust* and many others that gave me a chance to act as well as sing. One day I was sitting at the piano, playing the accompaniment and singing Mimi's death scene when, in her extremity, she turns to Rodolfo and sings, 'Have they gone now? To sleep I only feigned, for I wanted to be alone with you, love.' I was quite carried away and was in tears at the end. My mother came in, took one look at me and said, 'Tragedy Queen, that's you.' That remark stuck with me.

Mr Elliot had no sense of humour but his eccentricities made me laugh. He was a very small man, no more than 5 ft 2 in with a barrel chest which he'd developed along with his basso profundo voice. One day, quite out of the blue, he said, 'I am a tall man.' He strutted about while he spoke. 'Look at me, I am a tall man.' I couldn't see what he meant and I daren't titter. 'Yes, I am a tall man but I have short legs.' The subject was left at that; who was I to gainsay him?

Not long after I started lessons with him, he moved to a larger townhouse overlooking the River Kelvin, with an elegant first-floor drawing-room he used as his studio. It was a beautiful room that unfortunately was hung with his own paintings of Scottish landscapes; hills, lochs and heather painted in colours straight from the tube. His undoubted talents did not extend to the visual arts, but he was a great singing teacher and musician and one was carried away with his enthusiasm. Occasionally he would get together his sopranos, tenors and baritones for a musical evening of solos, quartets and duets. I was given a foretaste of what it would be like to sing in opera, but I never did.

16

It's good to be a great woman, but greater to be a good woman.

MOTHER

*T*he aunties' Thursday nights were still a feature of our week. That was also the night I had to 'do the stairs'. This involved giving them a good brush down, then applying the pipe clay. Pipe clay came in a bar like soap, only it was made of a kind of chalky material which, after you dipped the old rag of blanket in the hot water from the pail, you applied to the stairs in a smooth fashion. God help you if you got it streaky.

Streaky pipe clay was not acceptable. There was an artistic side to it. When the stairs dried, you took the dry chalk and made a little pattern with it down the sides of the stair. This indicated a caring attitude towards your neighbours and anyone else who had occasion to ascend the stairs. It was a respectable thing to do and also gave the impression that people's houses were in an equally clean condition. A dirty stair was a sign of a dirty house.

The Thursday nights usually had a theme. Sometimes it would be operations, including descriptions of exploratory surgery.

'They were up and down my "elementary canal" for four and a half hours and they still couldn't get to the bottom of it.'

Then there would be the comparing of scars. One night my mother produced her gall-stone from out of a box and told the tale of a woman up the road who had hers polished and mounted and made into a brooch. Another auntie described the amount of gravel her specialist had taken away from her gall-bladder. This was disregarded, as gravel didn't really count. The star turn was always Auntie Dorrie with her damaged walls.

Dorothy

I may sound as though I am minimising and deriding what were really serious illnesses that caused much suffering and worry to the family, but it was the way the stories were related, and how they made my father say things like, 'Christ, Harry, they've goat me sick wi' aw their operations' or 'Don't go in there the noo, Harry. They've goat their scars oot again.' As a young person I was quite fascinated, but when it came to anything gynaecological I was put out of the room as well, with the words 'Away you go into the kitchen. This is big people's business.' No doubt this was to protect me from the fear of childbirth.

When the subject was exhausted, I would be called in again to help with the second cup of tea and my mother would say, 'Get out your music, the aunties want to hear you singin'.' That was no bother to me, I had an audience. If Isabel was there with Auntie Lizzie, she would sing too, and then we'd do duets. I look back at those days and in a way, apart from the operations, the roll-ons and collecting the ménage money (a local credit system), it was probably much like a Victorian parlour evening.

My big brother, a keen hosteller, motorcyclist and hiker, was eager to sing a song at one of the youth hostel ceilidhs. He chose 'The McGregors' Gathering', a stirring ditty about Rob Roy and his followers, and asked me to play the accompaniment for him. Every time he sang, my father would complain about the noise. Of course the aunties had to be treated to a rendition. My mother would prepare him for his solo with encouraging words. 'Right, son, straighten your hump and don't force it.' Father and Uncle Harry were in the kitchen one night as usual; they were doing their football pools. When my brother started to sing in his rather tight tenor voice, Father shouted through, 'Is that you got the bugger singing noo? Whoever told that boy he was a singer's got a sin tae answer for.' Then, as we ignored him, he shouted, 'Shut that door, I can hear him.' Somebody shut the door, then he yelled, 'Ah'll shut the kitchen door because ah can still hear him.' He said to Uncle Harry, 'Christ, Harry, if a strangulated hernia could sing, that's what it would sound like.' There was much laughter from the kitchen at that remark.

My brother carried on regardless, and was reaching his crescendo when, whether for effect or just because he was annoyed, my father burst into the room as he got to the third stanza, when Rob Roy is defiant and rouses his men to carry on in the face of adversity, 'We're landless, landless, landless Gregalach, landless!'

Father got him by the throat and said, 'Son! I'll gie ye landless! If you don't shut up, ye'll be homeless.'

I fell off the piano-stool with laughter, my brother stomped off in the huff and my mother fell out with my dad for upsetting her son and giving her a showing-up in front of her sisters. I believe there was a slight rivalry between the two men. My father was only 20 years older than his son and there was a vying for dominance in the household, and of course my brother was the light of my mother's eye. He was also very handsome and a big hit with the girls.

Another fad the aunties went in for was the home perm: the Toni. It was advertised with twins sporting the same hairstyle and the caption read, *Which Twin Has The Toni?* With the advent of the home perm, That Wullie King was surplus to requirements. On an unforgettable Thursday night, after they had washed their hair in the kitchen sink, they all sat in a row in the big room waiting for the permer – who, of course, was me. Not only did they want a perm, they chose styles from a magazine. The 'Italian Boy' was all the rage and that's what they wanted. I was hard-pressed to achieve this, as good hair wasn't a family trait. The process involved soaking a strand of hair in a lotion that smelt like a tomcat's urine, then wrapping it in a small paper and rolling it up in plastic curlers. Multiply that by six heads and we are talking a night shift. After a while, and many test curls in between, came the neutraliser, which had its own peculiar aroma. There was a bit of ill-temper when I pulled someone's hair accidentally. The whole business was a nightmare and the results weren't great. In fact, there was a feeling of 'Come back Wullie King, all is forgiven'. When there was a lull in the proceedings, to keep them happy I would make a second cup of tea and pass it round. While they were having this, my mother said, 'Sit down at the piano and give us a song while we're waiting.'

I don't know how many hats I was supposed to wear, but on that one day I was an invoice typist, a stair-washer, a hairdresser, a purveyor of teas and a cabaret turn.

17

Men are always waiting in the wings to be discovered.
Women are always waiting to be found out.

COSMOPOLITAN

*I*sabel was now in show business while I was still studying singing, cycling every weekend and working in the Kraft Cheese. Her first summer season was in Bundoran, in Ireland, and of course Auntie Lizzie accompanied her to protect her little 'chick'. In Glasgow there was an advert in the local newspaper: 'Carrol Levis is coming to town'. He toured the Moss Empires with his show called 'The Carrol Levis Discoveries'. It was a parasitical way of making a living. He sent his cohorts on before him to audition local talent and get them lined up to appear every night with him. At the end of the show, the audience were asked to vote for the winner by applause. This was calculated on his 'Clapometer', a contraption like a wheel of fortune where the pointer reached its highest point with the most applause. A rather dubious way of gauging audience reaction.

In the run-up to the finals, on the Wednesday, I sang 'One Fine Day' from *Madame Butterfly* and won the heat. Saturday was the big night and the Empire was packed to the gunwales. While we were all getting ready for the show, one of Carrol Levis's sidekicks knocked on the door of the dressing-room I shared with a girl whose talent was playing xylophone and tap-dancing at the same time. This man asked me to come down and see Mr Levis in his dressing-room. I walked into the room and Carrol Levis was sitting in an armchair in his dressing-gown, with eyepads on, and his feet up. To me he was like a great white toad, with thinning hair and an amorphous shape.

'Sit down, my dear.'

I ignored this; I was getting a 'no-no' feeling. As he couldn't see me for the eyepads, I decided it was safe and stood near the door.

'You're very good, you know – lovely voice, and you could go far.' He expressed this opinion in a pseudo-American accent.

'Thank you very much, Mr Levis,' I replied, without conviction. 'I'd better get back to the dressing-room and get ready.'

Off came the eyepads to reveal the red-rimmed eyes of a lizard.

'No rush, my dear. Sit down, sit down.'

I didn't.

'Take a look at these photographs on my dressing-table.' There were framed pictures of two or three beautiful girls, dressed in evening frocks. They looked like models. 'These girls were nothing until I took an interest in them, you know. I put them where they are.' I wondered where they were. By now he'd got hold of my wrist. 'Now listen carefully, my dear. You play ball with me and I'll play ball with you. Because if you do, I can adjust the clapometer in your favour.'

I nearly laughed in his face, it sounded so ludicrous. What went through my mind was us playing a game of 'wee heidies' in a football pitch, but of course I knew exactly what he meant. I had to get out of this oppressive atmosphere. We did a kind of dance around the room while he held onto my wrist. I finally got to the door and made my escape, and as I walked up the stairs to the dressing-room I knew what the outcome of the talent competition would be. The clapometer did not swing in my favour, although my mother swore I got the most applause. I was not the least bit disappointed because I didn't want anything to do with that horrible little frog. Nothing was mentioned to my mother about the encounter with Carrol Levis. I would have been too embarrassed.

Then I did something which was a complete aberration. I left the Kraft Cheese and all my friends to work in Cooper's sausage factory. I honestly cannot remember why I did this. Perhaps it was to give the family a change of staff sales: my father was fed up with cheese. I went from a modern, airy office to a Dickensian office with great angled desks to hold enormous ledgers that had to be filled in by hand. There was a door between the place we worked and the actual factory, which was a lot cheerier, with girls round a table linking the sausages as they came out of the machine and singing 'They Tried To Tell Us We're Too Young', the big hit of the day. One of my duties was to walk through the factory to the drivers with dispatch notices. I held my breath as I passed the black pudding room – not the prettiest or sweetest-smelling place in the world. I stuck this job for about a year when I heard about an agent in Sauchiehall Street called Nellie Sutherland of the Gault Agency, who could possibly get me work in the theatre. Isabel was doing well, with singing jobs all over the country. She told me that she had been working with two painters who, on their fortnight's holiday, had played the theatre she was in at the time, the Corn Exchange in Dunbar. The two boys, the Alexander Brothers, were doing very well and were thinking of leaving the painting trade to take up the 'business' professionally. I had already performed in a few shows in a semi-professional capacity. One memorable appearance was in the town hall in Millport in a show run by Archie McCulloch. I was paid £1 for this, plus my expenses. I thought it was a wonderful fee for one night's work.

I took an afternoon off my work in the sausage factory and auditioned for Nellie Sutherland and her boss, Hamish Turner. I passed the audition and was immediately offered work: a weekend in the Roxy, Falkirk. I would get a fiver for the two nights. I was amazed at this amount of money and was even more gobsmacked when she added, 'Now it's not a lot of money, dear, but it's good experience.'

My mother thought it was a wonderful idea, so I handed in my notice at the sausage factory. Mr Campbell, my boss, was a man of strong religious conviction, what my mother used to call 'a Christian kind of person' – I think he was an elder of the kirk. He seemed sorry to lose me: 'You've been doing very well and I was going to promote you to lunch dockets.' These were kept in a tin and had to be handed out to workers, and if you got them wrong they would laugh at you and cause, in a nice way, a humiliation that I was not prepared to endure. 'However, if you are determined to go I can't stop you. Perhaps if you tell me where you are moving on to, I could give you some advice.' I told him I was going into showbusiness. He was speechless; to him it was a girl 'going to the bad'. If he'd been a Catholic he'd have made the sign of the cross. I was dismissed from the office without advice, for which I was very thankful.

Father was sorry to lose the staff sales; these were Cooper's products at half-price. He had always derided them with, 'Christ, hen, there's only one thing you need tae eat these sausages and that's confidence.' But when I told him I was leaving the factory, his reaction was, 'Ah'll miss thae sausages.'

It was Friday night in the autumn of 1956 when I got on the train to Falkirk. I remember clutching my music and a small suitcase with someone's borrowed evening-dress in it, wondering where the cycling club pals were going that weekend. My cycling and hostelling days were over. I had entered a new phase in my life and I didn't have a clue where it was going to take me. This was a test appearance and if I did it well, I was promised a new career.

I arrived at the dingy theatre and was shown to the dressing-rooms. They were on the stairs beside the stage where there was a toilet used by the audience. The star comic dressed at the side of the stage. The musical director was Jimmy Running. He was in charge of the band, a quartet, which sounded for all the world like Hoover bass and drums with piano. The act before me was a male singer in the Perry Como style. He seemed to be having difficulty making himself understood. The song he would perform was 'Memories Are Made of This', a current hit in the Radio Luxembourg top ten. Jimmy said to the other musicians, 'The boy says he wants D minor diminished musical bridge. Gie him a wee rummel, that'll dae.' The boy got short shrift and had to take what was available in the way of accompaniment.

Jimmy didn't have much time for sopranos either. 'Aye, hen, ye'll have a joab tae get a hearin'. Hiv ye goat yer music? Whit are ye gawnae sing?'

'I thought I'd start off with "I Found My Romance in Vienna".'

'Oh, Christ, boys, did ye hear that? Heh heh. Naw, naw, hen, ye'll no get aff wi' that here. Hiv ye anything else?'

'Well, I could do "Waltzing, Waltzing High in the Clouds".'

'Well, hen, please yer bliddy sel, it's no up tae me. How much o' it are ye wantin' tae dae? Chorus verse chorus or verse chorus chorus or eh . . . dae ye want tae scrub it aw thegither? It's bliddy hellish that song.'

I was in a state of nerves and couldn't decide. I replied, 'I'll just do a verse and chorus of that one.'

He then proceeded to get a very black pencil and scrub out much of the introduction with the remark, 'I'll jist give ye two oompahpahs tae get ye goin', ye know whit ah mean?'

I didn't, but who was I to say?

The comic was Tommy Loman, who was very kind to me and gave me encouraging words before I went on. 'Ye'll be fine, hen, jist give it laldy.'

It was my turn to go on stage, and I found that I had to run on as I was only going to get two oompahpahs before I started, so I was quite breathless before the first note came out. Then I felt as though I had a balloon in my throat that blew up with every breath I took, constricting my voice. I don't know how I got through the first song, all the while doing a little waltz movement that seemed appropriate at the time. When I finished with the stormer 'Ave Maria', I really got them and ended quite successfully. The next night I went on just as nervous, and when I started to sing a man in the front row brought out his sports final and started to check his football coupon. Tommy Loman said that I'd done very well and he would let Nellie know that. He was a lovely man.

I was asked to play the following weekend at the Roxy with the same cast. I was slightly worried about the insecurity of the dressing-room situation, although there was always someone around to mind your things if any of the audience went to the toilet in the middle of the show. However, £5 for two nights wasn't to be sneezed at and, as Nellie said, it was good experience. I went on the Friday night and got the raspberry from a member of the audience; fortunately some people who were enjoying my singing made shooshing sounds at the offender and I carried on. This time I finished with 'The Holy City' which brought tumultuous applause. After the show one of the musical acts received his pay packet and went into a corner to count it. He seemed to take ages flicking the notes then, satisfied with the amount, he pocketed it. It seemed to me that he must be getting lots of money, but Tommy pulled me aside and said, 'That's an old pro's trick. He asks to get paid in ten shilling notes and then he turns his back on everyone and doubles the notes up. When he flicks them it sounds as though he's getting double what he's really being paid.'

I was called up to Nellie's office to discuss my next date. There was a small waiting-room at the top of the stairs and some professionals were sitting around the bench against the wall, trying to look well off. However, I noted the cuffs of the camel coats were frayed and that they lit up half-smoked cigarettes. The talk was 'big' among the men. I heard one say, 'I had to turn down a film last week, Nellie wouldn't let me out of my contract in Dunoon. Oh, well, that's showbusiness, eh?' Another man boasted of how he'd 'torn' them up in Dundee. 'I'm telling you,' he said, 'a standing ovation, they wouldn't let me off the stage.' I thought I really was among the crème de la crème here. When it came to their turn to speak to Nellie, who appeared from a hatch with a sliding door, they were begging her for work.

Nellie was a turn in herself when she slid the hatch up and down. She was famous for her slack false teeth, which clacked as she talked. She was what was called in those days a maiden lady, very old-fashioned with her hair in sausage curls pinned with Kirby grips that were always dangling from an untidy strand. Her opening line to everyone was, 'Are you vacant, dear?' Then she would give out work or dash hopes of anything doing this side of the year.

'Now, dear, Mr Morgan [Tommy Morgan] was very annoyed with you and it was no wonder he sacked you. He said that you had taken a refreshment before the show and you were drunk.'

The shamefaced singer said, 'Och, Nellie, it was only a wee refreshment, I had the cold.'

'But you fell off the stage, dear, and nearly broke the drummer's neck.'

'I'm really sorry, Nellie.'

'There's no use being sorry to me, dear. Some people would give their eye-teeth to play the Pavilion and there you are a nice singer and a good mover and you're just ruining your career with the drink.'

'What should I do, Nellie?'

'If I were you, I'd just go to Mr Morgan and eat humble pie.'

'Okay, Nellie, I'll do that.'

He was exiting through the door to go down the wooden stairs when she called after him, 'Don't forget now, dear, humble pie.'

Dorothy

It was my turn and she asked the usual question, 'Oh, hello, dear, are you vacant?' I was definitely vacant. I was totally dependent on this agency to get me work. 'Now, dear, you did very well at the Roxy and we're going to send you out on a major tour. You'll start off at Stonyetts then Woodielea, Leverndale, Gartnavel Royal and a big gala finish in Carstairs.'

I said humbly, 'Are all these asylums, Nellie?' That was what we called these hospitals in those days.

She said, 'Yes, dear, but I think you'll find it very rewarding.'

In the cast of the major tour were Chic Murray and Maidie. I had never seen an act like theirs before and stood at the side of the stage every night to watch them. They didn't get much reaction from the audience as many of the patients were sedated for the concert, but the staff loved them and they got huge cheers. It was obvious that their style of comedy was unique and they were heading for the big time. Maidie, who was tiny, would come on stage with her accordion, which seemed huge. She would sing a few songs and then Chic would enter, stand behind her and harmonise. When she sang by herself, she would turn upstage to look at him then turn back to the audience; when she did that, he would make faces behind her back. One night during this routine someone in the audience shouted out, 'Away, get aff the stage, ya mug, and let the wee wumman sing in peace.' Maidie would walk off and leave Chic on his own and he would start his act. 'Have you seen Dumbarton Rock? I was standing there all day and I never even saw it move.'

After this major tour, I trotted up the same stairs again to Nellie's office. She said, 'Mr Turner's taken quite an interest in you, dear, and he's very pleased with your work.' No one actually saw Mr Turner as he always kept to the back office. If you were 'big' you got in to see him but a wee soprano like me only saw Nellie. She continued, 'Mr Turner thinks you're ready for one of our major venues' – she always stressed the second syllable. 'You're being placed in the Tivoli Aberdeen for the autumn season. Now, you'll need at least six costumes for the six weeks, can you manage that, dear?' Naturally I said yes. I always said yes to work and wondered later how I would come up with the goods. Then she said the magic words: 'Your pay will be £12 per week.'

Dorothy

I nearly fainted: £12 a week, this was beyond my wildest dreams. I couldn't wait to go home and tell my mother. After she picked herself up and brushed herself down, we both wondered how we were going to get six dresses and how much would they cost. Normally the soprano in the show wore a long evening-dress, but short cocktail dresses were coming into fashion. We sought the advice of my sister-in-law, Maureen, the model. She suggested that I came in and meet Mr Corrigan, her boss at the wholesale gown shop, Schubette Models, in Exchange Square. Mr Corrigan, a man who did me quite a few favours, gave me two very pretty dresses with the compliments of the company. One was a strapless white net with blue sequins, and the other was a yellow dress with a skirt of small frills. They were absolutely beautiful. I still had to find another four and a large case to carry them in.

My mother remembered that there was a woman down the Barras who dealt in second-hand designer frocks. She operated from a small lean-to shop at the bottom of Barrack Street and Gallowgate. We both trooped down there and looked through her stock. They had all seen better days but beggars couldn't be choosers. We got four frocks for £5 and she threw in an old case for ten shillings. It had seen a few ocean journeys by the look of it. We took them home, altered them and got them cleaned. One was a blue satin gown with a hoop which made it into a kind of crinoline. My mother said, 'There you are, hen,' and sang 'In her sweet little Alice blue gown'. I wasn't convinced that I looked wonderful.

There were digs to sort out in Aberdeen. The usual way of doing this was to phone the theatre and ask for addresses of theatrical landladies. My mother knew better. 'I'm no happy about you moving in with these theatricals, you never know what they're up to. Auntie Isa and me'll take a day trip to Aberdeen ourselves and see what's doing. A nice respectable place.' She had a totally wrong idea about theatrical landladies, most of them were the salt of the earth, but we didn't know that then.

They returned exhausted but they had secured a place for me which was miles away from the theatre, near the sands. 'It's a lovely place, hen, and it's near the seashore for you to do your breathing. The wee woman's lovely; she's a young widow with two children and

Dorothy

she'll give you bed and breakfast, tea and a light supper for £2 and
ten shillings a week. Cannae say fairer than that.' I thought this was
fine and I arrived at the digs on the Sunday night, ready for the first
rehearsal the next day; Monday morning at ten o'clock. I was a
sheltered 18-year-old who had never been away from home. The
landlady seemed a very nice woman and her children were lovely.
After tea, when she'd got the kids to bed, she started to tell me about
her life. She wasn't a widow at all, she was twice divorced with a
string of boyfriends, and I sat with my mouth hanging open while she
told me all about her sex life. I couldn't believe it. I was hearing things
I wouldn't have believed were possible. This was the 'respectable' wee
widow woman my mother had got me in tow with. If she'd known,
she would have died on the spot.

I turned up for the first day of rehearsal dressed – it was my
mother's idea – in a hand-knitted Fair Isle twin-set and a kilt, and for
spite my mother had knitted me a beret to match. I was given some
funny looks but the cast were very kind to me. The comics were
Johnny Beattie, Tommy Loman and Wally Butler. The comedy woman
– the name for the female comedy feed – was Maggie Milne. It was a
beautifully dressed show, as the costumes had come straight from
Tommy Morgan's summer season and the producer (in the variety
theatre artistic directors were called producers) was a wonderful
dancer called Jack Raines. There was a tap-dancing double act who
were very 'gay'. In those days gay people were very much in the closet
but backstage they could be themselves. These two fellows were
utterly charming and made me laugh with their antics.

'Oh, darling, what's that make-up you've got on? For God's sake,
you've put it on with a shovel!'

He was absolutely right: I used five and nine greasepaint sticks and
the bluest of blue eyeshadows. On the first night they dragged me
into their dressing-room.

'Sit down, darling.' When I hesitated, one of them said, 'For God's
sake, darling, we're queens – we know what we're doing.' They did
my make-up beautifully.

The opening chorus was 'Another Opening, Another Show', with
lots of movement. The two quarters at the Sunshine School of
Dancing had paid off. I was involved in the scenes that were musical

excerpts from the shows. In the first week, one was a Tyrolean scene in which the first number was 'Dance to the Music of the Ocarina', and I had to dance with Wally Butler who, much to my dismay, kept on his glasses. I mentioned to him that perhaps he would look better if he took them off for that scene. 'Oh, aye, I'll do that and I'll end up falling off the bloody stage.' I never mentioned it again, but I objected to dancing on stage with someone wearing glasses. My solo was another Tyrolean-type song, 'Strange Music in My Heart', then it ended in a duet with me and the tenor – believe it or not, it was 'Valdaree, Valdaro'. The tenor, a mature man, had to leave halfway through the season as one night, during his act, his varicose veins burst (strange, but true!).

It was great to be in the show but nerves spoiled it for me. They were so bad that I had to go to the doctor for something to calm me down. Beta-blockers hadn't been invented. The nerve bottle he gave me was green stuff with a large percentage of alcohol in it. It didn't really help, and I felt squiffy with it.

My mother and Auntie Isa came up to see the show and my landlady put them up. We were all in the same room: Auntie and my mother in the double bed and me in the single. Of course, I didn't mention anything about the landlady's proclivities, and they seemed very pleased with the digs. The only thing that amazed my mother was the local dish they had for their high tea: a haddock and an egg. We were on the point of sleep that night when my mother suddenly sat up in bed and said, 'A haddie and an egg? My God, Isa, I've never heard of that in my life. Ham and haddie maybe, but no a haddie and an egg.'

I loved the company I was working with, they were such nice people and, contrary to my mother's expectations, very respectable. I made a lifelong friendship with Johnny Beattie and Wally Butler, and Tommy Loman took the trouble to show me how to 'take a call' – the bow at the end of my act. I had great difficulty getting off the stage, but he showed me how to curtsy and walk off, then walk on again to take another bow.

Towards the end of the six-week season, I returned to the digs for my lunch and noticed a big man's coat hanging on one of the hooks in the hall. I'd never noticed it before. There in an armchair in the kitchen was a tall, cadaverous man with great staring eyes. The landlady introduced him as her fiancé. She explained that he was just 'out'.

I said, 'Have you been in hospital?' He certainly didn't look very well.

He replied, 'No – Peterhead.'

So much for my mother's respectable digs.

18

Fear comes from uncertainty. When we are absolutely certain, whether of our worth or worthlessness, we are almost impervious to fear. Thus a feeling of utter unworthiness can be a source of courage.

ERIC HOFFER

*I*n the days of variety, an artiste could work in theatre almost 52 weeks of the year. People went to the theatre a lot in those days and there were plenty of theatres around. However, sometimes there would be odd weeks out of work and in the profession these were called 'resting times'. I didn't like the resting times as it meant having to turn up at the 'broo', or the Labour Exchange as it was known then (now the DHS), and signing on. Jobs were plentiful, the way they aren't now, so I sought the advice of Mr Corrigan, my sister-in-law's boss. He said he could get me a job in one of the shops he supplied. He picked up the phone and got through to Mrs Laing, the owner of Reeta's Fashions in the Gallowgate, near Glasgow Cross. He gave me a big build up and Mrs Laing suggested that I go along and see her. It was quite a large shop with different departments: gowns, coats, suits, shoes, baby linen and wools. It is still a well-known establishment, run by the next generation of Laings. I was rather devious in that I didn't tell them I was a variety artiste looking for a temporary job, but I really wanted to work there because in a way I think I needed levelling. I was seeking the 'gravitas' of ordinary working life that didn't cause me to go off my head with nerves. Mr and Mrs Laing were charming people and they offered me a job as a sales assistant.

Having had the experience of comedy on stage, I was very aware

Dorothy

of the characters that came into the shop and observed them carefully
as I was selling them clothes. There was one 'big Mammy' built like
a Sherman tank who came in with her very thin daughter.

'Get us a seat, hen, she's goat me run aff ma feet.'

In those days the sales assistants showed the customer to a cubicle,
asked what their requirements were, and brought some of the stock
to let them have a look. First of all the girl said, 'Ah want a suit wi' a
cocktail collar.' I had never heard of this style but I knew of a suit on
one of the rails that I thought would fit the bill. It was one of the
better ranges with a high percentage of wool and had a shawl collar.
As the girl was built like a stick insect, it would look beautiful on her
– a bit of class. She tried it on and looked fantastic; she felt good in
it too. She turned to 'big Mammy': 'Whit dae ye think, Maw?'

Maw paused, screwed up her face like a squashed scone and said,
'Naw, ah, no strrr . . .uck.'

'Whit dae ye no like aboot it, Maw?'

Maw replied, 'Ah 'hink . . . ah 'hink it's awfu common lukkin'.'

I couldn't believe it: the best suit in the shop. The girl looked like
a princess. The mother relented, got out her Provident cheque and off
they went. I would come home at night and relate all the stories to
my mother and imitate the customers. These impersonations would
creep into the aunties' Thursday nights. Instead of my mother asking
me to sing, she'd say, 'Tell the aunties about that customer in the
shop.'

After a few weeks I got another job, a winter season in the
Palladium, Edinburgh, with Johnny Victory. Mr and Mrs Laing knew
there was something fishy but they were very kind and said, 'Just
come back any time you're free.'

I loved that job in Reeta's. The shop was well run and had the kind
of organisation that I felt was now missing from my life. Every
theatre job was an unknown quantity, a new beginning, taking it from
the top, learning the trade, which in the theatre is a lifetime's work
with no pension scheme, no security, a lot of discipline and hard
work, never being able to 'lean on your shovel'. You've got a cold?
Sorry, get on there, the show must go on. You're upset about
something? Sorry, the show must go on. Sorry, dear, the only way you
can get out of your contract is with a death certificate – your own. At

all costs the show must go on. You have to work six nights a week and if you're on tour you travel on the Sunday. Your social life is cut to a minimum. And there are the auditions, when you come away with your confidence in shreds because someone else has got the job.

The theatre is definitely a hard life but the advantages outweigh the hardships. You have to focus. You have to concentrate, use the mind, learn the lines, keep the body fit, do that voice warm-up, the physical warm-up. There is always the chance of the 'biggie', that job that will project you into the rarefied air of stardom, even if, statistically, there's very little chance of that happening. And there is the applause, the audience approval you never get as a shop assistant.

Johnny Victory and his entourage were a motley crew. They didn't have the style of a Jack Raines production or the kind of cast I had become used to working with. I was asked to appear in risqué sketches, and resisted with the excuse, 'I'm sorry, I can't appear in that sketch, I'm a soprano.' I must have been a bit of a snob. There was a man in the cast, a musical act, who was bald with just a little hair round the edges. He would rub black boot polish onto his scalp to give the appearance of hair. At rehearsals he was a quiet introverted little man, but at night, when the boot polish was applied, he became an extrovert, full of confidence, and he took to the stage with a certain panache. They complained to the management about my unwillingness to appear in the sketches, but I wouldn't budge. I only did the one season with them.

The hardest season of all during my time in the death throes of variety was the summer season in the Winter Gardens at Rothesay. A 20-week season, twice nightly, and with a twice-a-week change of programme. We rehearsed and performed 14 shows before we repeated anything. The stars of the show were Gracie Clark and Colin Murray, and they worked the hardest of all. Gracie was the boss and she was a hard taskmaster.

The show was a Fraser Neil production. Fraser Neil also had a company called Mutries, a costume-hiring company. Unfortunately, there had been a big fire in his store in Edinburgh and most of his lovely costumes had been destroyed, as well as his scenery. This was a great loss to his own shows as well as all the other productions at that time. We therefore started the season with the minimum of costumes and very little in the way of scenery. Miss Gracie Clark was not a happy woman. As it was, the audiences were poor and she took this as a personal affront. The star of the show was the one responsible for putting the 'bums on seats' as we called it, and having been such a wonderful success in the past, with the diminishing audiences she felt she had lost her grip. Audiences or no, Gracie was a very funny woman. Her sketches were first-class and would definitely stand up to today's audiences. I could stand at the side of the stage every night and watch her and still laugh at every performance. She was a natural. Gracie had started out in the business as a pianist and singer, a soprano. She met her husband, Colin, when they were in a season together; he was a light baritone. They pooled their talents and started up a double act. She accompanied him on the piano and sometimes they did duets. There is still archive film of this act. Through time Gracie's voice, with over-use, took on a fearsome vibrato, a 'tremola' as my mother called it. She started to get laughs. This led to them both doing sketches as second comics and then on to being headliners. They had enjoyed a number of years of great success but now they, along with many other comics, were seeing the numbers in the theatres decreasing. Television was taking a hold.

We started our season with all these disadvantages, which of course I didn't realise at the time. The producer of the show was a man who is still a close friend of mine, Billy Cameron. He did a double with his partner, Irene Campbell. Billy was a Fred Astaire type of dancer but was capable of all kinds of dance. Irene was also an all-rounder and had a sex appeal that came across the footlights in great doses. She was always in the throes of a love affair but at that time was engaged to the comic Jimmy Neill, who was doing a season in Dunoon. Irene was known as the Queen of the Number Threes. The 'number threes' were the theatres which were not quite the big time but gave a constant amount of work, then beginning to dwindle. The 'number ones' were the theatres like the King's in Glasgow and Edinburgh run by Howard and Wyndham, and the Moss Empires, which mostly brought up acts from England, the Glasgow Empire being known as the English comics' graveyard. The Pavilion could possibly be described as a number two theatre, but most first-rate

Scottish comics played there, including Clark and Murray. Our budget could only stretch to four Moxon young ladies – they were the number-three-type chorus girls, often with holes in their tights. Hugh McIlroy was the tenor, married to Nancy, the head Moxon girl. Hugh had a beautiful voice and was very witty. There were the St Dennis sisters, a singing double act who also played the banjo. We were all used in Gracie and Colin's sketches, which we were delighted to be involved in. One minute I'd be a nun singing Ave Maria in a scene and the next I'd be the young daughter of Gracie in her domestic sketch.

Billy the producer got the worst of her tongue that season, with me, being a newcomer, a close second. She had asked Billy to have a weekly theme in the shows, for instance, one week it would be an Irish theme, then a French theme and, of course, the inevitable Scottish theme, with tartan and heather on the hills. The one set of costumes that Fraser Neil could provide was kilts. We did quite a few Scottish shows. One morning the cast was rehearsing the Granny's Heilan' Hame scene which led up to Gracie and Colin coming on as Granny and Grandpa and doing a sketch with the white wigs and shawls. She entered down the stalls and called out, 'No, sonny' – she always called Billy 'sonny' when she was agitated – 'No, sonny, we can't do that without the cottage scenery.'

Billy replied, 'We haven't got cottage scenery, Gracie. It was destroyed in the fire.'

'What have you got then?'

Billy said, 'We've got a back-cloth with hills and glens.'

Gracie took him to task. 'And are Granny and Grandpa supposed to be sitting round the fire outside in the cold, sonny?'

'Well, I cannae do anything about it, Gracie.'

Then she would turn to Colin, who was ineffectual in her shadow. 'Colin – tell him we can't do the sketch without the scenery.'

Colin would start to say, 'But, Gracie . . .'

'Don't talk to me like that, Colin. Are you trying to defy me?'

'But, Gracie . . .'

'Change the scena, sonny. We'll just do the "doon fae the hills" sketch.' This was a brilliant sketch where Gracie played a gipsy girl looking for a husband and Colin played her father. Gracie would play a grotesque lassie, her eye lighting on Hugh McIlroy, who played the laird's son. The man she was supposed to get was a red-nosed, white-faced fellow, played by a member of the Duncan White Trio, the musical act. She would look at him and say, 'Aw naw, Daddy, ah'm no wantin' that glaikit wan – ah want this wan,' and she would make a grab for Hugh. It was one of my favourites.

Their double acts were best of all where they played husband and wife. Their double 'Agnes's wedding' found them standing at a bus-stop with her looking 'scunnered' and Colin wearing a semi-drape Italian suit and carrying his guitar in a case. The guitar never came out of the case, it was just a prop.

He would say, 'But it was a lovely wedding, Grace.'

'There was nothing lovely about it, Colin.'

'But Gracie, it was a lovely spread. Did you see the pansies at the top table?'

'Yes, I did, Colin, but I never spoke to them.'

'Do you not think oor Agnes was a lovely bride?'

'Colin, your sister Agnes was never a lovely woman and at the age of 53 she's got nae chance of being a lovely anythin'.'

Putting these lines on paper is nothing to the way Gracie worked them, with all her facial expressions. She was a genius and Colin was the perfect foil.

One of their musical doubles was 'Over the Mountains, Over the Sea'. Colin would start the song off straight, then Gracie would take up the chorus and sing with her godawful vibrato and have the audience in tears of laughter. Of course, although Gracie's singing was dreadfully funny, she sang as though she were playing it straight. The secret of good comedy: playing it for real.

Much as I enjoyed their work, I was terrified of Gracie. I got the feeling she didn't like me, but then she was going through a bad time and she was overworked. One week she was doing one of the 'Ah love ma daddy' sketches. This was where she played the little girl and Colin was the daddy. The running line in these sketches was 'Ah love ma daddy'. This was a play within a play as you might say, inasmuch as onstage was supposed to be a theatre with them occupying a box. I had to learn, in a couple of days, a song called 'Sing, Sweet Bird, and Chase My Sorrows', supposedly as a soprano of the old music-hall style, wearing and Edwardian dress with a tiara and a feather at the back of my head. In the dressing-room I said to Irene and the St Dennis sisters, 'Wouldn't it be quite good if I played this with a red nose and tilted the feather as though I was drunk?'

They all looked at one another and said, 'Yes – why don't you try it?' They let me do it without explaining what would inevitably happen. I went on stage with the red nose and tilted feather and got laughs. The more laughs I got, the more I hammed it up. I thought I was doing fine. Oh, the inexperience of it.

When I got back to the dressing-room I said to the girls, 'Did you hear the laughs I got?'

They concentrated on repairing their make-up and said, 'Yes, we heard.'

Then the wrath of God descended the stairs. Gracie was towering over me, her face contorted with rage. She shouted, 'Don't ever try that trick again, dearie! I am the comic in this show and don't you forget it. If anyone gets laughs, it's me. Do you understand?'

I sat there a quivering wreck, still with the red nose and the feather, and took the row she gave me. I had learned a lesson. Don't ever try to get laughs when you're on stage with a comic. The weather that summer in Rothesay was beautiful, but I didn't really notice it. We rehearsed every morning from ten o'clock until one or two o'clock, then learned words of songs and sketches, and did two shows per night at 6.30 and 8.30. The show was advertised 'Twice Nightly – Twice Brightly'. The bit of the afternoon I had to myself was spent lying down in the foetal position, almost sucking my thumb for comfort. At the end of the run I felt as though I'd been through hell, but I came out of it with a tremendous amount of experience. I had seen how Gracie could hold a laugh forever with just a look at the audience. Every character she played was a real character whom people could identify with. She was a hard worker and expected nothing less from her supporting cast, and I am eternally grateful for the opportunity to have served my time with her.

19

The teeth are smiling, but is the heart?

CONGO PROVERB

While I was out of town that summer, big things were happening in Glasgow. Scottish Television studios were being built in the Theatre Royal. They took over the theatre and made a main studio out of the auditorium. Roy Thomson, a Canadian who became Lord Thomson, owned the company; he brought over a man from Canada called Ray Purdie to help start up the television station on similar lines to the television enterprise in his home country. Men who helped build the studios, electricians and joiners, were then offered jobs as trainee cameramen or lighting directors. Experienced directors and technicians were brought up from London, but they too had to lend a hand with the building work. It was the start of a big bonanza for many people.

My friend of 40 years standing, Jimmy Nairn, was an actor who had just finished a season with the Citizens Theatre in Glasgow and was waiting for a train in the Central Station to take him up to an audition in Perth Repertory Theatre when, by chance, he met an acquaintance by the name of Ian Dalgleish, a television programme director. He told Jimmy that Roy Thomson was holding auditions for announcers up at the STV studios. Jimmy's reaction was, 'But I am an actor.' Ian replied, 'But at the moment, you are an out-of-work actor.' Jimmy had to admit this was true. Ian was a newly appointed director with the station; he suggested that he would set up an audition and Jimmy could take it from there. A few days later, Jimmy received a phone call to present himself at the half-finished studios the following day at 3 p.m.

There were hundreds of hopefuls at the auditions but it was fined down to a few, and in the shortlist were Jimmy, Arthur Montford, Jack Webster and Bill Tennant. They all got jobs; Jimmy was employed as station announcer, Arthur as sports announcer, Jack Webster as the newscaster, and Bill as a roving reporter with a programme they were going to call *Here and Now*. They were invited up to Roy Thomson's office, where their remit was explained to them. The main thrust of the conversation was that there was very little money in the budget and they would all have to pull their weight, all hands to the pumps, do as many jobs as they were asked to do. Money was always tight with Roy, who was sitting at the meeting wearing a bashed fedora, a rather dusty suit and all-in-all looking like a tramp instead of the multi-millionaire he undoubtedly was. That was Roy's style. This was the man who later on described his television company as a licence to print money. However, he was a much-respected man, and everyone was keen to be involved with this new commercial television. At one meeting a man called Charles Redding, one of the programme directors who had been brought up from London, was apprised of the opening-night format by Roy. He was telling him how they must save money wherever they could; he had given him the budget and it must be adhered to. He then went on to tell him that he would be placing OB (Outside Broadcast) vans in outlying parts of the country. There would be one in Wick, Dumfries, the Islands etc. Charles couldn't resist the question, 'But Roy, who's going to pay the bus fares?'

The big night was approaching. The station would open on 31 August 1957. Guests that night included Deborah Kerr, Jack Buchanan, Jimmy Logan, Stanley Baxter and a host of Scottish celebrities. Roy had hired Geraldo and his Orchestra to play for the big night. He was heard to say at one point, 'Ray, it's cost me a fortune to hire this orchestra and look, some of them aren't even playing.' Jimmy Nairn, as the station announcer, opened the station with the words 'This is Scotland,' and the celebrations commenced. The central belt of Scotland had its own commercial television station, using much home-grown talent; that was 45 years ago.

I had missed all this excitement because of the season in Rothesay, but when I got home at the end of September my father had it all sussed. 'Wait 'til you see this, hen.' Our television was at the right-hand side of the kitchen fire, opposite the window. Father then took an aerial in his hand, opened the window and jumped up onto the sink, 'Wait and ah'll show ye. Noo, if ah sit with ma arse outside the windae ah'll get a picture. See, quick, look at that – see it coming through?' All I could see was wiggly lines, then I could just make out a face. 'That's Larry Marshall, hen. A programme called *The One O'Clock Gang*. It's a lotta shite, mind ye. They're gettin' aff wi' murder.' That was my introduction to the Gang.

In the autumn of 1957 STV were holding auditions for a show called *Stars In Your Eyes*; yet another talent contest. I was a winner and was asked to sing in a show called *Jigtime*. I made friends with the director, with whom I was to work throughout the years, Jimmy Sutherland. He and his wife Mary had been actors in rep seasons together. At one point in the planning of my songs for *Jigtime*, Jimmy asked me to have a drink with him in the Topspot, the pub at the corner of Hope Street and Cowcaddens. We sat beside John Grierson, the award-winning documentary maker. Jimmy asked me what I'd like to drink and I said that I'd like a Babycham! He turned to John and said, 'Christ, John, a Babycham! It would be cheaper to buy her a pint.' After a chat, as I got up to go, John Grierson caught hold of my arm and said, 'My dear, if I were you I'd work in comedy. You're going to get fat.'

One of Jimmy Nairn's jobs was to introduce *Jigtime*, but I never actually got to meet him then. I was to sing two Scottish songs in the show and the night before I took a bad throat infection. Out came the old cure. My mother heated up some salt on a shovel over the fire, then poured the hot salt into one of my father's old socks and tied it round my neck. That night the family were getting mince and potatoes for their tea, but my mother produced a poussin for me. A tiny little chicken, all for me.

My father said, 'A chicken? When do you ever buy chicken? Whit aboot the rest of us?'

My mother gave him one of her looks and said, 'Are you a soprano singing on the television tomorrow night?'

My father rose to the bait and said, 'No.'

My mother said, 'Well, eat your mince.'

The hot salt in the old sock did the trick. I went on the television (live) the next night as my voice was fine. I was hoping to get a running spot in the show, but I didn't. However, there was a job going for two good-looking lassies to open the barn doors at the beginning of the show, as the camera entered the set. I was told about this by Helen Rae, a designer in STV. She had got the job, which to her meant an extra £2 10s per week on top of her designer's salary. I applied for the job and Jimmy Sutherland said, 'Aye, sure thing.' For many weeks Helen and I opened the barn doors then went off to the dancing in the Albert ballroom. At the same time as my door-opening job, I was again working in Reeta's. Mr Laing said, 'There's a girl awful like you at the beginning of that show *Jigtime*.' I didn't enlighten him. It was a great wee life.

STV brought out a 15-minute programme called *The Admag*. Many actors wanted a shot at this, as compared to rep money it was a well-paid job. The format was that the presenter would advertise about ten products and demonstrate them in a live show. It was a recipe for disaster. For instance, one actor was describing a certain champagne and started to undo the wire round the cork. The cork didn't budge, so he had to keep talking; still nothing happened. Finally he put the bottle down and went on to the next product. As he started, the cork popped, the bottle fell on its side and sprayed his flies with champagne. The poor fellow had to carry on with the front of his trousers soaking. The scripts could also be disastrous. For example, a new screwdriver was being advertised – this screwdriver could do all sorts of things. The presenter started off well enough. He was standing holding the screwdriver in a kind of threatening position: 'Now ladies, we're going to look at home improvements and I'm going to show you something that every woman can put up herself.' He looked at the screwdriver and nearly fainted with embarrassment.

I was called up to Nellie's office to meet an advertising agent who had seen my photograph and wanted me to do an *Admag* spot with Edith MacArthur, one of Scotland's finest actresses; she must have been seriously out of work at the time. Nellie asked me to wear something slimming, as the advert was for Nimble bread and I was to be an example of someone who had used the product to help her slim. I couldn't look slim because I was fat. Fortunately, the advertising agent had had a slight 'refreshment' before the meeting, indeed so 'refreshed' was he that he was falling off the chair. I used this situation to my advantage; I really wanted the job. I just kept my coat on, and when he asked me if I was quite slim, I opened half of the coat to let him see one half of me. He was fooled and I was in. I turned up at STV in a frock I'd bought at Reeta's, a very nice little floral number, but on camera I looked enormous. Edith, on the other hand, was tall and elegantly slim.

The script at rehearsals went like this:

> STAGE DIRECTIONS: DOROTHY IS MUNCHING ON A
> SANDWICH MADE WITH NIMBLE BREAD
> *Edith*: Dorothy, how can you eat so much and remain so slim?
> *Dorothy*: I eat Nimble [*chew sandwich*] of course. It's delicious
> and contains half the calories of any other bread.

There was a great hoo-hah coming over the floor manager's earphones; he was talking to the director in the control box and trying to keep everything calm. The floor manager suggested that the director, Liam Hood, come down onto the floor to sort the matter out. As he entered the studio he was saying to his PA, 'Where the hell did they get this lump of lard?' Edith smiled kindly at me and tried to start up a conversation about something else entirely. Liam Hood looked like the wrath of God. He said, 'We're going to have to change the script, dear.' I was nearly in tears but could hardly have disagreed with him. The upshot was that the script went something like this:

> *Dorothy*: Oh, Edith, what am I going to do? I'm getting
> married in a few weeks and I must lose some weight.
> *Edith*: Try Nimble! [*Offer Dorothy the sandwich*] It contains
> half the calories of any other bread and it's twice as tasty.

When it came to transmission, the script was going fine until I tried to chew the bread, which by now had dried out and was too chewy to bite cleanly. I ended up trying to chew the bloody bread and say my lines at the same time. They never asked me back.

I made a determined effort to lose the puppy fat. I was 19 when Nellie called me up to the office and asked me if I was vacant for panto. Fraser Neil was producing *Aladdin* at the Palladium Theatre in Edinburgh. I would be playing Principal Boy and because it was the title role I'd get £14 per week. This was more than the Principal Boy in the Empress got, my sister told me.

20

Mental health is an ongoing process of dedication to
reality at all costs.

M. SCOTT PECK

*I*n those days – 1957 – £14 a week was a man's wage. Perhaps not
a lawyer's or a doctor's, but at least a good journeyman's. This
enabled me to send money every week to my mother, which helped
the home-front finances as Father had by now taken early retirement.
This meant that he was still doing odd jobs for people. He had two
specialities apart from his work as an electrician. One was the
terrazzo doorstep – this was replacing the old wooden or brass
doorstep outside the front door of people's flats with a kind of man-
made conglomerate of marble and other stone. It cleaned with a wipe
and we pronounced it terrazzo. The other act of vandalism was the
alcove. Many a beautiful cupboard in a sitting-room was destroyed in
favour of this abomination in the sight of God.

My father being an electrician, he would get hold of perfectly good
ornaments and vases, make a hole in the bottom of them, wire them
up and make a lamp out of them. There was a popular figurine of a
little boy with a basket of fruit at his side, his hand held high and
dangling a bunch of cherries. Father had him wired up and dangling
three torch bulbs. We also had a 1930s-style lady with a wavy perm
and a floaty-floaty frock pulling, for some reason known only to the
artist, two greyhounds. My father wanted to wire her up and make a
lamp out of her, but couldn't think of a way of doing it. However,
he'd just put the idea on the back-burner for the moment.

Our cupboard in the sitting-room was the trial run for his new
career in the alcove business. He cut the door in half – it had already

had its panels flushed – retained the bottom half, then pulled out the shelves above. A piece of hardboard was bevelled round the back of the space to which he stuck a fabric which was studded with mirrors – pink mirrors. Not satisfied with that, he then put a hardboard pelmet about the space with a strip light behind it, to illuminate this mosaic of pink mirrors. He then sat my mother down for the unveiling of the alcove. He waited until dark, drew the curtains to exclude extraneous light from the street, and switched on the alcove. My mother was delighted. It was modern and that's what she loved about it, the same way she loved the interior grate; she now had one of these in the big room as well as in the kitchen.

The aunties all wanted an alcove; the neighbours all wanted one. My father had created a shrine. But a shrine to what? The woman upstairs was delighted with hers. She was an Irish Catholic and when my father had finished installing hers she ran down to my mother and said, 'Ah, sure, I love me alclove,' she hadn't got the word right, ''tis just the right place for me Child of Prague.' As far as we could see, the Child of Prague was a figure of a wee boy wearing a frock and a big hat. Not being Catholics, we didn't have a holy figure to put in our alcove but my father, who was going through one of his phases of being an expert on all things naff, had a wonderful idea. He worked away quietly for an afternoon, then called the family into the room. There she was in the middle of the alcove: the lady with the wavy perm, the floaty-floaty frock, pulling the two greyhounds with a light-bulb under her bum.

I was rehearsing for the panto in Edinburgh during this time. I had theatrical digs in a house in Grindlay Street run by a lovely woman who treated us with great care. I was sharing the digs with the Genie of the Lamp and the speciality act who had four poodles with her. I felt very well off with my £14 a week, and these digs were three guineas – slightly more than the norm, nevertheless I was a high earner. On pay day I was able to afford a 2/6d business lunch at Smith's tearoom near the theatre. I received a letter from my mother while I was there. She thanked me for sending the weekly money and told me that she had gone out and bought my young brother some underwear at Gall's the draper's sale. They were 'seconds' but they were warm. To this day my young brother tells how he, as a schoolboy, was always embarrassed when he took off his trousers at sports and revealed 'Imperfect' written across his underpants. I'm sure he wasn't the only one.

The panto was a great success and Fraser Neil had the most gorgeous costumes made for me. Dean and Dixon were the comedy duo, Mamie Dixon playing the Dame; Jimmy Neil was Wishy Washy, and his fiancée, the beautiful Irene Campbell, was Principal Girl. Although she was ten years older than me she didn't look much older. While I greatly admired her elegance and beautiful, velvet-toned speaking voice, I practised my gigantic strides even in the street. I wanted to be a superb Principal Boy. I had my hair cut short and dyed black with a pigtail stuck on at the back. For many years, when I spoke of the reviews, I always said that I was described as 'wooden'. Only recently a friend in Edinburgh went to the *Evening News* archives and looked out the review, and although it did say I was a bit 'stiff', it described me as 'the charmer of the evening'. I didn't remember that bit. I don't think anyone could ever have described me as being big-headed. I never ever had enough confidence for that.

I continued in the variety theatre for the next two years, doing seasons with different comics. I was billed in the programmes as our Silver Soprano, but the shows could not afford passengers; if you couldn't do the comedy feeding, you didn't get the job. I played a wide range of characters, from the young ingénue to old ladies, red-nosed comedy and slinky tarts. Then, of course, there was the opening chorus to learn with movement, sometimes dance, the first-half finale and the grand finale.

Variety folk had a language of their own. One of their words was 'scamson'. This was used when rehearsing sketches with certain comics. Most comedians jealously guarded their scripts, in fact they more often than not didn't give you a script. The cast would turn up at ten o'clock in the morning for music rehearsals; that's when we went through the scenas, first-half finale and so on. Around noon, the comic would turn up and dole out the characters we were to play the next week. As with rep, we were performing a show a night whilst learning next week's show during the day. The comic sometimes gave you your lines but didn't say his own so that you couldn't write them down and keep them. Rehearsing a sketch sometimes went like this:

'Right, hen, you come on as the daughter with a tin of Zebo in your hand, and you say "I got your Zebo, Daddy" and I'll say scamson scamson. Ye see?' You would take a note of your own lines but you hadn't a clue what he was going to say. 'The next thing you say is "Where will I put it, Daddy?" and I'll say scamson scamson. Ye see?' I would end up with a list of cue lines but not a clue as to what the comic would reply. It could be very confusing, but I learned to give the cues without knowing what the sketch was really about.

This didn't happen all the time – a younger comic always gave you a reasonable script. Jack Milroy was a scream to work with; he'd never give you a script, but he'd rehearse the sketch with his lines so after a few runs you knew what you were about. However, Jack was a brilliant ad-libber and when he had an audience he would change the script: for instance, if he caught sight of a woman in the audience with a funny hat. He'd do a whole number out front about this woman, then he would turn to you and say, 'Whit were you saying, hen?' I or whoever was feeding him that particular line would bring him back to where the sketch had been left off. In the meantime, of course, not only was the audience laughing but the cast as well, and if you couldn't get your lines out for laughing, he would just crack more ad-libs until you got on to the story-line again. Jack Milroy and his wife, Mary Lee, are two of my dear friends from variety days. They must have a story to tell about their experiences, which are legion, and if they don't get around to writing their book it will be a great pity and much will be lost from the history of variety. If I invite Jack and Mary for dinner I am sore by the end of the night. His stories about the war are wonderful and Mary chimes in with her version. Every so often, in the middle of Jack's stories, she will say, 'Away ye go ya glaikit auld thing, that's no whit happened', then she will interpolate her side of it. They are a sketch on their own. They are also one of the love stories of the theatre and are truly devoted to one another.

Jack is just a natural raconteur but this is not true of all the comics with whom I have worked. Many were very dour people off stage. I never worked with Lex McLean but I met him occasionally, and off stage you would be hard-pressed to get a smile out of him, far less a joke. He was also a shrewd businessman and although he was not ungenerous, if an act didn't go well on the Monday night, it didn't appear the next – sometimes not even seeing the second half. He took no prisoners, did Lex.

One of my happiest summer seasons was in Dundee. I was working again with Johnny Beattie, whose comedy feed was Alice Dale (Stanley Baxter's sister). Johnny's male feed was John Mulvaney, who was also one of his best friends. It was a very happy company and I shared digs with Alice. The crooner on the show was Larry Davis, who absolutely wowed the females in the audience with his act. Larry's wife was Kath Menzies (their married name) and she accompanied him wherever he went. Johnny Beattie's wife was Kitty Lamont, who was one of Scotland's top models. She was a startlingly beautiful woman and had a wonderful sense of humour. She occasionally came up to visit Johnny, bringing their first two children, Paul and Maureen (Maureen grew up to be one of the country's foremost actresses). Another visitor to our digs in Dundee was Alice's cousin, Alma, who was a civil servant working in the Board of Trade in Glasgow. We started up a hen party every week with Alice, Kath and Alma and another friend, Nancy. This group met regularly for years afterwards, until some of us went our different ways – Alice to Kenya, then to Australia with her lawyer husband, myself to Ireland – but whenever possible we try to get together.

Johnny Mulvaney was always a very nervous actor, although when he worked with Johnny Beattie they used it to good effect and everyone thought it was part of the act. Johnny M was first and foremost an actor and a comic second, but he had started off as a singer. His first season was in Donachadhee in Ireland. My favourite story of him was about the time he went to Nellie Sutherland and she told him that the job was 'al fresco', which Johnny thought was the name of the manager. He arrived with his kilts for the show, only to discover that it was an open-air theatre: not what he was expecting at all. Then he was told he'd have to 'bottle', which meant taking a collection from the audience before they started. This made Johnny very nervous, and by the time he was announced – 'And here we have

Scotland's Troubadour of Song, Johnny Mulvaney – he was in a state. His first song was 'Oh My Love She's But a Lassie Yet'. The pianist gave him his introductory bars and he started:

> 'Oh my love, she's but a lassie yet
> Oh my love, she's but a lassie yet
> Oh my love, she's but a lassie yet . . .'

The nerves were getting the better of him, but he continued,

> 'Oh my love, she's but a lassie yet . . .'

What was the next line? He'd forgotten, but he had to carry on:

> 'Oh my love, she's but a lassie yet
> Oh my love, she's but a lassie yet
> Oh my love, she's but a lassie yet . . .'

What time was the next train?

> 'My love, she's but a lassie yet.'

– Oh, bugger it,

> 'Oh my love, she's but a lassie yet.'

He finished the tune and was on the next train and boat home to Glasgow. The lassies never got any older.

All the while *The One O'Clock Gang* was continuing, the cast including Larry Marshall, Jimmy Nairn, Charlie Sim and Sheila Mathews. It was a daily television show, broadcast live from the STV studios in Cowcaddens, Mondays to Fridays, and covering the central belt of Scotland – Grampian and the Borders didn't have the pleasure. It was going great guns and was very popular. The public never admitted to liking it; Jimmy Nairn tells of a man who met him in the street and said, 'By God, big Jimmy, yer patter's duff.' Many people loved it, many hated it, nevertheless they tuned in and the ratings were spectacular. The format was that of a light entertainment show, including songs from Charlie and Sheila (Charlie had replaced a young singer called Brian Johnston, who had tragically died not long after the Gang had started). Everyone was involved in the sketch, which was placed in the middle of the show. Each day had a different theme. I remember that Tuesday was the day when recording stars came up to plug their records, and they had a competition called Tip the Top where the public had to guess which records would be in next week's top ten or something like that. Another day there was a school sketch, and another it would be old-time music hall.

The late summer of 1959 saw me working again in Reeta's, my haven of rest between engagements. My friend Kath was a great friend of Wally Butler, the fellow who had refused to take his glasses off when we did the Tyrolean dance in my first season in the Tivoli, Aberdeen. He was now a programme director in STV, in particular on *The One O'Clock Gang*. In fact, Wally, the two Johnnies, Kitty, Kath and her husband Larry Davis had all run about together when they were young, all belonging to the same church. Wally had been telling Kath that since Sheila Mathews, a great favourite on the Gang, had gone back down south with her husband Charles Redding, they had been very fortunate to have Marie Benson to take her place but Marie, although a top jazz singer who had been with the successful group The Stargazers, was an Australian and found it difficult to take part in the Glasgow comedy. Actually her laid-back Ozzie-style of comedy I found quite funny. Wally was on the lookout for a female singer who could do the sketches as well. Kath suggested me and Wally said, 'Of course, Dorothy would be absolutely right for the show.' I was invited up to Wally's house to meet the scriptwriters and let them have a look at me. Wally, an accomplished pianist, played for me while I sang some songs from the musicals – quite out of date now, but they were popular then. I was signed up for a six-week contract, and went on to be with the Gang until its demise six years later.

How can I describe my time in *The One O'Clock Gang*? I think it would be safe to say it was a nervous breakdown that lasted six years. How could a show going out live every day, with a sketch, songs, and other items, possibly keep up a good standard? Sufficient to say we had our good days and our bad days, but we kept the ratings up.

I'd been introduced to the Gang beforehand, when of course I'd got all dressed up and made-up to meet them. But that Monday morning I decided to go in without make-up, thinking that the make-up department would do a good job on my face. I didn't realise that I didn't get made-up until noon. I was sitting on the bleachers, where the audience would sit, waiting for my turn to do the band call. I must have been looking very worried, sitting there with my face all screwed up, because I was told later that Charlie had said to Jimmy, 'Who's that sitting there?'

Jimmy had replied, 'That's our new girl, Dorothy. Do you not recognise her?'

Charlie said, and this line was to be used in the play *The Steamie* many years later, 'My God, I didnae recognise her without her make-up. She looks as though somebody sat on her face when it was still warm.' I'm sure I didn't look as bad as all that, but it was a good line.

The Tommy Maxwell Quartet were the group who played in the show and they were all first-class musicians. Ron Moore, the guitarist, was a particular favourite because of his lovely smile. However, my first song on the Gang was piano-only accompaniment, 'Romance' from *The Desert Song*. It was a very high and a very difficult song, but I passed the test the first day.

A day in the life of the *One O'Clock Gang* started at 9.30 with band call for the singers. Whoever was in first got their numbers rehearsed, while the stagehands got the set ready. Marie Benson left the Gang around 1962 and an Irish singer, Moira Briody, joined us. She was a wonderful performer who sang and accompanied herself on the grand piano. The singers were Moira, Charlie Sim and myself, with occasional guests. Peter Mallan often came in to sing Scots songs, which he did beautifully. There were two or three sets, one being the den where Larry Marshall introduced the show and told the audience what was coming that day. He would also parody some light-hearted news items. There would be one or two song sets, often designed by my pal and fellow barn-door opener, Helen Rae. Someone once said that I got all the nicest sets because she was my pal. There would also be the sketch area, set up with any props necessary. Helen was given 3/6d per day for the sets, which meant she had to recycle everything.

Dorothy

If a desk was required, it would always be the same desk. The prop man must have been down to the Barras every weekend to get bits and pieces. It was all done on a shoestring but it never looked tatty. Colour didn't matter, of course, because it was all in black and white. There were bleachers where the audience sat and watched us. Cameras in those days were great big unwieldy things and needed much strength on the part of the cameraman. There were always three cameras.

At 10.30 we had a tea break and then went into the studio to do a 'dry run', or a stagger through, as it was sometimes called. We went through the songs and the sketch in the sets to let the cameras line up their shots. A dress rehearsal at 11.30 had to be flown through because 12.30 was make-up time, and at five minutes to one we had to be poised, ready for the show in front of the audience, which was by then seated. Jimmy would open the show with the words, 'Sit back and relax, it's *The One O'Clock Gang*'. Tommy Maxwell and the Quartet would strike up the opening title music, and away we went. We entertained the central belt of Scotland for 40 minutes, with two commercial breaks. After the show we'd have an hour for lunch, and then rehearse next day's show until five o'clock. After that the singers had to go away and learn songs, as well as the sketches. It all sounds neat and tidy, but it wasn't.

The poor scriptwriters, Jimmy McNair, Hugh and Jimmy Waters, and Tom Walsh (there had been others before them, but they had given up) had their work cut out to produce laugh lines every day. It was an impossible and sometimes thankless job. We'd get the basic sketch. We had good characters in that sketch, and where you have good characters, they sometimes write themselves. Charlie Sim was very inventive, especially with his little schoolboy character which was popular with children and adults alike. He based it on a little boy he knew who, when he couldn't find words, would make them up and he'd go into a whole nonsense conversation while holding his play piece, a banana. He called it his 'nana'. Everywhere Charlie went people would shout after him, 'Haw, Charlie, where's yer nana?' Old-time music hall depended heavily on songs, and of course there were many music-hall stars we could draw on: Marie Lloyd, Will Fyffe, Harry Lauder. The wardrobe mistress, Mrs MacDonald, and her

155

assistant, Margaret Chalmers, made some lovely costumes for that show. She even managed to procure some original Edwardian dresses and suits. However, some of the sketches just didn't come off. One day, during the afternoon rehearsal, we were really struggling to get a sketch together and I suggested the sketch Isabel and I had done in the telephone engineers' concert party. We did it the next day. That's how desperate we were at times.

There was one person who kept us all going through the good and the bad days, Johnny Farren, the Gang 'dresser'. He was a real star turn. Johnny had been a child performer with a troupe of entertainers in the '40s and was on the periphery of the variety business all his life. I first met him in the week I joined the Gang, when I was trying on costumes in wardrobe. His first words to me were, 'Humf yer boady through here, hen, and I'll take your measurements.'

I liked him immediately.

'Ah hear ye dae a bit of the opera? Well, whit dae ye think o' this?' He put on a kimono and said, 'Lieutenant Pinkerton, where the hell have ye went?'

Johnny brought everyone down to size. If I was having a bad day I'd say to him, 'Oh Johnny, I don't feel like singing that song. My voice is awful today.'

He'd say, 'Hen, it's awful every day, but get oan there and chant or ye'll be back in the ropeworks on Monday.'

Another day I was singing a song wearing a floaty-floaty dress. Helen Rae had a stagehand flapping a caption board beside me to make my dress look as though it was wafting in the breeze of a balmy night. Big Trevor was wafting away when Johnny said to him, 'Whit are ye daein', Trevor?'

Trevor said, 'I'm causing wind.'

Johnny turned to me, 'You're awright, hen, wi' your singing and his wind you're a great double act.'

There was a famous morning when one of the cameramen came in with a horrific hangover. As the morning progressed, he looked worse and worse. He made the mistake of ordering a bacon sandwich at tea break. By the time we got to transmission he was positively green. He managed to keep going through the show until the last song, which was mine; some light and airy musical ditty. When I got to my obligato the cameraman could contain himself no longer and, during a big close-up, he vomited in a projective fashion all over his camera. Bits of bacon sandwich landed on my frock. Of course I carried on, under great stress, and at the end of the show I said to Charlie, 'Wasn't that just awful? He's a disgrace, that fellow.'

Charlie said, 'Well, Dorothy, everyone's entitled to their opinion.'

We never took ourselves too seriously; we wouldn't have dared. My habit of making up my own words to songs got me in big trouble one day. I was singing 'I'm Always Chasing Rainbows'. Normally, if I forgot the words, I would manage to think up something appropriate. On this day I don't know where my mind was, because when I came to the middle eight I should have sung 'Some people look and find the sunshine, I always look and find the rain'. I sang, 'Some people find a friggin' rainbow'. I thought, 'Did I say friggin'? Surely not' and managed to get on to the right words again. After the show I went straight up to master control, who always kept a sound-recording of the show. I said to the controller, 'Did I say friggin'?'

He said, 'Yes, do you want to hear it?' I couldn't believe my ears. Then I did the old pro's trick of pretending to myself that no one would have noticed. We got letters in about it.

The Tuesdays when we did Tip the Top, the 'famous' came up from London to plug their records, and the bleachers were usually full on that day. Some days when we weren't so full, the floor manager would go to the doctor's surgery across the road in Cowcaddens and drag the patients in to see the show.

'Here, wait a minute, son, ah'm no well.'

The floor manager would say, 'Come on, this'll cheer you up.' There were times when we depended on that doctor's surgery.

Normally I would be thrilled to meet big names, but we didn't have the time to speak to them and they would leave straight after their interview. I remember Cliff Richard when he was quite a fat boy, being hustled in by his protective manager. Shirley Bassey was stunning; Frank Ifield was charming, and one day there was this wee fellow come up to plug what I thought was the most godawful record. This tiny man sat at the piano, and while he played he emitted strange but rhythmic sounds. After the show he said to me in his London accent, 'Would you like to have lunch with me?' I turned him down. He said offhandedly, 'Please yourself,' and walked away. I told Charlie, 'That wee fellow asked me out.' Charlie wasn't impressed either. I said, 'I've never heard of him. What was his name again?' Charlie said, 'Eh – Dudley Moore.'

Not long after I joined the Gang, we had a visit from Archie McCulloch who asked for a meeting with us. He put the suggestion forward that we take the Gang out on tour. Everyone thought this was a great idea and we went ahead and arranged it. The deal was that we wouldn't actually have a payment but we'd be on a percentage of the box office. Naturally we thought we'd be playing to packed houses; the venues were town halls in places like Dumbarton, Lanark and Motherwell. The first night was Lanark. Johnny went on ahead with the costumes and when we arrived he said, 'Ah've talked to the box office staff and they've told me how many bookings they've had.'

Charlie said, 'Are we packed out?'

Johnny replied, 'Naw, they've sold three tickets. Two Russian sailors and a whippet, and ah've got a date wi' the big wan wi' the blond hair.'

Charlie, quick as a flash, said, 'Is that the whippit?'

Johnny wasn't far off the mark. Hardly anybody came to see the shows. We could only assume that because they saw us every day, they didn't feel they wanted to spend money to see us 'live'. I can't remember what the advance publicity was, but I believe we were billed as 'The Gang takes to the road'. Not only did we not earn a penny from the tour, Jimmy, who was always good at the sums, worked out that at the end of the whole ghastly business we owed each venue between 2/9d and 3/8d. Having said that, a chain of furniture shops asked us, singly, if we'd like to open their new shops. We were all getting a wonderful fee and were delighted. The queues were enormous outside the shops where we were to make an appearance. So big were the crowds that mounted policemen were there to keep order. One morning, over coffee, we were comparing notes as to the number of people we had drawn. Charlie said to me, 'How many mounted policemen did you have?'

I replied, 'Three, I think.'

'Oh,' he said, 'I had four.'

Dorothy

I worked hard and I played hard. They were the days of wine and roses and I, being young and foolish, thought they would go on forever. I learned to drive and bought a new Mini. My mother was thrilled with her daughter, who was earning £40 a week. I handed in £10 to the house; my mother, never having seen regular money like this, invested in a house in Saltcoats which she ran as a letting concern and compounded her income. We would go on shopping sprees and I'd take her for lunches; I was so happy to see my mother looking and feeling well and not the careworn woman she'd been. Then, as a bonus, my father found a job that really suited him. He worked in the Palais de Danse, which was just around the corner from where we lived. His duties, apart from electrical maintenance, were controlling the lighting for the dance hall. There was an element of theatricality in this and he called himself a lighting director. When he'd been asked to take on the job, he said to my mother, 'I'm quite keen, Mae, but there's just one thing I don't like about it.'

My mother was ironing in the kitchen at the time. She said, 'What's that, Sam?'

He said, 'They want me to wear white dungarees with "Mecca" stamped across my back.'

My mother, not normally given to coarse talk, replied, 'I don't care if they stamp it on your arse. It's a job, isn't it?'

I broached the subject of moving out of the house and finding a flat on my own. By this time I was 22 years old. Mother clutched at her heart, sat down and said, 'You can dig my grave now.'

I said, 'But Mum, I want to have sophisticated parties.'

She replied, 'Are you trying to put me into my grave? Whit's wrong with having sophisticated parties here?'

I didn't fancy the idea of inviting my glittering coterie of friends to a party up a close in Whitehill Street. I was getting ideas above my station. Another subject that came up in that conversation was my having to clean the communal stairs. Up until my big break, my mother had paid me 2/- for this service.

'Mum . . . now that I'm a wee bit famous, do I still have to do the stairs?'

She said, 'Aye. But you'll no need the two shillings now.'

21

Life can only be understood backwards; but it must be lived forwards.

SOREN KIERKEGAARD

*T*he Head of Programmes in those days was Gerry le Grove. Roy Thomson had brought him up from BBC London to replace Ray Purdy, who had gone back to Canada. I was with the Gang for two years before I met him. Jimmy Nairn and his wife were friendly with him and they always said what a nice man he was, and how lonely he was living in a cottage by Loch Lomond. Apparently he talked to them quite a bit about me. One day I was called up to his office; I thought perhaps I was going to get my P45. He sat me down and very nervously – he was a man who blushed readily – told me he had had a request from Barlinnie Prison to bring me to the jail to entertain the prisoners; how would I feel about it? He hastened to add that he would take me there and bring me back. I thought it would be fun and agreed to do it.

It was quite an experience. There I was on the stage, in front of all those hard men. I sang my usual soprano songs, then asked if they had any requests. To a man they all called out for 'My Ain Folk'. I couldn't believe it. I said to them that it was very sad and were they sure? 'Yes, give us "My Ain Folk".' I sang:

> 'Far frae me hame I've wandered but still my thoughts return,
> Tae my ain folk ower yonder in the shieling by the burn.
> I see a cosy ingle and the mist abune the brae . . .'

Dorothy

During the song I was wondering how many of them actually came from a shieling by a burn, or had seen the mist abune the brae. I continued, 'With joy and sadness mingle as I hear that old-world lay,' and when I went into the chorus they all joined in:

> 'And it's oh how I'm longing for my ain folk,
> Tho' they be but lowly pair and plain folk,
> I am far across the sea,
> But my heart will ever be
> Back hame in Bonnie Scotland wi' my ain folk.'

It was amazing to see all these GBHs, razor-slashers and murderers sitting there with tears running down their cheeks. That was one of the most captive audiences I ever had. It was also the first date I had with my future husband.

Gerry came from Shipley, in Yorkshire, of a middle-class family. He had gone to art school before the war, but had been called up after just a year's study. His parents had given him, for his 17th birthday, a course of flying lessons; he was a fully trained pilot at the beginning of the war and was therefore called up for Bomber Command. It was a bitter disappointment to him to discover that he had red/green blindness, which put him out of that branch of the RAF. He spent the war in South Africa, as a flying instructor. After the war he entered the theatre and worked in rep companies. He started out as an actor, then went on to be an actor/director, then an actor/manager, and was eventually employed by the BBC in the Drama Department. STV brought him up in 1958 to be Controller of Programmes. He was a dignified and elegant man, with a great sense of fun.

When I was 24, Gerry and I got married. Less than a year later my first daughter arrived. That day Larry announced on television, with great joy and emotion, that Dorothy had had a little girl. I was inundated with beautiful presents from fans. My cup of life was full and running over. My mother took over the childminding when I went back to work. We lived in a beautiful big house in Helensburgh, and Father went to work on the electrics and the decorating; he even fixed the central heating, which was situated in an outhouse. He and

Gerry had great respect for one another. My father now had a son-in-law who appreciated his eccentricities and celebrated them. The outhouse was filled with water, which they both pumped out, then they went to work on the wiring; the heating system was old-fashioned and hadn't been working for some time. Gerry kept saying, 'Are you sure this is going to be all right, Sam? I mean, I hope it's not dangerous.'

Dad knew what he was doing, but he kept Gerry on tenterhooks. 'Well, son, we'll soon see. Maybe you'd better stand outside and a good way from the building when I switch it on.'

Gerry had visions of the whole place going up in a blue light, with Father inside. My father made a dramatic deal out of it and shouted out to Gerry everything he was doing as he went along.

'Okay, son, I'm switching it on now . . . stand back . . . I'm now going to put a match to the pilot light. Say a prayer, son, because if I've got this wrong you'll no see me again.' Gerry begged him to stop. 'No, ah've goat tae carry on and see this through.'

Suddenly, with a heart-thumping 'boom', the pump started up and Father walked from the outhouse, triumphant. 'There ye are, son, nae borra.' Gerry thought he was a genius.

We had posh neighbours who lived in big houses, and we had been in to visit the lady next door for sherry. She had three maids and her husband, who had been a shipping magnate, was now suffering from senile dementia. (One of my mother's spurious remarks was, 'Aye, the clever wans go daft first.') We returned her hospitality by inviting her to our house for drinks. My father was working on something in the kitchen at the time and had his old dungarees on, and having been under the floor was in a mucky state. My mother told him to get cleaned up and he said, 'Ah'm no comin' tae yer party. Ah'm jist going tae get on with ma work.' The matter was left at that and Gerry, my mother and I were to entertain the guests. Gerry, a well-educated and sophisticated man, was deep in conversation with Mrs Can'trememberhername, my mother was smiling benignly and enjoying every minute of the sophisticated occasion, when in walked my father with a glass of sherry in one hand and a piece of shortbread in the other, dressed in the dungarees and his face pot-black. 'Dear lady, forgive the cut of me but eh've been doon below the flair and eh'm fair mocket.' I thought my mother was going to faint on the spot. Gerry thought it was hysterical and asked him to sit down. 'No, ah'll no dirty yer suite. I just wanted to make my presence known to your neighbours. Ah'll away noo and get on with the work.' He made his exit with a sweeping bow to them.

I tried to start up a conversation with the shipping magnate while my mother got over her embarrassment. I turned to him and said, 'We're going to Monte Carlo next week. I'm sure you must have been there.'

The shipping magnate replied, 'Yes, the Reynolds were indeed very nice people. They installed the central heating, you know.' The conversation was going nowhere.

The next week we did go to Monte Carlo, for the International Television Festival, an unforgettable trip. Roy Thomson had a house just outside Monte Carlo and we were given the use of it for the duration of our stay; I was thrilled to discover that at one time the house had been owned by Greta Garbo. It had an outdoor heated swimming-pool and an orange and lemon grove. The gardens were beautiful, and there was a pathway leading down to the Mediterranean. Although it was January it was quite warm, so we'd sit on the balustraded terrace before lunch and drink freshly squeezed orange juice and champagne served by the housekeeper/cook; her husband was the chauffeur. Gerry was there to buy programmes but at night we attended wonderful parties and of course we made a few trips to the casinos. The culmination of the festival was a grand ball at the Sporting Club in Monte Carlo, where we were guests of Prince Rainier and Princess Grace. I'd never seen anything like it. As we entered the Sporting Club we were rubbing shoulders with famous film stars. Jane Fonda was there; she had the longest legs I'd ever seen and everything about her face and figure seemed sculpted. Catherine Deneuve was there and Gina Lollobrigida. They really were the beautiful people. When we were all seated, Princess Grace and Prince Rainier made their entrance. Grace Kelly was exquisite. She wore a simple blue evening dress under a tapestry, fur-trimmed cloak. The cloak was removed and she stood poised for a moment to let everyone have a look at her, then took her place alongside her husband. I couldn't believe I was really there. On my return to the Gang, Larry interviewed me briefly about the trip. I have a recording of that interview and while writing this, I listened to it. Oh dear, I came back speaking very, very posh. I think the grandeur must have rubbed off on me. When I look back, I do believe I got quite carried away with myself at times. We were all riding high in those days, but life had a way of knocking you off the mountain just when you think you are reaching the top. Circumstances changed radically for Gerry and me.

If we go back to the start, briefly: ITV had been set up by a Conservative government and when it opened in 1955, a Conservative government minister opened it, Dr Charles Hill, then Postmaster-General. He had been the BBC's Radio Doctor during the '40s; he kept a nation advised on good health and on one occasion, during a broadcast, urged us all to keep our bowels open and our mouths shut. The ITA (Independent Television Authority) was determined to prove it could produce quality programmes as good as the BBC's. Quality programmes were at first one-off dramas and then news programmes. STV didn't have the facilities to produce drama, but news programmes could be attempted. Ray Purdy had been good at light entertainment but when Gerry le Grove became Programme Controller in July 1958, he soon started *Here and Now*. Later he introduced *Star Feature*, a film review programme with Jimmy Nairn; the light entertainment programme *Francie and Josie*, with the much-loved Rikki Fulton and Jack Milroy, and of course, the popular *One O'Clock Gang*. This state of the station continued for some time. The public was happy, the advertisers were happy, the revenue came in – but it was not to last.

By now Lord Hill was the head of ITA, the body set up to raise the standards of independent television. Light entertainment was put in the background in favour of drama and news. In addition, Ampex had invented video recording and this was to change everything, as programmes could be made more cheaply anywhere, at any time. There was no longer a place for lunchtime entertainment. *The One O'Clock* show from Tyne Tees was dropped; *Lunchbox* from ATV also bit the dust. Only *The One O'Clock Gang* survived. STV mounted a defence of its lunchtime programmes and the head of ITA was invited to Glasgow. The fateful day was 17 June 1964; a Wednesday. Had we on the Gang known he was coming, I'm sure we would have pulled out the stops to put on a better show, but no one told us. Why didn't Gerry tell me? I don't know. It was one of our spectacularly bad days, but I wonder if it had been a good Gang day, would it have made any difference? Of course not. The decision had been made. As far as I can make out, and these are only gleanings, ITV had to mind its Ps and Qs under the new Labour Government. The ITA had to show its teeth in promoting public service broadcasting. This meant news and drama.

At the end of the day, Lord Hill told the managing director of STV that this show, *The One O'Clock Gang*, was 'disgracefully parochial' and things would have to change if they wanted their licence renewed.

Things did change. Gerry was asked to clear his desk and the Gang members were given their notice. Gerry was 'out' immediately, but we on the Gang worked out our contracts. We finished at the end of December 1964. The Gang members were employed in other shows, but eventually the work petered out.

Eventually, when Gerry and I found ourselves seriously out of work, we had to rethink the big mortgage we had taken on. I could still work but it was rotten for Gerry, who had been at the top of the tree and now found himself unemployable – a common problem for many people nowadays.

My daughter Dorothy was two then, and my mother was complaining of extreme fatigue, so I brought in a local woman to help her look after my daughter. Mother was spending five days a week at Helensburgh and going home at weekends. At nights I'd come home and make the dinner and let her put her feet up, but she didn't seem very well. She took an infection and spent two weeks in bed. She would gaze out the window of the lovely blue bedroom upstairs, overlooking the estuary of the Clyde, and one day she said, 'I can go now, Dorothy. I'm really happy.' I told her not to talk nonsense and just relax. We'd had the doctor in but he said that she was improving. She went home one weekend and phoned me to say she wouldn't come down that next week. I went to visit her in Whitehill Street. Doctor Brown had said that she'd suffered a very slight heart attack but with rest she'd be fine. I arranged to take her down to Helensburgh the following weekend to look after her. We were sent for on the Sunday morning, and when we arrived my sister was at the door. I knew by her tear-streaked face that my mother was dead. The life of worry and hard work had overtaken her, and I thought I would never get over it. As I looked at her, I realised all the opportunities she had given me so that my life would be easier than hers. She didn't know about education, but she understood music and what a gift it was and had encouraged it in me. The person lying there was the wee girl who at the age of 14 was in service, away from her brothers and sisters at the other end of Glasgow, working 16 hours a day, washing, ironing, cleaning and running a house for a minister and his wife. Then she'd been a cleaner in the Royal Infirmary, scrubbing out wards. She had married and brought up four children. This wee woman was worn out. My father said, 'Hen, she ran about after everybody,' and that was the truth. My father and Auntie Lizzie were with her when she died, and she turned to Auntie and said, 'Oh, Lizzie, I thought I wouldn't be frightened, but I am.'

She was 59 years old. At her funeral a neighbour turned to me and said, 'Your mother was a good woman – she put out a lovely washing.'

I don't know how I got through those days after my mother died. Many people will know the feeling of the loss of a dear mother. It has to be borne, but when you experience it you understand that life is never the same again. It cannot be, and you have to accept that fact and go on living with part of you missing. I isolated myself in Helensburgh, and just grieved for her. She used to teach my daughter to sing little songs and one of them was 'I Know I Won't Forget You'. I had a recording of them singing it, which I played over and over and cried and cried. I just couldn't get over the fact that this strong woman who had loved, guided and sometimes dominated me would no longer be there. At the same time, I had to be strong for my husband in his situation. He was difficult to live with because of being out of work. It was the old story of 'the higher you climb the harder you fall'. In fact this was the beginning of the end for him. He was never well after he left STV. The doctor diagnosed it as 'nerves', but to use an old-fashioned expression, he had gone into a 'decline', and his blood pressure was dangerously high. I was 27 then and Gerry was 45. The 18 years between us was shown up in high relief. Perhaps if he'd been younger and fitter he would have been more resilient. I did try to be strong, but I had fallen apart, too, and found it almost impossible to carry on.

The Roy Thomson Foundation was opened in Newton Mearns in Glasgow. It was a college where men and women in the television industry from Commonwealth countries came to learn all aspects of television. Gerry was sure he would be asked to head the organisation, and he was disappointed when the post went to a man called Guy Bloomer. Guy was a good man, who had the experience of working in television overseas, and Gerry was employed as senior lecturer. It would have been too far for Gerry to travel from Helensburgh to the south side of Glasgow, so we sold our house, our 12-room and kitchen as my mother used to call it, and moved to a bungalow in Newton Mearns. The following two years were the unhappiest of my life. I have never been a 'suburban' type, preferring areas where there is a diverse population. Helensburgh was certainly a rich area but there were the hills to wander and sea to walk by. Newton Mearns had a sameness about it that was uninspiring. Gerry travelled abroad with his new job and often I would welcome the quiet times I spent with my little girl. We entertained many of the students to dinner, and those evenings were fun. One night a girl from Pakistan cooked us a curry, which she ate with her fingers; I tried it but I made a right mess, whereas she ate daintily, without dropping a morsel. That evening there was also a Nigerian princess who had the most wonderful personality. She offered to do the washing-up afterwards, but I had to stop her; she had never in her life done dishes and she splashed the water around so much that it looked as though we had a burst pipe. Another student I've never forgotten was a man called Rawalpindi, who read palms. I always remember he called me 'a onceful person'; I suppose that could be interpreted in many ways, but he saw a long career for me, if a hard one. I doubted that very much, as I believed my days in the theatre were over. Gerry put out his hand for his palm to be read; fortunately someone was speaking to him at the time, and Gerry turned away, because the look that came over the man's face was one of horror. He quickly changed his expression and told Gerry that everything was going to be fine, but he didn't tell him much more. He had seen the break in Gerry's lifeline.

At this time I was involved with a group of spiritualists who operated from a house in the Mearns. They were good people who did much healing, and I witnessed some amazing cures. I believe in what someone once said, 'There is a little truth in everything.' It was a year after my mother's death and I was thin and ailing in my mind. I even had some of her frocks in my wardrobe that I kept so that I could just cuddle them when my grief got unbearable. A dear friend, Nancy, took me to the famous spiritualist Albert Best, and told him how I needed a healing to try and get over my bereavement. This is a very strange story.

About a fortnight before this meeting, Gerry and I had been sitting at the fireside and our little girl was upstairs in her bedroom, sleeping. I heard her laugh in her sleep and Gerry and I went upstairs quietly to investigate. The child was sound asleep but she was laughing out loud. I whispered to my husband, 'I think she's seeing a g.h.o.s.t.' I actually spelled out the word, not wanting to admit to myself that it was true. It seemed so bizarre. When we came back downstairs Gerry said, 'It must be a good ghost if it's making her laugh.' No more was said about it.

When I went to see Albert two weeks later, he was already in a trance as I entered the room. I sat down quietly so as not to disturb the moment, and with his eyes closed, his first words to me were, 'Your mother is here and she's laughing.'

I got a terrible shock and was quite shaky.

He continued, 'She tells me about the night when you and your husband heard your daughter laughing in her sleep and you said, "I think she's seen a g.h.o.s.t.".' He repeated the words exactly as I had said them. I could hardly believe it. He said, 'Your mother will always take care of Dorothy, as she did in life. She was there that night to play with her and comfort her, so don't worry about it. It's quite natural.' I would have thought it was supernatural but he didn't think so. After he had told me more amazing things, including some advice as to how to deal with Gerry in his unhappiness, he asked me if I wanted to ask my mother any questions. I couldn't think of any; all I said was, 'I want my mother to be in Paradise.'

He replied with a gentle smile, 'We all have to work towards that, my dear. Your mother will be a shining light.'

This encounter was a great comfort to me and the wonders he told me about were certainly not the trivial kind I had heard before. Seeing him helped me a great way towards feeling better, and I became much stronger after that.

22

To know God better is only to realise more fully how
impossible it is that we should ever know Him at all. I
cannot tell which is more childish – to deny Him, or to
attempt to define Him.

SAMUEL BUTLER

Gerry was offered a position in a similar organisation in Ireland; a
teaching college for priests and those in Holy Orders in a place
about eight miles south of Dublin. Gerry went on ahead to establish
himself and look for a house for us. We had gone initially for a visit
and had fallen in love with Ireland. My daughter and I returned home
to sell the Newton Mearns house. In between times I was offered a
part as Renee Houston's wayward daughter in a BBC sitcom called *Let
Me Do The Talking*. I didn't tell Gerry I was doing it until later. He
wanted me at home, which is surprising since he had been an actor
himself and you would have thought he'd have had a sympathy for
actors wanting to work. I think he was so concerned about his child
that he didn't want anyone else to look after her.

The script was not wonderful but I was working with Renee, a
legend, and another actor whom I adored, Willie Joss, who had played
Uncle Martha in the 1940s–'50s BBC radio series, *The MacFlannels*, a
great favourite in its time. They were the sort of really good people
who, as my mother used to say, come along in your life and influence
you for the better. I have often thought that this is so true. Of course
there are many who have the opposite effect on one's life and with
hindsight and experience, not to mention a wee bit of the physics, I
have learned to recognise them. I think it is true that we bring close
to us and attract the people we want to be with. Sometimes I've had

to question my motives for inviting those people into my life who have brought me nothing but trouble and grief. From the great height of the age I am now, I am able to see that light attracts light. I am oversimplifying what is a very deep subject, and what I have said is only the bare bones of a belief I have held for many years. Renee Houston, whom I was thrilled to be working with, looked at me one day and said, 'My God, hen, I'm sitting here looking at you and I'm trying to remember who you remind me of, and now I know. You're just like me when I was young.' I was so delighted with the compliment. Renee was the very soul I needed at that time. She was motherly towards me and let me tell her my troubles. We went to a publicity luncheon together and I watched her making her speech. She had a beautiful deep voice and I marvelled at how she handled the press; she had that star quality. When we were alone together, her accent was quite Shettleston, Glasgow. At 66 she was still a fine-looking woman and had a lovely smile. On the way back to rehearsals, sitting in the taxi, I scolded her for not eating the lunch provided. 'You'll be hungry later, with all the energy you expend.'

I nearly fainted when she took out her teeth and said, 'See these, hen, they're only props. I cannae eat wi' them.' That was Renee. She was completely down to earth. She was a 'real' person for all her fame and talent. She told me a story about when she made the transition from variety to the legitimate theatre. She had received an award for a West End play and had to make a speech. She talked about her life and how thrilled she was to be part of the legitimate theatre. She mentioned legitimate theatre quite a few times until she finally said, 'Come to think about it, I've never felt such a bastard in all my life.'

Gerry found a lovely little bungalow to rent in Killiney, six miles south of Dublin; an idyllic spot on a hill overlooking Killiney Bay. He was enjoying his new job and his health seemed very much better. We had another child on the way. Ireland was a new beginning for us and we set about looking for a house to buy. There was a small estate being built on a hill and we chose an open-plan house with a garden that had to be created from scratch. Our furniture had been brought over and we moved in. One day I looked across the road and noticed that one of the neighbours had all her bits and pieces out on the front lawn. Something told me that this slightly disorganised woman was my kind of person. I made an excuse to go over and visit her and sure enough, my instinct was right. Helen became a great friend and a buffer for what was to come. She was pregnant too. I settled down to being a wife and mother and enjoyed the role.

Lisa was born in a nursing home in Cabinteely on 29 October 1968; 2 days before my 31st birthday. My sister phoned the nursing home at 8.40 p.m., at the precise moment the baby was born; I couldn't believe she was so tuned in to what was happening. We brought our new baby back to our new house. At the christening party most of the guests were nuns and priests, so the child was well blessed. Gerry was not so. His health was failing again. I tried all roads to get him to take the doctor's advice and go into hospital for tests, but he was adamant, saying that he would live without pills and doctors and take his chances. Like my mother he took a minor heart attack, but after a few days he was back at work. Gerry died in the house when his youngest child was only five months old.

My sister came over right away to comfort me and help with the arrangements. It all passed in a kind of dream. I automatically fed and cared for the baby and my little five-year-old, who was completely confused, shocked and unable to understand that her daddy had gone forever. Had it not been for my sister and my friend Helen across the road, and a new friend who entered my life at that time, I don't know how I would have managed to get through the days. Because of our connections with the Church, Monsignor Murphy in Glasgow had phoned his niece in Glasthule, down the road from Killiney, and asked her to visit me and look after us. Again I experienced the 'light' coming into my life through someone being sent to me who was to have a great influence. Maire Murphy, a stranger at the door, walked into our house and took over much of the responsibility of arrangements and organisation. Her parents, Lily and Noel Murphy, were to become like grandparents to my children and I bless the day I met them.

The moment came when it was all over. Gerry was buried and everyone had their own lives to get on with. My sister, having spent a fortnight with us, had to get back to her family and I found myself alone with my two little girls. That was the hardest part, but when you have children, you have to get on with it and therein lies the recovery. We were invited over to London to visit Gerry's best friend, Dorothy's godfather, and we did a lot of talking, crying and laughing with him and his wife. We also visited friends in Tunbridge Wells, Ian and Rita Yates. Ian had been sales manager with STV at the same time as Gerry was head of programmes. We talked about our days with the company and Ian, a very witty man, put the whole thing into perspective for me. He was the kind of man who had an optimism that Gerry didn't have. Poor Gerry, he had been my husband, the father of my children and my university. I would have to continue alone in the education of my children and myself. His knowledge was lost to us.

Ian Yates taught me that if you set up ten opportunities for yourself, one of them has to come up. He had been asked to leave STV too, but within a few months he had moved down south and had a job with a German firm. That was the July of 1969, the time when the first man landed on the moon. My daughter Dorothy was allowed to stay up to see this wonderful event on television in Ian and Rita's house, and I couldn't help thinking of all the conversations Gerry and my father had had about space and time and the future. I was heartbroken that Gerry hadn't witnessed the 'landing'.

We came back home to Ireland to find that the little garden I had created was in full bloom. This augured well for the future. I spent a lot of time with the Murphys, who were so kind to me. I also had friends in Killiney, John and Pat Dixon, and of course dear Helen, my artistic and sensitive friend. I had plenty of company and the summer passed pleasantly. By the September Maire Murphy suggested it was time I got back to work. I laughed and said that the theatre was a thing of the past as far as I was concerned. She made it her business to get me names of contacts and left it up to me to get in touch with them.

I thought about it long and hard, and decided to make an appointment with the Eamonn Andrews Studios in Dublin. I was to see a man called Fred O'Donovan, who put the shows in the Gaiety Theatre in Grafton Street, and his personal assistant, Ursula Doyle, an ex-dancer and widow of the famous Irish comic Jimmy O'Dea. I sang some songs for them and they asked me if I'd like to play

Principal Girl in the panto that year, *Robin Hood*. The top comedienne in Ireland was Maureen Potter, who had worked for many years as an actress and second comic and was now a big star. She was highly respected by everyone in her profession and I was very fortunate to have the opportunity to work with her.

As always, I said 'Yes' to the offer and then worried how I was going to manage it. With the help of my friends and an au pair, an Irish orphan who had been brought up by nuns, I went into rehearsals. It was a terrifying experience. I had been away from the business for so long that at one point I thought I would have to tell them I couldn't do it. Mr Haining's voice came back loud and clear, 'You said you could do it when you wrote in.' I couldn't let the side down but I thought, 'This is ridiculous. What am I doing here? I should be at home with my children.'

The panto was wonderful; it was what Nellie Sutherland would have described as a 'lavish production'. This was a number one theatre and in the end I played my part quite well. It was a strictly disciplined theatre. There was a green room where you could chat together whilst waiting to make your next entrance, but no one was allowed to sit down in their costumes. There was a bar in the green room, something I'd never come across before, but of course no one drank alcohol until after the show.

Maureen was very kind to me and on Friday and Saturday nights we'd sit chatting after the performance. She'd tell me stories about the theatre in Ireland and the films she'd made; one of them was James Joyce's *Ulysses*. I would make her laugh with stories about the Scottish theatre and about my father. She had many well-known actor friends who came in to see her. My mouth hung open when in walked Cyril Cusack, an actor whom I'd admired for years. Michael Mac Liammóir was a pal of Maureen. He held the floor of the green room and talked of his performances. A very subdued Richard Harris occasionally paid a visit, and Noel Purcell was a regular. One night Jack Benny and his wife Mary had been to see the show and came round afterwards. On another occasion the telephone rang in the green room and I overheard a conversation Maureen was having with a friend. It went something like this: 'Ah sure, darlin' girl, don't be bothered with them . . . No . . . you just tell them what you want . .

. A devil bit of it. No . . . no . . . ah, now you're talkin'.' The conversation went on like this and it was obvious that the friend had phoned to get Maureen's advice on some matter. When she came off the phone, she told me she had been speaking to a friend in Hollywood. The friend was Maureen O'Hara.

Maureen Potter was a one-off. She was married to a captain in the Irish Army. She was what we called, in the Scottish variety business, a production comedienne; that meant that most of her work was in sketch form. She would play the wee Irish women with a fellow comic, Danny Cummins, but also a huge range of comedy characters. If I were to compare her to anyone, it would be Gracie Clark without the hassle. She was exceptionally talented and at the end of each show would do a 'front cloth' stand-up act which was heavy on political humour. There was a very warm heart in Maureen and she and I would often talk about our families and how difficult it was to run a house and work in the theatre at the same time. Of course she had the full responsibility of the show on her shoulders, but she had a humility about her that to my mind is the mark of a truly great artiste.

One afternoon, during a matinee performance of *Robin Hood*, Maureen mentioned to me that Hal Roach was out front. The name rang a bell with me – Hal Roach.

I asked Maureen, 'Is he a comedian?'

'Of course he is. He's the star turn at Jury's Hotel.'

Jury's Hotel in Dame Street was where they did the Irish cabaret for tourists. As we in Scotland have a heather and haggis show in Edinburgh hotels, so the Irish have a shillelaghs and Irish dancing extravaganzas. Then I remembered that years ago, in the Gang days, I'd had a letter from Hal Roach asking me to do a summer season with him in some Irish holiday resort. Somehow or other I had forgotten to reply to him. So here I was working in an Irish theatre, and Hal was in the audience. After the show I was frightened to meet him in case he remembered me. He did. We were just coming off the finale when this man shouts from the side of the stage, 'Where's that Dorothy Paul?' Maureen introduced us and his first words to me were, 'Ah ya hoot, you never wrote.'

I loved the people I worked with in Ireland. They were colourful and genuine folk and I was made very welcome. I did a few weeks in Jury's Hotel, where I was singing lovely Irish songs, and watched Hal as he charmed the audiences with his sometimes irreverent humour. 'Ah now, I can see all the nuns are here tonight. Some of them don't wear the gear but they're here. Ah look now, there's one sitting beside the good Father . . .

'They're very devout, the folk in Ireland, ye know. Up in the hills of Donegal a new priest arrives by the way, and Casey and his wife were going to the church to hear him for the first time. But Casey's wife took the flu, so Casey went along to hear him on his own and he was very good. He said many marvellous things to impress the people but one of the things he said was, and I quote, "The happiest times in my life were spent in the arms of another man's wife: my mother" . . . and so on. So when Casey got back to the little cottage, the wife said, "Well, what's the new parish priest like?" and Casey said, "My God, I've never heard the like . . . he said things you wouldn't believe. He told us that the happiest times of his life were spent in the arms of another man's wife, and he told us her name, and I can't remember it now."'

Hal told story after story all about Irish rural life, and he had the audience eating out of the palm of his hand.

Tourists came from all over the world to Dublin. Sometimes we had dinner or coffee with members of the audience. One night I was talking to a charming couple from Hollywood, Arthur and Claudia Hamilton, both very good-looking people. Arthur asked me what I did in the cabaret and I said, 'I'm the soprano.' I asked him what he did for a living and he told me that he was a songwriter. I was most impressed by this and thought to myself, 'A songwriter from Hollywood?' Then, as gauche as ever, I asked, 'Have you written any tunes I might know?'

He replied, 'I've written many "tunes" but you may know the one I wrote for a film called *The Girl Can't Help It*, it's called "Cry Me a River".'

I nearly fainted on the spot.

Another feature of my life in Ireland was playing the organ in Ballybrack church. I wasn't very good at it but I enjoyed the practice. I'd go along of an afternoon and play the organ to my heart's content. On Sundays I'd sit in the organ loft and play for the congregation. My eldest daughter, who by this time was attending the Dublin School of Music and showing quite a talent, would stand beside me and nudge me whenever I played what she called 'a bum note'. Her nudging didn't make me play any better. On this particular Sunday I'd been asked by a neighbour if I'd take her little girl to mass as she, the mother, had a cold. There I was with my own two and this other little girl who had been to see the panto the day before. All through the service this little girl was going on, in a loud voice, saying what a good actress I was. 'Oh, Mrs le Grove, I loved the panto . . . you were very good . . . you're a very good actress.' She would not be quiet and between her going on and my eldest daughter's nudges, I was getting a bit agitated. At the end of mass the priest announced the last hymn; he had given me the hymn just before the service so I had to sight-read it. I played the introduction and started the verse. No one sang. I looked through the mirror at the priest who was waving his arms and looking up at me. I didn't know what the arm-waving was supposed to indicate. My daughter was nudging and I was quite confused. Finally the priest announced, 'The organist is playing the wrong tune, so I'll just start you off myself.' He sang and the congregation continued unaccompanied. I was humiliated and the situation wasn't helped by my daughter saying in my ear, 'See, that was you, Mum, you did it wrong . . . Mum . . . Mum . . . You did it wrong.' The other Miss Chatterbox was struck dumb by this débâcle. After the blessing, the congregation, mostly my neighbours, made their way out of the gallery and down the stairs. They each gave me a little smile as they passed. I was sitting there with egg on my face. Then in a great loud voice my little charge says, 'Mrs le Grove, you're a very good actress but you're not very good at playing the organ.'

I closed the organ and took the children to the car. There was always a queue of cars leaving the church and the priest stood at the gate and bid everyone good morning. When I reached him I said, 'Father, I'll never play the organ in your church again.'

He said, 'Ah sure, don't be upset. Anyone can make a mistake.'

I informed him that I had not made a mistake, he had given me the wrong hymn. An argument ensued, holding up all the cars. I said

Dorothy

loftily, 'Father, it may only be a hymn to you but to me, an artiste, it's a performance.'

My daughter didn't help as, in all innocence but with veracity, she put her fourpenceworth in, 'She's not very good at it anyway, Father.'

The other little girl came to my defence. 'No, but she's a very good actress.'

I had Maureen Potter in fits telling her about it.

In 1970 I was starting to get a lot of fun out of my life that I had missed in my 20s. I had a lovely house two beautiful daughters, a career in the Irish theatre, although – it has to be said – not a very well-paid one. Gerry had not left me destitute. The insurance had paid out and I had a widow's pension. I missed my friends in Scotland but many of them came over to Ireland to visit, as did my father and sister. There was an old-fashioned quality about Ireland that I loved. Everyone baked their own bread, which I learned to do and have since forgotten. The meal of the day was always a high tea. High tea at Mrs Murphy's house was a great treat. Her kitchen was plain and scrupulously scrubbed and above the fireplace was a picture of the Sacred Heart. One day my daughter asked me why the man had a big strawberry on his chest. Ever after the picture was called the Holy Strawberry, but not in Mrs Murphy's hearing.

There was a priest from the local church who used to come to visit me, Father Conlan. When he entered my house around 4.30 in the afternoon, he always asked for a bit of toast and two boiled eggs. I was delighted to make this for him, as he was a charming and very holy man. He asked me why I was taking my children to church and not receiving the Holy Sacrament myself. I told him I wasn't a Catholic. We talked at length about this and he suggested I go to the nuns in Ballybrack to hear what conversion was all about. I did so. Being in a highly emotional state in those days, I decided that the Catholic Church was for me, but I went into it for the wrong reasons and many years later I decided it had been a wrong decision. I now feel that there are many roads towards right thinking, and that the Catholic Church is only one of them. I still have many friends in Holy Orders and I admire them greatly. Certainly the priest, Father Conlan, was a truly wonderful man who not long afterwards went to work in the mission in South America, a place where the clergy don't have a

Dorothy

history of longevity. I never heard of him again and I often wonder if he is still alive.

Fred O'Donovan asked me if I'd like to do the summer season in the Gaiety. I said yes, and we started to rehearse a show which ran 16 weeks during the summer. Maureen, of course, was the star of the show and it played to packed houses. I fed Maureen in the sketches and sang in an Irish scena. The song I sang was 'Teddy O'Neale'. Sometimes to this day I'll sit at the piano and sing that song and I can never finish it without tears in my eyes. Perhaps that's because I don't have a soprano voice any more and I can hear myself. The deeper reason is that the days I spent in Ireland were heightened emotionally because of the tragedies that had occurred. There was a bitter-sweetness to my life. In that show I had to dance quite a bit and I was never fitter. We rehearsed in a school playground in the summer evenings. I felt good, and when I look back at the photographs, I think I looked good. Perhaps I was in my prime. It was the year of the World Cup and we all made our entrances in the opening as different football players. The songs all had a football theme. The costumes were wonderful and I was having a ball.

Work was thin on the ground between shows, however, and many months would go by without much income. When I look back I could have managed, just, but my eldest daughter had now started school and I discovered that it was compulsory for her to learn the Irish language, the Gaelic. Was this a good idea, and would it do any good to burden her with this extra subject? The cost of living in Ireland was escalating at a fast rate, and there was no NHS. I was beginning to wonder if we could afford to stay there. Children are always back and forward to the doctor with colds and 'throats', so the cost of consultations and antibiotics was running away with a lot of money. The other consideration was that, although it was wonderful to work in the theatre in Ireland, the pay was only half what it was in Scotland. I was starting to feel the pinch.

I did another panto with Maureen in the Gaiety, this time playing the Fairy; a lesser part than the last time. The following spring Ross Bowie, an agent/producer in Scotland, asked me to do the summer season for him in Largs, with a much higher salary than I would have got in Dublin. I accepted. In professional terms I would be going from a number one theatre in Ireland to a small seaside-resort theatre in Scotland. Still, I thought it was a good decision at the time and it would get me into Scottish theatre again. It would also let me see how I felt about living back home, compared to the Ireland I had grown to love.

23

The world, like an accomplished hostess, pays most attention to those whom it will soonest forget.

JOHN CHURTON COLLINS

I returned to Scotland with my two children and I thought I would take up where I left off and that I would still be a wee bit famous, and it didn't happen. I was back to being just another variety turn in a small seaside theatre. Two unknown comics headed the bill and we did nothing at the box office. Halfway through the eight-week season the two comics were sacked and two others were brought in, and we still didn't do the business. If, when I was younger, I had been involved in the death throes of variety, then this surely was the mortuary.

Digs were very hard to find with two small children, but Ross Bowie had a hotel in Largs and let me have a room there, and I made an arrangement with one of the staff to babysit for me at nights. As Howard M. Lockhart would have said, 'You've come a long way.' Yes, I had come a long hard way from glittering Monte Carlo to Largs and the Moxon girls with their famous holey tights.

I met up with some old friends in the cast, Jackie Farrell and John Shearer, and the tenor was Don Gordon. There was a trio of boys who did a singing act and four Moxon girls. I had to have the children with me at rehearsals, and in the afternoons I would take them to the beach and try to keep my eyes open so that my two-and-a-half-year-old wouldn't run into the water. We all had tea together, I'd put the children to bed and go off and do the show. I was a very tired lady. The bonus was that Johnny Farren was doing wardrobe again and also waiting at tables in the hotel, so laughs were guaranteed. Sometimes he would take the children away for a walk in the afternoons just to let me get a little rest.

One day Johnny and I took the children to a café for afternoon tea. Lisa was sitting on Johnny's knee and Dorothy beside me. We were all tired, it was a hot day. A woman came up to us and said, 'Oh, Dorothy, I remember you from the *One O'Clock Gang*.' I gave the usual smile and pretended she was the only person who'd ever said that. Then she went on: 'Oh, these are your two wee girls.' She cooed over the children for a moment then turned to Johnny and said, 'You must be Dorothy's husband.' Johnny never said a word and the woman moved on. Then he turned to me. 'Dorothy's husband! What does she think I am, a big lesbian?' I don't know what I would have done without him on that season.

Another day the children and I were on the beach and I was so tired I could hardly keep my eyes open. I was lying down and holding the youngest child's hand to keep her beside me when up came two men who looked down into my face. They were Roddy McMillan and Johnny Greave, having a wee day out at Largs. Roddy said, 'My God, hen, you look exhausted.' I told him I was in the middle of the season and it was hard going. Roddy said, 'Just you have a wee sleep to yourself and Johnny and I'll take the weans for an ice cream.' Off they went for an hour and I fell sound asleep. I was very grateful to them.

It is so essential to be fit in our business, because tiredness can make you blank out on stage and you can forget your lines so easily. One night I was finishing off my act with a song called 'Macushla', a sad Irish song which Johnny used to call one of my 'womb tremblers'. The words in the song were all to do with colours, for instance, 'Macushla, Macushla, your red lips are calling', and 'Macushla, Macushla, your white arms are reaching'. At the end of the song I didn't know where I was, and sang, 'Macushla, Macushla, your red . . . no . . . white . . . no blue arms are reaching . . .'

I came off stage in a state of embarrassment, and Johnny said, 'Why didn't you just say striped?'

Johnny had a partner whom he lived with in Glasgow, his tall dark man. During the season Johnny got word that his partner had decided to leave him and go to Australia. I have never seen such devastation on a man's face as I saw in Johnny's. He was heartbroken. My heart went out to him and all of us tried to comfort him, but it was like a death to him. They had been together for many years and any time I was in their flat I saw a genuine, loving relationship. Wee Johnny, as he was always known, never got over it. He died two years later. Being a pro he kept going for the sake of the show that year, but his heart was no longer in the business he had always loved.

After the last night of the show, when we were all set to go our separate ways, someone had a party in their digs. We all got dressed up and went along. During the evening, one of the dancers who had been having a romance with one of the singing trio boys discovered that he had been deceiving her, to use an old-fashioned phrase. She was in a dreadful state; tear-stained and not a little unsteady. Johnny and I decided to take her home in a taxi to her digs. I said, 'Would you like to come to our hotel and have a wee coffee before you go home?' I was thinking that she could talk about it and get it out of her system. The end of a show is always a sad time. It was a wet night and the rain was horizontal along the prom. We got out of the taxi to discover that the manager had locked up the hotel and probably taken a sleeping tablet. We banged and banged at the door but there was no answer. I was thinking that my children were in there and I couldn't get to them; was the babysitter still looking after them? At the same time this poor lassie was crying her eyes out and I was giving Johnny a row for not having organised a key. The rain was lashing down on us from all sides and finally, after much banging at the door, Johnny shouted, 'For Christ's sake let us in . . . it's Baron Hardup and the two ugly sisters.' Eventually we were able to waken the manager.

While I was in Scotland I had made enquiries about work. I even went to visit Nellie, but poor Nellie had gone to that major venue in the sky. I realised that although I could work in theatre in Ireland, there wasn't much hope for a Scottish artiste working in Telefis Eireann. Someone else told me that there was a lot of work going in the clubs. I weighed up the pros and cons. On the one hand Ireland was a lovely place to bring up the children and I had a lot of friends there. But on the other, my family were in Scotland, there was more work, the children would not have to learn Irish and there was the NHS. Scotland won, and in November 1971 we moved back to our own country and Glasgow.

Dorothy

When I looked back at the days in Ireland I felt there was a kind of unreality about them. We had lived in such a beautiful place, but Gerry had died and was buried there. I had never given myself time to think or make plans. I had just plunged into the theatre once again. It was the only work I knew, apart from invoice typing and serving in a shop. The Gang had given me ideas above my station in the talent department and I realised that I was as yet unskilled in many aspects of my profession. I had learned everything I knew 'on the hoof' and that was in variety, but times were changing and sopranos, unless you were one of the greats, were becoming out of date in the shows I was involved in. I had to work if I wanted any kind of good life for myself and the children, and I needed the kind of work that gave me time to be with them. The clubs seemed the ideal solution; I could work four nights a week, Father would mind them at nights, and I would be home the rest of the time. Brigadoon had been left behind; this was reality. I had to start again and build up some kind of reputation in a new entertainment medium. I didn't realise what I was letting myself in for.

In the theatre you have people sitting out there who have paid their money and are willing to sit, watch and listen while you perform. There is a commitment from the audience. Not so with the clubs. The bingo and the bar were the two important elements of the evening, the 'turn' was secondary. My first venue was Broxburn Athletic Club. I arrived to attend what I thought would be a band call. I wasn't expecting Scotland's top musicians, but I did expect them to be able to read music.

'Whit are ye wantin' tae dae, hen? "I Feel Pretty?" Heh heh . . . How dis that go?'

I said, 'It's written, here's the music.'

The keyboard player – I won't call him a pianist – said, 'His it goat chord symbols?' The music did have chord symbols but by its very nature the music had to be played. Jimmy Running in the Roxy Falkirk was a virtuoso compared with this man. Then he told me he could only play in the one key, of course it was a key that didn't suit me, so after much arguing I said, 'Just try to follow me.' I had to do two 20-minute spots and I was terrified. I asked about the microphone and the convener said, 'Don't worry about the mike, hen, it's very good – we call the bingo with it.'

Dorothy

I died a death in Broxburn. I got the raspberry from some wag in the hall and, of course, this got laughs. I carried on singing, but instantly realised that my kind of singing was not right for the clubs. I had to change if I wanted to survive. I was heckled rotten: 'Haw, hen . . . is Larry Marshall still alive? Haw, Dorothy, let's see ye in yer wee school uniform . . . Where's Charlie's nana?' If ever I was going to leave showbusiness, this would have been the time. I do not know why I kept going back for more. I must have thought little of myself at that time.

During the summers of these years, I managed to get summer seasons and had to change my daughter's school so that I could have her with me and my little toddler. Father and Auntie Nellie took turns looking after the children, and the children adored both of them, especially Grandpa. One season in Ayr we had to take a cottage in Mauchline, which meant I had to travel 44 miles a day back and forward to the digs. The children played in the kirkyard which our windows overlooked, where Robert Burns's relatives and friends were buried. There was also a bookie's shop adjacent to the house. It was many years later that Dorothy told me Grandpa would send her down with a line to put on. What did I do to my poor children? However, they did have their mother with them most of the time, and they haven't turned out too badly.

For years I couldn't get work in panto so in the autumn and winter I was back to the clubs. One famous night I was in the Trades Club, Kirkcaldy. By this time I had dropped my voice an octave and started to do country and western numbers, which went well; the more banter the better – 'Lay the Blanket on the Ground', for instance. I always finished up with a big soprano number. However, there were Catholic and Protestant clubs and you had to know which songs to omit. Religious intolerance was alive and thriving; I would never sing an Irish song in a Masonic club nor would I sing 'The Star of Rabbie Burns' in a Catholic club. I absolutely hated the idea of this kind of prejudice. The way to deal with it was just to laugh in the face of it. But back to the Trades Club. This was the MC: 'Order, please . . . order, please . . . come oan noo, quiet down. If you're wantin' your bingo tickets you'd better get your arses in gear and get into the convener's office or they'll aw be finished. Right . . . I have one or two announcements to make. It has been brought to my attention that some of you have been using the exterior of these premises as a toilet. And I've been told that some of you have been avoiding your yoo . . . your yoo . . . making your water in the car park.' He seemed to choose what he thought was the more delicate way of putting it, but then he went on, 'The committee are very annoyed about this and only last week somebody shat on it as well . . . so here she is, Dorothy Paul.'

I couldn't believe it, but I went on as no one seemed to make the connection with me and the perpetrator of the unseemly behaviour. During my act a slight fracas broke out in the bar behind the audience. I could see something was going on, but didn't hear anything. I was belting out 'The Holy City' at the time. Just then the MC grabbed the microphone from my hand and called out, 'Point of order, point of order! Come on, youse two gentlemen – if you've any differences to settle, please settle them out in the car park.' This car park seemed to be a busy place. 'There's a turn on here . . . and this hoor's come aw the way fae Glasgow.' He turned to me, handed me back the mike and said, 'Okay, hen, carry on.'

That was enough. I was out of there. I walked off the stage and into a small room where I'd left my bits and pieces. I was just ready to leave when the convener himself came into the room. He said, 'Well, hen, I suppose you'll be wanting a return booking.' I assured him that I did not. 'Aw come on, hen, this is the best wee club in Fife, everybody wants tae come back here.' I wasn't interested. He went on with an offer that perhaps many couldn't refuse. He said, 'See if you come back, I'll tell you what I'll do. D'ye see that blackboard there with all the names of the turns that are coming in the next few weeks? See that?' There were names scribbled on a blackboard. 'I'll tell ye whit ah'll dae wi' ye, hen. If ye come back, I'll write your name in three different colours of chalk.' I was overwhelmed by his generosity of spirit, nevertheless I told him that perhaps I belonged to an élite society of performers who would definitely not want to return. He took the hump at this remark. 'Aye, well, you please yersel. But see you, Dorothy Paul . . . See you? If I'd been you, I'd have quit while ah wis ahead.'

There was nothing more to be said. I swept aff.

Dorothy

Stories of the clubs are legion. An act went round the circuit called Paul Gerard, the Voice in the Night. This man was one of the first to have a radio mike. That meant he wasn't tied to an amplifier with wires, but could wander anywhere with this cordless mike. The reason for the title of his act was that he would place himself behind the bar and sing his opening few words of the song:

'You smile, the song begins,
You speak, and I hear violins – it's magic . . .'

The magic being that no one knew where the voice was coming from. Then he would appear and walk through the tables and sing, 'Oh, oh, oh, it's magic' and so on into his act, where he would eventually take the stage.

One club he played had fire-doors and a fire-escape behind the stage. He thought this would be a wonderful opportunity to work the magic. He told the convener that he would go outside, round the back of the hall, up the fire-stairs and wait outside the fire-doors and open them up after the opening bars of his song. The convener agreed that there would be an element of surprise that would get him off to a good start. Paul Gerard was a very well-dressed act: white suit, shoes, the fashionable frilly shirt and an immaculate hairstyle. As arranged, he went round the back, the band struck up the chords, he went into 'You smile the song begins, you speak and I hear violins – it's magic'. He then turned the handle of the fire-doors, only to find them locked. The convener was busy at the time, no doubt sorting out some fight or other, when one of his committee approached him and said, 'Did you tell that boy in the white suit that we'd open the fire-doors for him?'

The convener said, 'Aye, ah did. Have you got the key?'

'Ah've no got the key.'

The convener said, 'Well, you'd better find somebody who's got it. The boy's standing out there waitin' tae get in.'

By this time the voice in the night had sung two songs outside on the fire-stairs. Then the rain came on. By the time the two organisers had found the key he had got through a further two songs, he was soaking wet, furious, and much of the magic had gone out of his act.

Some of the clubs had theme nights. Being innocent of this kind of business, one night I found myself party to what I can only describe as 'mob fantasy'. This involved ordinary people dressing up as cowboys and cowgirls, and acting out their ideas of what the Wild West was like. I've no doubt that during the day these folk went about their business as miners, shopkeepers, factory workers; normal everyday members of their community. On one night a week they were gunfighters in the OK Corral, the Clanton Brothers, Doc Holliday, Jesse James, Butch Cassidy and the Sundance Kid, or any other figure of American history. What I found particularly dubious was the women who were dressed as squaws, going around greeting people with 'How'.

I arrived at this club and was immediately shown into my dressing-room, a ladies toilet. The bingo session was in progress, so I thought that I'd peek into the hall and take a discreet look at the audience. I'd never seen anything like it. There were cowboys in leather chaps, big Texan hats, high-heeled boots, spurs a-jingling, checked shirts and gunbelts with six-shooters at the ready, all with their heads down over the bingo.

I thought to myself, I'd better be good tonight and, if not, I'd better be quick and keep ahead of the posse.

At the end of the bingo session, a big cowboy with an east coast accent took the stage. 'Testing, testing,' he said through the mike before he started. People always blow on a microphone, much to a good sound-person's annoyance because the moisture in someone's breath causes damage to the head.

The big man gave his opening remarks, 'Can you hear me at the back there? Aye, right. Welcome amigos to the Carlanden Corral. Ah've a wee message from bonnie Jean in the caterin'. She's a good lass, Jean, and she's done her best to keep prices doon but as from tonight, there's another 2p on the wagon wheels.' This was a wee joke to warm up the audience and a smattering of laughter ran round the hall. 'Noo, ye'll no ken me but I'm yer host for the evening, Wild Bill Hickcock frae Pumpherston. The usual boy, the Methil Kid, couldnae make it the night, ken, he's got the cauld. So I'll be doin' your introductions and that. Noo you've hid the bingo and then we'll have the turns and then we'll come to the highlight of the evening.' Here there were a few chords on the electric organ and some Wild West type catcalls from the audience, just to build up the sense of occasion. 'Aye, it's the grand final of the Quick on the Draw contest.' There was a roll on the drums and Wild Bill Hickcock continued dramatically, 'Aw the way from Pittenweem, we've got Buckshot McSweeney and he'll be shootin' aff against yer own yer very own' – the drums got louder and there were more hi's and ho's from the assembled cowhands – 'Yes, Club Foot Paterson.'

The audience went wild at this announcement. I was introduced and I sang to a frenzy of indifference. I left town before the shooting started.

In 1974 I had a regular Sunday summer job in Butlins in Ayr. Of course I took the children and Father with me, as there was plenty for them to enjoy at their age. Band call was at 3.30 p.m. and I had much organising to get everyone ready. My girls remember me dashing about with an electric hairdryer on, the kind that had a tube leading from an electric machine which hung round the shoulder and a hood that blew up with hot air. The rollers were in place under the hood. They loved it when I put on the hood, switched it on and it ballooned up. They always said, 'Mummy, you have lift-off.' At the same time as my hair was drying, I was serving up lunch. 'Right, girls, Dad, do you want fish-fingers and chips or egg and chips?' The orders would be taken and furnished. One day my father, who had asked for fish-fingers and chips, looked at everybody else's plate and said, 'Oh here . . . ah could have went an egg.' It sounded so daft that I burst out laughing. My eldest daughter said, 'Mummy, I know why you're laughing. It's not I could have "went" an egg, it's I could have "gone" an egg.'

We would all get into the car and take off for Ayr with costumes, music, toys and Grandpa's telescope. Grandpa said to the girls, when we got in sight of the beautiful island of Arran, 'See that? Goat Fell through the telescope.'

One of them would answer, 'Did it?'

Then we would get, 'Mummy, Mummy, stop at a "layabout", I'm going to be sick.' It was probably the egg and chips.

It all seemed like hassle in those days but, like many mothers, I would give anything to have one of those days back. I would do the band call and Father and the children would go round Butlins playing on the rides and eating candyfloss. I would meet them between the shows and take them either for a picnic, if I'd been up in time to make one, or for tea at the awful Butlins dining-halls. You would wait in a queue and by the time you got to a table the food was cold. It was always fried food, so we might expect another 'sick' stop on the way back. One teatime Grandpa made an awful face when he ate a chip.

'Whit the hell's in these chips for God's sake?'

Lisa said, 'Mummy, Grandpa's shaken sugar all over his chips!' He'd lifted the sugar-shaker instead of the salt. It was sometimes like taking another child out for the day, but he loved the days out as well. My father was always willing to accompany us on the summer seasons and would fall out with Auntie Nellie if it was her turn to come with us. I had to divide up the 'minding' fortnightly.

One of the happiest summer seasons was in Dundee. I rented a little flat above a post office in Invergowrie, amidst beautiful countryside. When it came to the fruit-picking season my sister came for a fortnight and we got an extra job as 'pickers'. We got 10p for picking a punnet and were able to buy as many punnets as we needed. There was much jam-making that year and a good outdoor exercise for all. It was almost like history repeating itself, with me taking a house and then relatives joining us, only we weren't as crushed as my mother's houses had been.

I was now beginning to do television dramas. All the years of belting out comedy lines, not to mention the smoking, had had an adverse effect on my soprano voice. I was doing less singing and more acting and realised that I loved it. However, at that time I was combining two aspects. After doing a play in which I had a rather steamy bedroom scene, with a man dragging me into bed and going into a big clinch, I found myself back in Ayr for another summer season. One Saturday afternoon I was doing the weekend shopping in William Low's and all the while telling the children to behave and that no, they weren't going to have Smarties before their tea – just the usual kind of thing with children. We were at the check-out when my daughter noticed the actor with whom I had done the play. He was in the next check-out getting his shopping bagged and paid for. Suddenly, in a great loud voice, my eldest daughter shouted, 'Mummy, Mummy, look . . . there's the man you were in bed with.'

Everyone looked round but what could I do? The words hung in the air and couldn't be withdrawn.

24

They know enough who know how to learn.

Henry Adams

*W*riting was always something that was uppermost in my mind. I wrote sketches for comedians with just a small part for myself. In those days, the 1970s, few women were taken seriously as lead comedy actresses. Come to think of it, few women are taken seriously as lead comedy actresses even now. There is certainly little commissioned work given to women, and men normally write for men, with a few exceptions. I believe I would have entered lead comedy parts sooner if I'd had someone in a position of power who believed in me. Fortunately, I did eventually get my chance. Over the years I have had to be slightly devious and take part in a panto which for all the world was a straight part and then make it so funny that the director had to keep it in.

In 1974 I got one of the biggest disappointments of my professional life. I submitted a television sitcom script, based on my life as a club singer. I wrote the piece with follow-up scripts, and the title music (helped by my daughter Dorothy), and played the lead along with a first-class team of actors: Tom Watson as the father, Mary Riggans as the father's girlfriend, the late Helen Norman as the auntie – Helen was another performer who came to the straight theatre via variety. The programme was performed in front of a live audience and got huge laughs. The show was shelved and never shown. It was a bitter affront and made me feel so bad that I lost confidence in writing. My associate writer on the show was Jack Gerson, one of Scotland's best television writers who is now a well-known novelist. He could not for the life of him understand why it never got a showing. I supposed when we are creative we set ourselves up for failure as well as success. As that old imperialist Rudyard Kipling said, 'Watch the things you gave your life to, broken, and stoop and build 'em up with worn-out tools.'

I was quite filled with resentment over that treatment, but life goes on. I was determined not to go back to the clubs; I would rather have taken in stairs to wash. Come to think of it, I was probably more skilled at that than 'laying the blanket on the ground'.

In 1975, in the middle of a summer season down at Ayr, Jimmy McNair, the former *One O'Clock Gang* scriptwriter, came down to see me and offer me a job as a chat-show hostess. I was amazed. How on earth did he think I could do something like that? Of course I said yes. Then I wondered how I was going to cope with it. Would I get found out this time? As a matter of fact, I did. I phoned my friend Kath and asked her what she thought. Her comment was, 'Yes, I think you could do it, but you better watch you don't swear.' Me? Swear? *Quelle idée*! She continued, 'You know how when things go wrong, you always say "Oh, shite"!'

The girl who had been doing this live afternoon show was overworked and wanted a break for four months. However, it was mentioned that if I did it well, I might take over the job altogether.

They asked me to dye my nice brown hair blonde in order, they said, that I look different from the way I looked in the *One O'Clock Gang*. I got my hair dyed and took up an attitude. I would talk posh and the viewers would think I was clever. I knew I wasn't clever because I didn't get my Highers at the school, but I would pretend I was. I appeared live at 2 p.m. every day, with guests. The show was called *Housecall*. On a Monday it was a medical and keep-fit programme; Tuesday was fashion and a guest from showbusiness, someone who was playing one of the Glasgow theatres; Wednesday was a programme for OAPs – I also sang a song on that day, accompanied by a dear friend, Peggy O'Keefe – and Thursday was anything goes, with recipes.

It was like being back in the *One O'Clock Gang*: a daily dose of nerves. I tried very hard to be interested in what everyone was saying and talk posh and keep my mouth shut when appropriate, but I just couldn't manage it. On the Monday programme we had a regular doctor who led the way and who brought with him a specialist on the particular subject to be discussed. I took every disease they talked about. Every week I had something different. On the Tuesday I was a little better, as I knew a bit about showbusiness and found that if I gave the guests funny cues it would get them started. The most frightening was Victor Borge. I went to see his show the night before, which was no hardship because I love the man's work. At the hospitality lunch before the programme, he was very quiet and subdued. He hardly spoke to me at all, and I felt he disliked me or just didn't want to be there. Jimmy NcNair thought it would be a good idea to have him sitting at the piano, with me beside him on a high stool. His instinct was correct because the minute the cameras were on Victor Borge he came to life, and using the piano as a prop he had me and the entire crew in stitches. I asked him if he had played 'to all the crowned heads of Europe'. He replied in his lovely Scandinavian accent, 'Yes . . . but I usually prefer it when their bodies are there as well.'

The failures outnumbered the successes. For instance, I interviewed a red-hot feminist talking about her book, and she made mincemeat out of me. I realised that I really didn't know what feminism was all about, although as a single parent I had to father and mother and 'ballsy' when necessary. I took note of yet another gap in my education. Then there was the head of Twinings Tea, a charming man, who nearly ended up hitting me on camera. The trouble was that I hate tea, and he was there to plug all his different products. At the lunch beforehand he asked me if I would take part in a tea-testing session on the show. I said yes, of course, thinking that I was going to have to bite this bullet and drink something that might make me sick: sacrifice for my art. If I hate tea then I hate cold tea even more, and by the time he put the tea in a cup that looked like a shaving mug, swirled it around and handed it to me, it was frozen. I had about ten teas to go through before it was all finished. As we went through the tea-tasting business, he was talking all the time and asking me what I thought about them.

'What would you say to Earl Grey?' I would honestly have said 'Boak', but I smiled and said it was lovely. Then Lapsang Souchong and something else and something else – they all tasted awful to me. I kept up the oohs and ahs and yes it's lovely, without much enthusiasm, hoping I wouldn't throw up. Then we came to the last one and I thought, thank God. I think it was Orange Pekoe and, running out of compliments, I suggested that it might be nice with a slice of lemon.

He got nasty. 'What do you mean, a slice of lemon? With my tea? My Orange Pekoe?'

I said I was very sorry, but it was only a suggestion. The captions went up on the end of the show with the title music and the man still berating me for insulting his tea.

I hit the ladies and vomited.

I have recordings of all these shows, made by Frank, a friend of mine in Edinburgh who was one of the first people to have a video. I don't know where I got my idea of style. Every frock I wore on that show looked as though I had gone into a shop and said, 'Give me something that doesn't suit me.' With my blonde curls, my awful frocks and posh accent, I was a disgrace to my profession.

A woman director, Tina Wakerell, who had made her name in London and was very talented, came in to direct the programme. Her first words to me were, 'Why are you speaking in that dreadful accent? You're neither one thing nor the other. Speak naturally and you'll make it so much easier for yourself. You're tying yourself in knots.' I decided that she had a point. I went on one day with 'Good efternoon and waylcome to *Housecall*' and the next day I was saying 'Hullo rerr.' I was called by the Head of Programmes, dear Tony Firth. He said, 'Now Dorothy, what can I say? You are doing very well, my dear, but the accent . . . just a little too, well, Glasgowish. I wonder if you could give it a little bit more . . . shall we say . . . cut glass?'

I went back to 'waylcome to *Housecall*'. I wasn't caring anyway, because I knew I wasn't going to be retained in the position. Not long before I finished in the show, one Tuesday we had a hero's spot. The hero in question was a wee Glasgow man who had been instrumental in saving people during a Glasgow hotel fire. The conversation was as follows:

> *Dorothy*: Good afternoon and welcome to Housecall. Today we have a mixed bag and I'm Dorothy Paul. We're going to

have a yoga session and I'll be tying myself in knots, ha ha ha. Our cook is going to do something interesting with doughnuts, and I'll be speaking to Jimmy Ferguson, who was the night porter when there was a big fire in a Glasgow hotel. But first let's meet our fearless firefighter, Jimmy Ferguson. [*Turn to Jimmy*] Hello, Jimmy.

Jimmy: Aw, hullo rerr.

Dorothy: And tell me, Jimmy, at what time did you discover the fire?

Jimmy: It wis aboot four o'clock in the mornin'.

Dorothy: Indeed . . . and where were you when you discovered the fire?

Jimmy: I was in the toilet actually when I smelt it.

Dorothy: Really . . . indeed . . . and who did you have in the hotel that night?

Jimmy: It wis a big party of woman schoolteachers from Wisconsin in America.

Dorothy: Oh, really . . . from the USA? Mm . . . ah . . . and what did you do when you discovered the fire?

Jimmy: Well, basically ah jist went round the rooms and knocked up aw the women.

At this point the camera started to shake. At least when it came to the doughnut spot I didn't make the same mistake as Bill Tennant, a man who was excellent as a chat-show host. However, even the best can get it wrong. He had Fanny Craddock on, demonstrating how to make the definitive doughnut, and as he was winding up the show, he said, 'See you tomorrow, but in the meantime I hope all your doughnuts turn out like Fanny's.'

Altogether I did *Housecall* for four months. At the end of it, the *Sunday Mail* got hold of a story that I was being sacked. I wasn't being sacked, I was just not having my contract renewed, but this worked in my favour because the *Sunday Mail* gave me headlines: 'Dorothy Paul axed from *Housecall*'. Sacks of mail landed in the *Housecall* office objecting to my being taken off. The thrust of the complaints was that I should be kept on because I had a 'warmth'. It was very nice of people to write in and say that, in fact one man wrote and said, 'Don't give glamour the hammer'. I may have had warmth but I didn't have the skill for the job and I knew that myself. The viewers' complaints were noted by those 'above' and I got a phone call from my dear old friend through thick and thin, Jimmy Sutherland. STV were starting up a soap opera called *Garnock Way*, and I was offered a part in it. The part was of a good-hearted barmaid called Sandra Beattie, who meets up with Cully, played by another pal I had worked with in the past, Jackie Farrell; he was the local bookie whom Sandra eventually marries. This soap ran from January 1976 to 1979, when we arrived for rehearsals one day to find some of the top men in STV in the rehearsal room. Coffee and biscuits were being served. The presence of the high heid yins and the coffee and biscuits indicated that the P45s were about to be handed out. *Garnock Way* was terminated and *Take the High Road* was brought in. I was sure I would get a part, but I wasn't invited. During that time I walked down a very dark road, which led to a place in which there is a door. That door in my memory is firmly closed and I have thrown away the key.

I tried and tried to get work but nothing was forthcoming. I wrote to every film company, every television company; I even wrote to the director of *Doctor Who*, but Glasgow aliens weren't in the script at that time. By now I was in my 40s and it is said to be a difficult age for actresses. This is not true; many actresses in that age group are working. It was just a bad age for me. I did get some work in the odd theatre play, but nothing of any import.

One day I was in Byres Road and met a woman whom I knew slightly; she was an ex-model and still a stunner. She kindly asked after the children and I told her that my daughters were doing very well at school (I've always been boastful about my children's educational successes, much to their chagrin – probably a reaction to my own failure in that department).

This woman said, 'My, my, your children *are* doing well. Your husband must have been clever.'

Her statement went straight to the heart. I took her to task. 'My husband must have been clever?' I repeated it with even more vehemence, 'My husband must have been clever? How dare you! I was the one who brought up my children. I was the one who helped with their homework, I was the supporting cast . . .' I went on and on at her, but I was really talking to myself. The woman must have been delighted to get away from me and go on about her business.

I went home and told my girls of the encounter. Lisa told me that her best friend's mother, Maureen, who had become one of my closest friends, was going to college to do her Higher English. She said, 'You're clever, too, Mummy – you could do that.' I phoned Maureen and got the details about Clydebank College. I had missed the course halfway through. It was explained that if I did history and English along with two O-grades, I would qualify for a grant. I applied for the grant forms, filled them in and took them up to the appropriate office in Glasgow. I thought I was back in Nellie Sutherland's office. There was a sliding window, but when I knocked on it, instead of Nellie it was a boy with a very bad case of acne who stuck his head through. The poor boy's face was one big spot. I hoped he would grow out of it. He took the papers away and came back with a negative answer.

'Ah'm sorry, you'll no get a grant.'

'What do you mean?'

'Well, you see, you've been living in Edinburgh for three years and you came back to live in Glasgow on the 1st of July. Now if you had come back to Glasgow on the 30th of June, you would have got it, but you're one day short of the specified time so you cannae get the grant.'

I said, 'Maybe I got the date wrong. Maybe it was the 30th June I came back. Now that I think about it, it was the 30th of June.'

'You've put down the 1st of July and signed it. Ah cannae change it.'

I asked nicely, 'Surely you have discretionary powers?'

His reply was, 'Whit?'

'May I speak to your superior?'

'Naw.'

I was losing the rag; unfortunately the short fuse was alight. I said, 'Look here, young man, I am now going to my MP. I have rights, you know.'

His reply was, 'Please yersel,' and he closed the window on me.

I was dying to shout through the window, 'I would wish a pox on you but you've already got one.' I didn't, but thought it was a very good line.

Dorothy

I wrote to my MP, a Mr Tuppie, who very kindly took up my case with the 'authorities' and managed to get me the grant. I was back at school. Hurrah! I was the happiest woman alive. I was going to get further education at last and I felt that a new life was opening up for me. My girls were studying hard and I was studying along with them. The house was a tip but I didn't care. This was a great opportunity and I wasn't going to blow it. In history I studied the period between 1848 (the year of the revolutions) and 1918; special subject, Bismarck. The period included the unification of Germany, and the unification of Italy. I was getting to know all about Garibaldi (whereas before I'd only known about his biscuits), The Crimean War, the Franco–Prussian War, Pope Pius the IXth when he lost his temporal power and 'upped' his spiritual power. I was enthralled. The special subject was riveting. My teacher, Ian Mitchell, had written a textbook on Bismarck and was extremely interesting in his teaching. My English teacher, Ben Docherty, was erudite and his long chalky fingers and gentle voice betrayed a passion he had for his subject. He was wonderful. I did O-grades in art and fashion and fabrics. I had been sewing and cutting out patterns for years, and drawing and painting were hobbies, so I managed to cope with those. It was very hard work to keep up with the rest of the class, who had been there since September, but I was determined. In the classes were young people, late starters, who were getting a second chance at higher education, and women of my own age who had brought up families and wanted to get back into education, like myself, feeling that they had missed out when they were younger. Many of them had already applied for university places, including my friend Maureen, who went on to do a degree in the Social Sciences and now has a job which is both fulfilling and makes a useful contribution to society. I found myself at lunchtimes talking and sharing the ups and downs of our lives with fellow students. Our common ground was a thirst for knowledge and a desire to widen the spectrum of our lives. It was a life-changing experience, and one that I would wish to see more women involved in. We were what is known as 'returners'. As the course went on, I was aware of a new-found confidence among us. I wouldn't have missed that time of my life for anything.

The girls and I were sitting exams at the same time; Lisa had a maths exam the same day as I did the history. I couldn't believe I was getting this marvellous chance. Then it was over, and I had to wait six weeks for the results.

I was offered a lead part in a touring production, and I met up with an actress for whom I had great respect, Anne Scott Jones. She is a delight to work with and we have been friends ever since. In the July we were up in Inverness; she had her daughter Louise on tour with her and I had Lisa. A telegram from my elder daughter arrived at the theatre one night. It said: 'You've passed exams. Higher History, Higher English and two O-grades.' I couldn't believe it. I just clutched the telegram and Anne said that I let out a deep moan and in a very quiet voice said, 'Oh fuck, I'm clever.' I'd done it! If ever I was proud of myself, that was the time.

Rejoicing, I went on to do Highers in art, with Maggie Ramage, and French with John Moriarti. He was a first-class teacher and had high hopes for me, but I couldn't be there the full year, so although I managed to achieve the art Higher, I only got a compensatory O-grade for French. *Ça ne fait rien*, as they say in Bridgeton.

Armed with my certificates, I could have gone on to university, but I didn't.

25

As likely as not the patient will report, 'I have no idea
why I am depressed,' or will ascribe the depression to
irrelevant factors. Since patients are not consciously
willing or ready to recognise that the 'old self' or 'the
way things used to be' are outdated, they are not aware
that their depression is signalling that major change is
required for successful and evolutionary adaptation.

M. SCOTT PECK

I approached a crossroads in my life on a dark night, when the
signpost was obscured. I made a quick decision and took the
wrong road. There is in me – and I don't think I'm alone in this –
something that says, 'You don't deserve to have it all good.' A
negative voice, which is part of my own psyche and which, if I allow
it to have its say, can destroy all the good work I do on myself. Very
few of us have it all good: chaos comes into our lives, blocks our
paths, and we have to find a way through. I have always found it hard
to put the past behind me; memories of deep unhappiness still haunt
me and colour my life at times – as my mother said, 'the tragedy
queen'.

We can't expect to have everything, but we can work on good areas
of our lives and enhance them. I have a great ability to punish myself
just when I am starting to do well. This happened when I went into
the business that failed, and it took many years to get back to the
right road again. It put myself and my family in penury. I shall now
rephrase that. *I* put myself and my family in penury. We were quite
close to that mythical place 'the grubber'.

Sufficient to say I worked my way out of it by taking all sorts of jobs, sewing, PR, and market research. The latter involved house-to-house knocking on doors, asking people to answer questions on everything from washing-powders to politics.

One day I was interviewing a young man outside his door in a housing scheme, a delightful young man who seemed to have an inner grace. As he was answering my questions, a woman's voice shouted from the kitchen, 'Come and get yer soup.'

The boy replied, 'Jist comin', Mammy.'

I went on with the interview, writing down his answers as quickly as possible, when the disembodied voice sounded again, even louder, 'Come and get this bliddy soup.'

'No be a minute, Mammy.'

Just then a gross, foul-mouthed woman appeared, whom I thought couldn't possibly be the mother of this lovely boy, and who shouted and swore at both of us. She had a pot of boiling soup in her hand and was about to throw it in my direction when the boy promptly shut the door and saved me. What was I doing to myself? I've thought it all through, and of course taking this kind of job was self-punishment for my stupidity. I served the sentence which I'd imposed on myself, and decided to find another road out of my difficulties.

Our lovely flat in Kirklee had to be sold and I bought a larger flat with a studio, the flat with the inbuilt angel that gave advice. They say that no experience is lost. I would add to that, that no encounter with people is ever lost if you are born with the powers of observation which I seem to have. The flat was in a state of dilapidation after years of neglect. It had '60s black walls and ceilings. Some friends even said that perhaps it had been used for satanic rituals. My 'psychics' would have told me if this was true and it wasn't. The flat had a good feeling about it, even though it was dirty and dismal. It was on a hill with a beautiful view from the front windows towards the east. When the sun set, the buildings were illuminated in a golden-red glow which made even the broken-teeth effect of the multi-storeys look attractive. Yet another new beginning.

I have read that intelligence is a combination of learning from experience and problem-solving. I can only assume that I was half-intelligent, as I was able to solve problems but was unable to learn from experience. I seemed to continue making the same mistakes, dashing into situations without sufficient thought. However, this move was around the time when I was finally 'getting it together'. I was able to use my experience in the theatre to start teaching others, and I gained a certain self-esteem as I watched the young people respond. STV and BBC began to approach me for children to play parts in dramas. The kids were delighted, and some went on to greater things in the theatre. Saturday was the day when all these colourfully dressed little people gathered to perform, improvise and generally enjoy the interaction. I encouraged them to write their own work and one day we did a reading of a playlet that one of the children had written. I sat him beside me as the writer, I as the director and the others reading the piece, explaining that this was the way it was done in the professional theatre. From then on they felt that they were part of the real theatre. At the end of a term we would video-record some of the work. I wrote a revue for my adult classes with monologues and little scenes about Glasgow life and characters. Some of the scripts have been used in schools.

At the same time, I was doing my other jobs to keep the wolf from the door. I heard that STV were auditioning for newsreaders. I thought this might be a good regular employment. The theatre had given me up for lost, so why not give television a try? It couldn't be that difficult just sitting there, reading the news. Oh no?

For a start I was wearing a dress that was a swathed affair which on camera just looked untidy; I had caught sight of myself on the monitor. I was given a script to read that on the face of it didn't seem too difficult. It was about a road accident, a murder and an archaeological dig. News has to be read impartially and straight, and I couldn't do it. I was all over the place, I couldn't keep my head still, I couldn't put two words together coherently, and at the end of it the floor manager, a bloke I'd worked with on dramas, was smiling and saying, 'Very good, very good.' He wasn't actually smiling, he was trying to control his laughter. I said to him, 'Was that duff?'

He said, 'No, it wasn't duff. It's just that eh . . . eh . . .' He was fumbling around for words to describe my performance.

I helped him out. 'Be honest, John. I was like Noddy with a stutter, wasn't I?'

He was about to agree but just said, 'Your personality is just a bit big for the news.'

Ever since then I have had the utmost respect for newsreaders; their control and containment is a discipline all of its own. So, back to the drawing board.

I had to redecorate the flat. I had painted the studio white; the children would have hated black walls. It was a huge flat, with enormous rooms, so I had to get some help. My friend Maureen had already helped me knock away a lot of the sugary plaster on some of the walls, and together we did a fair bit of replastering. A real pal is someone who stands beside you up a scaffold, and gets themselves filthy putting their back into the work on your behalf, and of course it was in her spare time while she was studying for her degree. I phoned a wee man out of the *Evening Times* to do some of the papering and painting. The ceilings were very high and beyond my skills. They were so flaky, every time you banged a door bits fell down like confetti.

The man I contacted described himself in his advert as the Lone Ranger. That should have given me a warning signal. He arrived at the door, Reginald Cowboy Joe and his boy Shooey, a floppy young man with long lank hair and a lovely tooth.

'Hello, missus, ah'm Dougie the painter and this is the boy Shooey. Wipe yer feet, Shooey, before ye come intae the wumman's hoose. My God, whit a size o' a hoose, eh? A big loaby, eh, Shooey?' The boy Shooey nodded and grunted. 'I take it, missus, ye'll be lowering yer ceilin's.'

I said no, I wouldn't be contemplating unbalancing a perfectly well-designed Victorian structure.

'Ah 'hink yer daft, missus – it'd save ye heat. See, ah've this pal Jimmy that does the ceilin' lowerin'. He pits up the framin', he wallops up the gyprock and his ither pal Eddie, he dis the Artexin'. Beautiful work. Any pattern ye want. He'll show you the books. Ah'm telling ye, missus, he done this wumman's hoose in Thornliebank an ah'm tellin' ye you went intae that close, up the stair intae the hoose and ye wid a' thought ye were in a Spanish hacienda, 'n that right, Shooey?'

'Grunt.'

Dorothy

'Yer no waantin' that?'

I said, 'No.'

'Ah well, Shooey, hacienda that, eh?' I had to laugh. 'Ah well, please yersel.'

We moved to the sitting-room.

'Zis yer lounge? Look at that, Shooey – yer maw could get her hale hoose intae here, couldn't she, Shooey?' Another grunt. 'Naw, right enough, she widnae get her bad leg up they three stairs. Wait a minute, hen. Dae ah no know yer face fae somewhere? Wait a minute, ah'll get it . . . eh . . . Am ah right or am ah wrang? Behind the coonter in Henry Healy's in Argyle Street, under the Heilan' Man's umbrella? . . . Naw? Eh, the hambone shop doon the Gallowgate? Naw? Well, ah know yer face fae somewhere.'

He then got this dog-eared book out and a blunt pencil which required to be licked before applying it to the paper.

'Right, missus, you'll be waantin' it wallpapered. Are ye goin' furra Anaglypto, a lotta toffs go fur 'at. Or dae ye favour the wid chip that comes in thick wid and thin wid, whitever ye like, or maybe ye wid prefer the blown venile? An' I take it you'll be pickin' oot yer cornices in a contrast? Ah could dae that in colour that wid bring oot the flooers fur ye. Whit's that yer waantin'? Done in monochrome . . . monochrome? Whit colour is that exactly?'

I told him I wanted it all done in the one colour.

His reply was, 'Ah missus, ah don't 'hink ah'd like that.'

My thought was that if he'd liked it, I would have been seriously worried. He then did some calculations on his notepad and came up with a sum in telephone figures. The sum was to be paid in cash. I asked him to leave.

'Are ye no waantin' us tae dae the joab?'

I said no. I saw them out of the door and heard Butch Cassidy's remarks as they were going down the stairs. He said to the Sundance Kid, 'Cheeky bitch that wan, eh, Shooey? Mind you, ah know her face fae somewhere . . . ah bet she wis quite a good-lookin' wumman in her day.'

The minute they left I wrote down the whole conversation. I had a sketch.

Dorothy

Around 1986 I found myself keeping a diary of good days and bad days. The bad days saw a picture at the top of the page of dark clouds obscuring the light. Sometimes I even drew lightning through the clouds. On some of the pages I had written, 'I search for the light'. The few good days were indicated by a childlike drawing of the sun. This was the onset, in my mid-40s, of a thorough-going clinical depression. I had lost my life-savings in the 'business' I had invested in, but the real reason was not the money but the shame of the failure. I kept reminding myself what a fool I had been, until gradually over the years I went further and further down. On one level I was functioning: teaching, looking for work, cleaning, cooking, but the rest of me was miserable. My poor children had a dreadful time with me. Fortunately they had each other.

One day I had an insight into my problem and realised that the loss of fortune couldn't surely be the whole cause of my depression. My father was in and out of hospital; he would stay with me for a while and then I'd send him home. He was acting very strangely, inviting the most unsuitable people up to his house and getting into trouble. Eventually I got him into a home where he seemed very happy. He even found a girlfriend there.

The word 'light' was uppermost in my mind and it seemed so important to find it. Was this a place? I didn't know. Many years before, I had met a woman who had impressed me with her gentleness and kindness. She had many gifts, one of them being a beautiful soprano voice. By chance I heard that she was running yoga classes in a nearby library. I sought her out, attended her classes, and became friendly with her. She introduced me to her friend who also did yoga and I realised that these women, married women with families, took time out of their lives to help others. I had sought the light and had found it in two inspiring women. In addition to my other true friends, I had their help in my darkness. I also realised that if I wasn't to go under, I needed to understand myself more fully. I approached the Garnethill Centre in Glasgow and began in psychotherapy with another wonderful woman, who took me through my life bit by bit. The course was hard going and I faced much that I didn't want to see or know about myself. I have always been able to see the worst in myself. I have no illusions on that score. I remember my psychotherapist asking me why I was always smiling, even when I was discussing the most awful aspects of my life. Smiling is a habit with me; keep the face up, don't show your feelings, you're in the public eye, nobody loves a crier, crack a joke, see the funny side. In private I was falling apart.

The depression didn't occur overnight and neither did the recovery. I lay in bed one night and tried to make myself stop. I concentrated on not being there any more and in this kind of meditation I was aware of my body functioning. I wanted out but the body wouldn't let me. It was a strange experience.

With the help of my Angels I made a slow but steady recovery. When you eventually come out of a depression, it really is like coming out of the darkness into the light. I can pinpoint one night when my daughter helped me through. I was sitting at home, no make-up on, not like me. I was going over the let-downs I'd had over work. I had been promised a panto in Paisley Town Hall, only two weeks' work but nevertheless very welcome. At the time I was working in the STV wardrobe department. This particular night my daughter said, 'Mum, get your coat on, there's a Woody Allen movie on in town, *Broadway Danny Rose*. You know you like him.'

Your children always get the worst of you. I said, 'Nobody could make me laugh just now. Just leave me alone.'

She physically pulled me out of the chair and put my coat on and pushed me out the door and into the car. I fought her all the way. I was wearing one of my oldest coats and I must have looked a sight. At the end of the movie, which I enjoyed, she oxtered me out of the cinema and quoted one of Woody Allen's lines: 'You see, Mum . . . one day you're a bum and the next you're a hero.' Just at that moment I could almost see a bright doorway. It was as though I had been encapsulated in a grey fog and I now saw a way out.

I believe it was her power of healing, along with that of the other good women in my life, that hauled me through. There was a kind of magic at work and I recognised it. The kind of magic I believe in is the magic that comes from giving life your best shot; hard work. I had been worked on by other people through this dreadful time; my friends and family and my therapist helped me along the way. I had sought help and I had received it. A burden was lifted and I knew I would get better.

Dorothy

Next day I got word that the panto was on. I also got a small part in one of Andy Cameron's television shows, and then a part in three episodes of *Taggart*, which I would do the following January. I had a lot of help but I had to take the final step myself.

Nowadays I sometimes feel sadness overwhelming me but I just let it happen and know that it will pass. I have never again entered that dark place. If it looms up on my path, I recognise it and take steps to avoid it. In many ways, the recovery from the depression has helped me in every way. 'Lack of self-esteem' has never left me, but one can learn to have a healthy respect for oneself. I can recognise it in others, I can pick out the smiling depressives; I can also recognise Angels.

I know I have a dark side to my nature which manifests itself in anger, selfishness and sloth. I hate the last one more than anything. I face my dark side and realise that one of its aspects is my hustling nature when it comes to business. Nobody can be Mrs Nice all the time, and who would want to be? Mrs Nice couldn't write and perform one-woman shows without drawing on her darker self. The depression taught me a lot, and when I look back at the aunties, I think much of it was genetic.

26

Fame is a bee.
It has a song –
It has a sting –
Ah, too, it has a wing.

EMILY DICKINSON

My agent phoned me one day early in 1987 to tell me that auditions were being held at the Adam Smith Centre, in Kirkcaldy, for *The King and I*. This would be right up my street; dancing, singing and acting. I gave up smoking for two days, thinking that that would make up for all the years of ruining a beautiful voice with the terrible weed. I practised my singing exercises and drove up to the audition full of confidence. This really was something different and something I'd always wanted to do: a musical.

I auditioned for the artistic director/manager and thought I had done well. When I sang 'Hello Young Lovers', his entourage were moved to tears. As I have slowly but surely lost my singing voice, I have managed to improve my way of selling a song. I believe that is more important than technique in some areas of music. I drove away from the audition, for the first time in my life, thinking that the job was 'in the bag'. Two days later, my agent phoned me to say that someone else had been offered the part of Anna. I was stunned. Didn't get the part? Who did they think they were? How dare they! That part was meant for me. I flew into a rage. I kicked the fridge and dented it badly. I was the wrath of God. My children came home that night to find Mrs Hyde cooking their dinner.

A couple of days passed and I was still angry when my agent came on the phone again. 'Hello, dearie – Wildcat Theatre Company are taking up Tony Roper's script, *The Steamie*, and they want to see you for a part.'

My reply to this was, 'Well, this is another job I'm not going to get.'

Earlier that week I had been in Boots the Chemist and met Elaine C. Smith. She had heard my voice asking one of the assistants if they had any Slimmachoc. She had grabbed hold of my arm and said, 'That'll no do you any good, Dorothy.' We both laughed at this and recalled the fun we had had doing Liz Lochhead's play *Sweet Nothings* way back in 1982, a TV play written for women, set in a bra factory. It had been a lovely play and all of us had strong parts in it. She reminded me about the stories we all told each other about our experiences in the theatre. Elaine was just making her name in those days, and she used to listen avidly to the older actresses recounting their tales. She had a wee story to tell but was afraid it wouldn't match up to the raconteurs. She told her story and it got huge laughs. Apparently I had said to her, 'Here, hen, come you and sit up here with the big girls. You're good.' That day in 1987 she had told me about the casting for *The Steamie* and that she'd put my name forward. I thanked her but thought she was just being kind.

So there I was, going up to Wildcat's base, Jordanhill College, to audition for the part of Magrit. I still had the anger about me when I entered the office to find Alex Norton, the director, and Dave Anderson, the musical director and songwriter on the play.

Alex Norton volunteered, 'Dorothy, I'm so glad to meet you. I used to run home from school every day to see you on the *One O'Clock Gang*.'

I said, 'Oh really?' I was being reminded of my age by this fella. 'So you want me to read? I'll read. Where's the script?'

This was Mrs Not Very Nice talking, and I couldn't help myself. Years of rejection finally took their toll. I couldn't have given a bugger about this part. It would only be another in a long line of 'Sorry, dearie, you didn't get it'. Sod the lot of them. I read Magrit angry. Of course, the part of Magrit was that of an angry woman. Then Alex asked me to read it another way. I said, 'Certainly. I'll read it any way you like. I'm an actress.' I read it again and they thanked me for coming along.

Dorothy

Alex said, 'It's the first time I've been nervous auditioning someone.'

Was he being funny? Who cared? My God, was I surly? I walked away from the audition without a hope of getting the part.

The next day, 'Hello, dearie, Wildcat want you to play the part of Magrit.'

I couldn't believe it. I had been churlish to the point of rudeness and I had got the part. It didn't make me think that I should continue in that way, but it had worked that time.

Rehearsals were hard, because as well as yards of script we had to learn solo songs, duets and ensembles. I was terrified; it had been ages since I had been in a stage play. The script was wonderful, with very diverse characters all thrown together in a steamie, a public wash-house, on a Hogmanay circa 1953. Dolly, played by Elaine, was in her 60s. Elaine was 28 then, but her love of the character shone through and was absolutely believable. She was the wee simple woman with a big family who loved the world and everyone in it. Dolly wasn't the brightest of women but therein lay her charm. Dolly sang 'The Big Clock on the Steamie Wall', telling of the hard work women had to do in those days before leisure time was invented. Doreen was played by Kathy Murphy. She was the young married woman who had dreams of getting a house in the country, Drumchapel, where she and her husband would love each other, bring up their family, and have a lovely bathroom. Her song was 'Dreams Come True', which extolled the joy of living in a new housing estate in the place that Billy Connolly was to describe as a 'desert wi' windaes'. There were shades of the girls' get-togethers in the Kraft Cheese here. Mrs Culfeathers was the old lady, at death's door but working, taking in other people's washing right up to the end. During the play there was always the thought that she might not see the last scene. She did because of the support of her 'Pals', the title of a song sung as a quartet. Ida Schuster played Mrs Culfeathers in the first tour. Magrit was a bitter, disillusioned woman with a drunken husband and two adored boys. She started the play angry and finished the same way. There was a big heart in Magrit, but only now and then did it show. Her sympathy was for her fellow-women and for the lot they had all been cast into by being born women. When I look back at that part, I realise there was great release of emotion for me in playing Magrit. I'd known these women, I'd experienced all of the characters first-hand. I understood them. I was from that background.

As with any play, you go on the first night full of nerves, not knowing how the audience is going to receive it. This was a new, untried work. The set was beautiful, a partly stylised but mostly practical area to work in; designed by Malky McCormick, the famous cartoonist. Each actor had their own 'stall' – as Dolly sang in her song, 'Aye and we're the donkeys'. We also had a token man, Andy, played by Ray Jeffries. He was the maintenance man who saw himself as a bit of a sex symbol and who would slowly get drunk during the play.

We got laughs from the word go. Halfway through the first act people were wiping tears from their eyes. They also shed tears of sadness over Mrs Culfeathers and her reminiscences of when she was young and how her world had changed: her husband no longer her partner, but a poor old man it took her all her time to nurse; her children having abandoned her.

The second half went from strength to strength, culminating in the famous mince scene which involved the telling of the same story twice, a dangerous thing to attempt in a comedy. The second telling got even more laughs. 'Was it Galloway's mince that Mr Culfeathers liked or was it Jackson's potatoes?' An inane story but with the writing and the playing combined it was huge.

All the songs were written by Dave Anderson, with the exception of Elaine's big number at the beginning of the second half. That had been written by a young man called David Hicks, who had died just before the play opened. This lent an extra poignancy to Elaine's performance of it. Dave Anderson wrote all the rest and they were brilliant, and different. He gave me a gift of a song, 'The Labour of Love', in which Magrit sings of her drunken husband, her weans and how she would spend Hogmanay, waiting for 'him' to come home drunk and spoil her preparations, the shortbreid, the black bun and the fact that she'd got 'aw dressed up an' aw'. We finished with 'Aw the Best When it Comes'. We sang of how we'd never get out of the 'bit'. We were the workers of the world and we never tasted the cream:

Dorothy

Aw the best to you and yours,
Today ye'll no remember,
How you worked tae an early grave,
May until December.

The last chorus in harmony said:

Someday we'll say what became of the slums,
Aw the best when it comes,
Here's tae the day when we get more than crumbs,
Aw the best when it comes.

I remember that when we toured the play, we played an actual steamie in Govan, and to a woman we all had tears streaming down our cheeks and were choked with emotion at the end when we sang that song because we looked down at the audience and there they all were: wee, grey-haired, weary women who had been the characters we played. The women who never had and never would have any more than the crumbs. They were the mothers who had reared families on nothing, like my own mother, who had been through the Depression of the '30s with the threat of the Parish, the war, all the hardships that we had played out on the stage but had never experienced. It was amazing that on that makeshift stage we had all had the same thoughts.

The end of the first night saw us lined up receiving a standing ovation. It was one of the great highlights of our careers. We knew we were involved in a 'classic'. We toured all over Scotland and hardly any publicity was required. The word went round like wildfire that this was a play not to be missed. Even when we played big theatres with many dressing-rooms, we all dressed together; this was to get into the camaraderie of the characters. We'd laugh and joke while we dressed and made up and by the time we made our entrances we had warmed up. It was an unforgettable time of my life. I think I could speak for all of us in saying that we all felt the specialness of that play.

When we came to perform the television version of *The Steamie*, Elaine was seven months pregnant. Scottish Television was concerned that she looked too young, naturally, for the part, even with the addition of latex. It was also felt that her pregnancy was too far advanced. Eileen McCallum took the part of Dolly and played her beautifully, while Sheila Donald played Mrs Culfeathers. The television play was excellent but I never felt it had the same magic as the original stage version.

27

The father of every good work is discontent, and its
mother is diligence.

LAJOS KASSAK

A s always happened in our business, the work comes in clumps,
and sometimes you are doing two and three jobs at a time. This
happened in the autumn tour of *The Steamie*. I was in a television
'three-parter' called *The Bookie*, where I played Maurice Roeves' (the
Bookie's) ex-wife. It was strange to be playing a bimbo, *nouveau-riche*
type of woman by day, and a work-worn, bitter housewife every
night. I went on to be involved in other Wildcat productions: *The
Important of Being Honest*, then *The Celtic Story*, rehearsing the latter
while touring with the former.

I got word that my father had broken his hip and was in the Royal
Infirmary. We visited him every day until eventually pneumonia, the
old man's friend, took him away. I left the hospital on the night of his
death at two o'clock. I had been given a plastic bag which contained
his belongings. That was all that was left of his life except his electric
organ, which he left in the home. The funeral had to be postponed for
a few days because I had an opening night on the Wednesday. I didn't
want to rush him under the ground. I wanted the full monty, with the
service, him buried beside his mother, and the hospitality in my
house. My brother bought him a new boiler suit to be buried in, as
he'd wished, and had to find Granny's grave in Riddrie cemetery.

Father had been rather abandoned by some of the family after my
mother's death, but they all turned up for the funeral. Many
neighbours who had known him were there. There was also a
policeman who had visited him regularly just because Father was a

character. We asked the minister from Rutherford Church to take the service and he did it very beautifully. I chose the text that I thought said it all about old Sam: 'Consider the lilies how they grow. They toil not neither do they spin. Yet I say to you that not even Solomon in all his glory was arrayed like one of these.' I saw the beautiful soul in my father. As a human being he was a 'one-off'.

After the service we all went up to Riddrie cemetery to bury him and as the minister was reading, I started to think of all the funny things my father had said about funerals and death. He had come to my house one day and said, 'They buried Uncle Archie last Tuesday.'

My natural reaction was to say, 'Is he dead?'

Father had replied, 'I hope so, they buried him last Tuesday.'

As I looked around at the other graves I remembered going round the old Glasgow Eastern Necropolis with Dad when I was a wee girl, when he had told me that he'd seen a gravestone once that said: 'Here lies the body of Katy McMurny/She fell aff a train and broke her journey.' I couldn't help these lines going through my head even at that solemn occasion. Perhaps it was a defence mechanism, or it could have been Father trying to lighten the situation. My mother would have said, 'Look at that, Lizzie. All these gravestones saying "Here lies my beloved husband". Where do you think they buried all the bad yins?'

As they lowered the coffin into the grave, it looked to me as though it was all to the one side and I heard myself saying, 'Wait a minute, you'll have to straighten him out.' This took a minute or two but finally the coffin was properly horizontal. I didn't want him lying on his side for all the years to come.

We all went back to my house for the meal. I kept thinking that I would have to go on stage that night and be funny. My daughters did the catering, not steak pie but a very acceptable buffet and a wee hauf. The day went well and we celebrated his life and all his carry-ons, as my mother would have called them. My terrible regret was that during the time he was in the home I was in the clinical depression place and I couldn't take what my father reminded me of. I seldom visited him there, and it wasn't until he was in the Royal that I could face seeing him. Fortunately, the good folk who ran the home said that he was happy there; he did wee electrical jobs for them and played the organ for community singing. It transpired that he had had two or three girlfriends during his stay. Father always managed. Whereas my mother had to have the back-up of her sisters and desperately needed her place in the centre of the family, Father needed nothing like that. He was basically a loner who could relate well to strangers. My daughters look back and see my dad as good fun and totally eccentric. They spent many happy days with him and the wee 'tricks' he got up to were harmless. My father was a big boy all his life and, to me, a lovable big boy.

The Celtic Story was a very complicated show and I didn't hold out much hope for its success. I was afraid it would be a celebration of bigotry. I underestimated Dave McLennan and Dave Anderson's writing. It was a wonderful show, which told the story of a hundred years of a football club. I played many parts in it, including a member of the family of fans, and Queen Victoria. I was heckled every night during that scene, as I was playing her with as near as I could get to a 'royal' accent. The audience shouted and swore when she came on, until one night I stayed in character and added the line, 'One is only acting.' This tickled the folk and elicited a round of applause.

In the middle of the first act, I played a young Irish woman who was sitting at a chenille-draped table with a paraffin lamp, writing to her husband in the trenches. One night a middle-aged woman, much refreshed, took her seat in the stalls. She was wearing a Celtic shirt and made quite a fuss as she squeezed along the row of seats, tramping on people's toes. Once they found their own seats she brought out a can of lager, opened it with a loud squish, and turned to her husband: 'Oh Christ, Wullie, it's that Dorothy Paul . . . ah cannae stand her.'

I was rattled but carried on. 'Ah, my dear Thomas, I am writing to tell you how your team got on . . .'

Her voice from the stalls, 'Here, Dorothy . . . yer Irish accent's shite, by the way.'

I didn't think it was too bad, and carried on and finished the scene. Towards the end of the show I was singing about one of Celtic's big successes, 'Oh Hampden in the sun, Celtic 7, Rangers 1' – there she was again, 'Away back tae sleep, Wullie. See that's her again.'

Dorothy

The show ran for eight weeks to packed houses. It was a great, hard-working cast and I'm so sorry Celtic FC never made a video of it.

During my next play, *Harmony Row*, I met up with Barbara Rafferty and we hit it off right away. She is such a lovely woman and a beautiful actress. I played the mother who is fighting against the poll tax and she played my daughter. I always remember we played the Adam Smith Centre, Kirkcaldy, and I told her the story of *The King and I*. Even as I told her about the rejection I was still angry, until she said, 'Dorothy, don't you understand you were never meant to get that part?'

I said, 'What do you mean?'

She replied, 'If you had got the part as Anna in *The King and I*, you would not have played Magrit in *The Steamie*. They were running at the same time.'

Of course she was right. I had been taken down the right road and I hadn't even noticed. I started to realise that there were signs given and you had to be vigilant in recognising them. I remembered Kirkcaldy and the Trades Club. 'This hoor's come all the way from Glasgow.' That had finished my career in the clubs. Instead of thinking that Kirkcaldy had been the scene of my worst nightmares, it was in fact the place of my Nemesis. I have a lot to thank Kirkcaldy for. The next time I played there it was with my one-woman show. The folk in Kirkcaldy loved it.

Work had been steady up until January 1991, when the diary looked a bit bare. I had a lot to make up after the loss of my savings. It's easy to lose money but very hard to save it. I had much to be thankful for, my girls were doing well and I had got over a bad spell. I had learned many lessons and hopefully would never make the same mistakes again. I had heard the voice and acted on its suggestions, and my friend Michael Boyd believed in me; not many people had. I had started writing the script, which was mostly narrative, telling the stories as I have told them to you, dear reader. I first of all visited Liz Lochhead to ask for advice. She read what I had written and told me that it was most certainly written from the heart – Liz had always told me that that's where the most successful writing comes from –

but that it wasn't quite right. 'The stories are good but it needs structure.' Then she added, 'Who's going to direct you?'

I told her I had thought of John Bett. I had seen him acting on stage in Shakespearean plays, and in the big Wildcat historical plays at the Tramway, where he had played many different parts. He'd done films and television and lately he had directed the second production of John McGrath's *The Cheviot, the Stag and the Black, Black Oil*. He was a consummate actor, director and prolific writer. He was also highly respected amongst his peers. I wondered what he would think of what I'd written so far. Liz agreed that I couldn't get anyone better to help me. I thanked her for being a pal and went off home and wrote immediately to John.

John received my letter at 8.30 the next morning and by ten o'clock he had read my script and was on the phone. He told me that he had had a warm glow when he read it. 'There is so much humanity in the story you've written. For anyone who is working class, it will be instant recognition, and people who have not experienced living up a close will find a rich vein of humour.' He added, 'I think you have done well.' He believed in me, too.

I was overjoyed when he invited me to his home in Fife to discuss how we were hoping to present it. I travelled joyfully, somehow knowing that I was in the right hands. I was welcomed by John and his lively wife, the actress Sarah Collier. It was only afterwards that I asked her if at that time she knew what she was getting into. She said, 'No, I didn't, but none of us knew where it was going to lead.'

John and I set to work right away. He suggested that I dramatise all the events instead of narrating the story; play all the characters. I ended up playing myself as a child, the doctor, all the aunties, my father, Nellie Sutherland the agent with the slack false teeth, Mr Inwood the choirmaster, the dubious Carrol Levis, the girls in the Kraft Cheese and even the wee woman in the audience of the Pavilion who shouted out, 'Yer Irish accent's shite, by the way.' Johnny laughed at them all. He makes a great audience of one.

Many times I'd say to John, 'John, I don't think that's funny.'

He would say, 'But Dorothy, you're not sitting where I'm sitting. It's hilarious, trust me.'

I did trust him. I knew him to be a total professional who would never let me down. We worked long and hard at the script, rewriting, structuring and knocking it into shape. We had a few bookings. We would open in the Ayr Civic, then the Tron Theatre, with two nights in the Arts Theatre in Paisley – altogether nine nights' work. It had to be paid for, and I had to use my meagre savings, but I was assured that we would break even if we did 50 per cent business. The expenses went up and it looked as though we'd have to do 60 per cent capacity. When it reached the point where, in order to get my money back we would have to do 75 per cent business, I could see my wee bit of cash flowing down the Swanee. I didn't worry unduly, for the simple reason that I was too involved in rehearsals, and the thought of a 'showing-up' was the threat I put myself under and that was worse than losing capital.

Ayr Civic was full. A good start: we would cover the costs. My daughters came down to see it, my wee stalwarts. They've always come to my opening nights and I always get good 'notes' from them. They haven't been around the theatre all their lives without knowing what it's about. I felt I was under-rehearsed because of the time we spent on the writing. John was confident.

'You need an audience. Once they are out there, you'll be away.'

He is such a good director and he calmed me down, although when he met Sarah, who had driven down to see the show, I feel sure he said to her, 'She doesn't know a bloody word of it.'

The curtain was to go up at 7.45 and at 7.15 we were still rehearsing. The make-up was thrown on and at 7.40 I was blow-drying my hair. The show started with my now famous 'cleaner' character making her way through the audience, warming them up with her gross repartee. She got huge laughs and, as John predicted, I was 'away'.

It was the first time I'd ever been on stage by myself (with the pianist) for two hours. I was a success. I didn't give myself a showing-up. We opened in the Tron Theatre, Glasgow, on the following Tuesday, 12 June 1991. At the end of the show the audience were on their feet. I was receiving a standing ovation. I just wept. Look, Mum, I'm drawing attention to myself! What do you think, Mum? How did I do? It's as much your story as it is mine, and you were great. Oh Mum, if only you had been there to see it.

Dorothy

Contrary to our expectations, we did 110 per cent business and Michael said, 'We can advertise the show "by public demand" for the following week, if you can do it.' I did it. We did a full autumn tour with that show, then two tours the following year, ending up with the television version. It was a BAFTA and was shortlisted in the 15th International Celtic Film and Television Festival. John and I went on to write and produce another three one-woman shows, all of which have been televised. Many awards have followed, including the Great Scot Award for entertainment and the Glasgow Lord Provost's Award for my contribution to the Arts. Not bad for a rejected soprano.

28

She was an ageing singer who had to take every note
above 'A' with her eyebrows.

MONTAGUE GLASS

*T*here have been many articles written about me. Journalists have
picked out areas of my life which make good copy: the loss of
my husband; bringing up my children on my own; the crash of the
business; the fact that I had been a big name one minute, and
forgotten the next. I call these 'God help me' stories. Poor me – look
what life had done to me, and yet I have struggled on. This is untrue.
Life has not been bad to me; I have been very fortunate and was given
many choices. The trouble was, I think, that I was ill-equipped to
make some of them.

Hodding Carter said: 'There are only two lasting bequests we can
hope to give our children. One of these is roots, the other, wings.' I
was held too close to my mother and have never really got away. I can
see this now. I loved her too much. She has been dead for 32 years and
yet I still seek her approval – not healthy. She withheld my wings, not
out of malice but out of love and need. The relationship was a tight,
mutual dependency. Of course she didn't realise what she was doing.
I don't realise when I talk about 'my girls' that I am doing the same.
Fortunately, 'my girls' have their own lives, completely separate from
mine. We meet up, discuss things, laugh together and get on with our
own lives. I do try to let go.

When I look back, I see my life as a long road with signposts. For
much of the way I seem to have taken the directions marked 'hard'.
It didn't have to be like that, but those are the roads I chose. My
mother used to say, 'Aye, there's some folk that come in and touch the

world lightly'. You could describe such people as 'pond-skaters'. I looked under the surface, and even dug up things that I needn't have touched. But if I hadn't looked that bit deeper, I wouldn't have noticed all the characters that I've played.

It really annoys me when people dismiss actors as 'airy fairy'. I want to scream out, 'But don't you realise that what we say on the stage is the truth? Real life is where we role-play, fitting our scripts to the given situation. Take any work situation, and you'll find role-playing.' I once described to someone outside the business how, on a first night, the blood pressure goes up and the nerves are uncontrollable. As I complained about this, the person said, 'I wish I could get that kind of buzz from my work.' I realised how right he was. It is a tremendous feeling to be at the outset of something new, to create a role no one has ever played before. After all, a play can be beautifully written, but it takes the actors to bring it to life.

I still write down things I overhear, for use in a script at some later date. Only the other day I was walking down Byres Road and heard a very young mother chastising her child outside Hillhead Library; it made me think that Glasgow language hadn't changed so very much since I was a wee girl. This harassed mother shouted, 'Stop that, Jason. Aye, ye can laugh, but if you don't stop your carry-on you'll laugh on the other side of your face.' Even now I don't know what that expression means.

I have called my story 'the revelations of a rejected soprano'. A whimsical title, yet there is a little truth in everything. I mean it in fun, but I still remember the rejections. I've turned most of them around and made a laugh out of them; it's the only way to stop them from eating into your soul.

We are all born with a certain optimism and sparkle, I'm sure of that. Just as my father was denigrated for his being 'different', so all of us have suffered that smothering of our natural exuberance at some time. There are few really free spirits amongst us – most of us have been brought up to conform. I now try to feel free. I am getting better at saying 'it disnae suit me' when faced with demands on my time. Another expression I have tried to lose is 'hivtae'; you hivtae do this or you hivtae to do that. No, I don't hivtae. I can do what I like now.

The men in my life, apart from my late husband, are conspicuous by their absence in this book. I haven't mentioned the good ones to save any embarrassment. I haven't mentioned the bad ones to protect the guilty. However, if I were asked to name the one man I would be happy to spend the rest of my life with I would say, without a doubt, Harrison Ford.